A Fingertip Guide to Scots Criminal Law

A Fingertip Guide to Scots Criminal Law

Sixth Edition

Peter Hamilton

and

J Ross Harper

Edited by Kristopher Donnelly

Bloomsbury Professional

Bloomsbury Professional Limited, Maxwelton House, 41–43 Boltro Road, Haywards Heath, West Sussex, RH16 1BJ

Bloomsbury Professional, an imprint of Bloomsbury Publishing Plc

A CIP Catalogue record for this book is available from the British Library.

ISBN: 978 1 78043 242 7

Typeset by Phoenix Photosetting, Chatham, Kent

Preface

A Fingertip Guide began life more than 30 years ago as a result of a civil service industrial dispute which had brought Glasgow Sheriff Court to a halt.

The benefit to the public was a dramatic reduction in crime as police went back on the beat instead of whiling away time at court, waiting to give evidence, but for the authors, something had to be found to occupy unexpectedly idle hours.

It was decided to write a 'basic' Handbook on Criminal Law for students. The three column format (which, it is thought, remains unique) was adopted, and two final year students recruited as research students.

It tells us much that since then one of those students became Lord Advocate and is now Dame of the British Empire and the other, now, sadly, no longer with us, was a leading silk at the Scots Bar.

None of those involved in its original creation would ever have expected a 'basic' handbook to prove useful enough to be now in its sixth edition.

Changing constitutional, social, and forensic circumstances mean that each new edition required substantial updating and the energetic vitality of Scots Criminal Law means, I think, that this is particularly so on this occasion, providing a challenging assignment. Without the indefatigable editorial resourcefulness of Kristopher Donnelly that assignment could not have been accomplished and my gratitude to him is immense. At Bloomsbury Professional, the publishers, Paula O'Connell's legendary patience and charm has made an arduous task a happy activity.

The reader should remember that, as the title makes clear, the book is meant to signpost the busy court practitioner into the appropriate pathways to more in-depth research into the day-to-day issues of criminal court practice.

Peter Hamilton
Glasgow
January 2013

Contents

Table of Statutes

References are to Page Number

Table of Statutory Instruments

References are to Page Number

Table of European Legislation

References are to Page Number

Table of Cases

References are to Page Number

A

B

C

D

E

F

G

N

O

S

T

Y

SUBSTANTIVE LAW

OFFENCES OF DISHONESTY

THEFT

Theft is the **felonious appropriation** or taking of the **property of another** without his consent with the **intent to deprive** him of it permanently, temporarily or indefinitely

COMMENTARY	CASE LAW	STATUTE LAW
Felonious appropriation – dealing with property as if it were one's own.	*Dewar v HMA* 1945 JC 5. Felonious appropriation results when the accused forms the intention to deprive the owner of his goods or his rights as owner of the goods; a fact which may be inferred from the surrounding circumstances. *Held*, a crematorium manager selling coffin lids intended for cremation as coffee tables amounted to felonious appropriation.	
	Kivlin v Milne 1979 SLT (Notes) 2. *Held* that the intention to deprive the owner of his property could be inferred from the abandonment of that property.	
	Black v Carmichael 1992 SCCR 709. Wheel clamping, private car park, notice demanding payment for release; held theft and extortion, 'even if debt due', enforcement by other than legal process showed *mens rea* for theft despite the owner's property not being physically removed from his possession.	
Felonious taking – amotio required I.e. removal from container, room or within an open space showing an intention to steal	*Peter Anderson* 1800 Hume 172. Removal of article from till.	
	Cornelius O'Neil 1845 2 Brown 394. Window raised from outside, clothing moved with stick nearer to window.	
Appropriation by finding.	*Lawson v Heatley* 1962 SLT 53. Mother receiving £1 from son knowing must have been stolen and making no attempt to track owner.	Civic Government (Scotland) Act 1982, s 67. Duty on finder to take reasonable care of found property and to hand it to police or other designated (sub-s (3)) official ibid s 73. No right of ownership conferred by finding.
	MacMillan v Lowe 1991 SCCR 113. Possession of cheque books found four hours previously; no attempt to hand them in, and attempt to conceal them from police.	
	Kane v Friel 1997 SCCR. Piping and sink abandoned on waste ground; theft connection quashed – no evidence of previous owner's intention to retain.	
Property – private or public ownership. Must be both moveable and corporeal. Information therefore cannot be stolen.	*Dewar* 1777 Hume I 75. and *HMA v Mackenzies* 1913 7 *Adam* 189. The 'stealing' of trade secrets and trade recipes did not amount to theft.	
Res nullius – eg wild animal must first be brought into ownership.	*John Huie* 1842 1 Brown 383. Fish, once netted, are fisherman's property.	
Escape from captivity.	*Valentine v Kennedy* 1985 SCCR 89. Rainbow trout previously enclosed, escaped despite adequate precautions were still owned.	
Of another impossible to steal one's own property (*Hume* 1.77)	*Sandlan v HMA* 1983 SCCR 71. Jewellery, money, sales records of company of which Sandlan was director.	

COMMENTARY	CASE LAW	STATUTE LAW
	Hamilton v Wilson 1994 SLT 431. Theft of illegitimate child by father who did not have custody rights: permanent deprivation intention unnecessary.	
Belief that property is one's own.	*Dewar v HMA*, above. Belief that removal of coffin lids common practice at crematoria entirely fictitious.	
Permanently.	*Kivlin v Milne* 1979 SLT (Notes) 2 Stolen car abandoned where owner unable to find it.	
Temporarily.	*Hamilton v Wilson* above. *Smith v Dewar* 1977 SLT Sh Ct. 75. No *mens rea* in taking a moped to have 'a shot'. *Milne v Tudhope* 1981 JC 53 dispute about payment for finding work: tradesman stripping items from property to force payment. *Sandlan v HMA* above. *Kidston v Annan* 1984 SCCR 20. Goods received for repairs estimate; refusal to return unless repairs instructed.	
Indefinitely.	*Fowler v O'Brien* 1994 SCCR 112. Bicycle taken without permission and used openly.	
		Criminal Procedure (Scotland) 1995, s 11 – enables prosecution in Scotland quoad property stolen elsewhere. Schedule 3, s 8(4) provides for alternative verdicts – reset, fraud.
Preventive Offences. Criminalises behaviour taking place prior to the commission of a crime.		Section 57 of the Civic Government (Scotland) Act 1982: criminalises being found in or on premises from which an intention to commit theft may reasonably be inferred. Section 58 of the Civic Government (Scotland) Act 1982: only applies to individuals who have two or more previous convictions for theft and criminalises the possession of 'tools' from which an intention to commit a theft may be reasonably inferred.

Aggravation of theft

Theft may be aggravated by the way in which it is perpetrated: **opening lockfast places, theft by housebreaking and** housebreaking **with intent to steal**.

COMMENTARY	CASE LAW	STATUTE LAW
Opening lockfast places. Anything apart from buildings secured by a lock.		
	McLeod v Mason 1981 SCCR 75. Lockfast car: unnecessary to establish whether intent to steal car or contents or both.	
Breaking open must precede and be for the purpose of theft.	*Jas Stuart and Alex Low 1842 – I Brown 260*. Chest stolen before being broken open. See also: *McLeod v Mason* 1981 SCCR 75.	
Housebreaking 'House' = any roofed building which is shut and fast against intruders.	*Hume* i. 103	
'Breaking' = any means of surmounting security of building, including unusual entry.	*Burns v Allan* 1987 SCCR 449 Dismantling of alarm system = housebreaking. *Lafferty v Wilson* 1990 SCCR 30. There must be evidence that the premises were previously secure prior to the alleged housebreaking taking place.	
Intent to steal. Housebreaking itself is not a criminal offence. It must be coupled with a theft (as above) or an *intention* to steal.	*McClung v McLeod* 1974 38 JC 22. Window broken = housebreaking with intent to steal established, despite premises not being entered. *Burns v Allan* 1987 SCCR 449. If a theft is not committed a charge of housebreaking with intent to steal may still be competent, if the intent to steal can be reasonably inferred from the facts. *Held* that the dismantling of an alarm system whilst carrying 'housebreaking tools' is enough to be convicted of housebreaking with intent to steal.	

RESET

Reset is taking **possession** of, or **being privy** to the **retention** of, property **dishonestly appropriated** by another, **knowing** it to have been so appropriated and **intending** that the owner be deprived of its recovery.

COMMENTARY	CASE LAW	STATUTE LAW
Possession is the control of the property and occurs as soon as there is **retention.**	*Robert Finlay* 1826 Alison i 133 Stolen property was thrown on bed by thieves and covered over by one of the accused who was convicted of reset. 'If he once acquiesce in the placing of the goods there under circumstances inferring his guilty knowledge, and still more if he lend any aid towards their concealment ... his guilt is incurred.' *HMA v Browne* (1903) 6 F(J) 24 B participated in arrangements for banking of stolen money. Per LJ-C Macdonald: 'Not necessary ... that the property passed into the personal possession of the receiver.' Accused convicted.	Criminal Procedure (Scotland) Act 1995, s 11(4)(b). Any person who, in Scotland, receives property stolen in any other part of the United Kingdom may be dealt with in like manner as if it had been stolen in Scotland.
Privity Where the dishonestly acquired property has not been handled, it requires an overt positive act in connection with it to demonstrate privity or connivance.	*McCawley v HMA* (1959) SCCR Supp 3 McC a passenger in stolen car. *Held* thereby privy to its retention and convicted. *McNeil v HMA* 1968 JC 29 McN a passenger in car transporting stolen property and convicted. 'Reset consists of being privy to the retaining of property that has been dishonestly come by.' but compare: *Clark v HMA* 1965 SLT 250 C present at, but not participating in, negotiations for the sale of stolen cigarettes. *Held*, a misdirection that non-reporting of dealings in stolen property could constitute connivance in its retention. Per LJ-C Grant: 'It was a direction that connivance could be inferred from mere inactivity and I do not think it properly can.' *Girdwood v Houston* 1989 SCCR 578 G convicted of reset of number of articles. When police first questioned G, he denied all knowledge of theft. Subsequently made statement that he knew where articles were and knew who had stolen them. Took police to hiding place. *Held* that as reset could be committed by being privy to retention of stolen goods and in light of G's initial denial, sheriff correct in convicting.	Road Traffic Act 1988, s 178(1)(b): driving or allowing oneself to be carried in a motor vehicle taken away without lawful authority.
Dishonestly appropriated Reset was at first restricted to reset of theft, then extended to robbery and now by statute extends also to property appropriated by breach of trust and embezzlement, or by falsehood, fraud and wilful imposition.	*Isabella Cowan* (1845) 2 Broun 398 *Daniel Clark* (1867) 5 Irv 437	Criminal Procedure (Scotland) Act 1995, Sch 3, para 8(2). May be a conviction for reset where the property was obtained by robbery, theft, breach of trust and embezzlement, or by falsehood, fraud and wilful imposition.

COMMENTARY	CASE LAW	STATUTE LAW
		Criminal Law (Consolidation) (Scotland) Act 1995, s 51. Criminal resetting of property shall not be limited to the receiving of property taken by theft or robbery, but shall extend to property appropriated by breach of trust and embezzlement and by falsehood, fraud and wilful imposition.
But the dishonest appropriation must be complete before reset can occur.	*Robert and Agnes Black* 1841 Bell's Notes 46 RB convicted of theft, not reset, because intention to appropriate pocket-book found by AB not formed until she had taken it home to him. RB could not reset property not yet stolen although physically in possession of AB. AB also convicted of theft.	
Reset and theft are mutually exclusive.	*Backhurst v MacNaughton* 1981 SCCR 6 B charged with reset of a number of articles. Gave evidence admitting theft of some of the articles. Convicted of reset of them all. *Held*, on the concession of the Crown, that person admitting to theft of articles cannot be guilty of resetting them. Conviction quashed quoad the articles admittedly stolen.	
Knowing Guilty knowledge is the first of the two constituents of the *mens rea* of reset. If possession is innocent at first, there is no reset until the property is known to have been dis-honestly appropriated. Once this guilty knowledge is known the subject cannot wilfully blind himself to this fact.	*Latta v Herron* (1967) SCCR Supp 18 L, a solicitor, bought two guns at 11 pm at a price about one-third of their true value. The transaction was arranged by a former client of L. In the case stated for appeal, LJ-G Clyde stated 'although I was inclined to believe that when [he] purchased the firearms he was not conscious of the fact that they had been stolen... after a reasonable time for reflection ... he must have come to realise that they had been dishonestly obtained'. Conviction upheld.	
The courts may infer the guilty knowledge of the accused from the circumstances of the case.	*Friel v Docherty* 1990 SCCR 351 F obtaining prima facie valid HGV MOT certificates by means other than standard procedure. Convic-ted on the grounds that he must have known them to be stolen. Appeal. *Held* the sheriff was entitled to find as he did on the facts. *Forbes v HMA* 1994 SCCR 471 Guilty knowledge. Lowry painting found in F's car sandwiched between sheets of cardboard, painting partly visible. *Held* on appeal that given the possession and the awkward account given for the presence of the painting and the cardboard, sufficient for guilty knowledge. See also: *Nisbet v HMA* 1983 SCCR 13 Awkward explanation of acquisition of goods enough when corroborated by statement of the thief. *Davidson v Brown* 1990 SCCR 304 *McKellar v Normand* 1992 SCCR 393 *Murray v O'Brien* 1993 SCCR 90 *Hamilton v Friel* 1994 SCCR 748	
Intending An intention to prevent the owner recovering his property is the second of the two constituents of the *mens rea* of reset. Therefore, if it is absent, there is no reset.	*Cook's Case* 1917, unreported; Macdonald, p 67 C, a law agent, negotiated with a thief to buy stolen property from him. However, since he was doing so on behalf of the owner, who was his client, he was acquitted on a charge of reset.	

COMMENTARY	CASE LAW	STATUTE LAW
If the intention is present there need be no motive of personal profit from the possession of the property dishonestly appropriated.		
Husband A wife cannot be charged with reset for receiving or concealing stolen goods brought in by her husband, with the purpose of protecting him from detection or punishment, unless she made a trade of the crime and has taken part in disposing of the stolen goods (Alison i, 338).	*Smith v Watson* 1982 SCCR 15 Accused was wife of man sentenced and imprisoned for robbery. Received money from the robbery through the letter-box and retained it awaiting husband's release. *Held*, sustaining an appeal by the Crown, that accused should be convicted, and that wife's exemption should be restricted to cases where (a) the property is brought into the matrimonial home by the husband and (b) the wife conceals it to protect her husband from detection. Decision in *Clark v Mone* 1950 SLT (Sh Ct) 69 doubted.	
Doctrine of recent possession: Applies to both theft and reset, permitting an inference of guilt upon the accused to be made if the goods in question are found in his/her possession soon after the theft or reset.	*MacLennan v MacKenzie* 1987 JC 99 No strict definition of the term recent or the required time-frames exist. *Held* 2½ months was too long for theft but not too long for reset.	

References: Hume I, 113; Alison I, 328; Macdonald, 67; Gordon, 683; Gane and Stoddart, 612.

SENTENCING POLICY

Bennett v Tudhope 1987 SCCR 203—B, first offender, convicted of resetting shotgun and of possessing it without a firearms certificate. Sheriff took view that danger of shotguns getting into wrong hands was such that offender should be dealt with severely. Sentenced to three months' imprisonment, upheld on appeal.

Rankin v McGlennan 1990 SCCR 607—Convicted of resetting £200, sentenced to 240 hours' community service. Order breached and three months' detention substituted. Appeal.
Held that appellant could now pay a fine. £300 substituted.

Macleay v HMA 2000 G.W.D. 29-1148: *Held*, that 15 months' imprisonment for M, with one minor analogous conviction in 1978, for obtaining four paintings by fraud, and reset of various items including vehicles, machinery, a quantity of shellfish and a painting, committed over nearly five years, was not excessive, having regard to the nature and timescale of the offences.

ROBBERY

Robbery is **theft achieved** by **personal violence** or **intimidation**.

COMMENTARY	CASE LAW	STATUTE LAW
Theft must be completed.	*Purves v McIntosh* (ark. 1846, 178) Watch later dropped, pulled from victim's pocket, *amotio* effected theft.	Criminal Procedure (Scotland) Act 1995, Sch 3, para 8 provides for alternative verdicts.
	O'Neill v Lyma JC 1934, 88 Handbag taken after owner pushed against wall.	
Achieved by personal violence Violence must precede, or be contemporaneous with theft.	*A. McGinnes* (I Broun 1842, 231) [Violence] committed entirely 'for the purpose of plunder' and not discrete assault.	
	Reid and Barnet (2 Broun 1844, 118) Not robbery to use violence to 'retain' already stolen article.	
	Jas Fegen (2 Swin. 1858, 25) Watch chain grabbed from pocket, pulled again as victim fell.	
	O'Neill v HMA JC 1934, 98 The physical violence does not have to amount to an assault in law. See also: *Morrison v HMA* 2010 HCJAC 16	
	Cromar v HMA SCCR 1987, 635 Handbag pulled from complainer, handle snapped as she tried to hold on to it.	
	Flynn v HMA SCCR 1985, 580 Conviction by jury under deletion of all reference to use of violence *not* robbery, only theft.	
Intimidation Any threat of immediate injury which includes handing over of property.	*Matthias Little* (Alison I, 1830, 231) Threats of instant death, valuable property handed over.	
The victim's will must be completely overborne either by violence or intimidation.	*Harrison v Jessop* 1991 SCCR 329 'There may be robbery without any wounding or beating of the person. ... The law means only to oppose this sort of taking as against the will of the owner to that which happens privately or by surprise ... and understands it therefore to be violence if the thing is taken by means of such behaviour as justly alarm for the personal and instant consequences of resistance or refusal'. (*Hume* i,143)	

SENTENCING POLICY

Davidson and Anor v HMA 1981 SCCR 371. Use of loaded shotgun and bayonet, £4,500. Although sentence reduced from 14 to 11 years 'public interest required a very substantial sentence'.

Graham v HMA 1996 SCCR 105. Two robberies with loaded pistols within 2 hour period. 15 years reduced to 12.

FRAUD

Fraud is the **achievement** by **false pretence** of a **definite practical result**.

COMMENTARY	CASE LAW	STATUTE LAW
Achievement There must be a **causal connection** between false pretence and the practical result.	*Mailler v HMA* (SC(V)) 1914, 184 Cheque dishonoured *after* delivery of goods not fraud. If cheque had been issued to *obtain* goods there would have been an offence.	
False pretence – must be an essential, not collateral matter.	*Tapsell v Prentice* (6 Adam 1910, 354) Misrepresentation by T that she would be buying considerable amount of provisions from shopkeeper who bought from her a rug in excess of its true value. *Not* fraud as misrepresentation not related to provisions.	
By implication.	*Turnbull v Stuart* (Ark. 1847 361) Mixture of grains and oats made up to look like pure oats.	
	James Paton 1858 3 Irv 208. Bulls which were entered into a livestock competition had air pumped under their skin and their horns artificially lengthened in order to make them look better, This was held to amount to an implied and fraudulent representation.	
Explicit	*Turnbull v Stuart* (25R (J) 1898, 28) Claim that house being sold had been owned by people experienced in matters relating to houses.	
	Stuart v MacPherson (JC 1918, 96) Card cheating; pretence by cheaters that they were strangers to each other.	
Non-disclosure	*Buchmann v Normand* SCCR 1984, 929 Application for private hire licence space in form *Quoad* previous convictions left blank.	
As to future conduct	*Richards v HMA* UC 1971, 29 R caused third parties to misrepresent that they wished to buy heritable property for private residential use, truth being that R wanted the property for his own uses.	
Practical result: The recipient of the false pretence must actually be deceived by it bringing about a practical result to constitute a fraud.	*Adcock v Archibald* 1925 SLT 258. A miner deliberately attached his name tag to a bag of coal dug by his colleague. Deceived, his employers recorded him as having dug more coal than he had in fact dug constituting a fraud.	
Almost any practical result of the deception will suffice in constituting a fraud. Thus there is no need to prove an actual gain by the accused.	*William Fraser* 1847 Ark. 280 per Lord Cockburn at pp 312 'the practical result need not be a pecuniary or financial advantage but any deceit that injures and violates the rights of another.'	

OFFENCES AGAINST PROPERTY

MALICIOUS MISCHIEF

Malicious mischief is the **damaging** in part or in whole of **another's property.**

COMMENTARY	CASE LAW	STATUTE LAW
Damaging May be achieved intentionally,	*Forbes v Ross* (1898) 2 Adam 513 An appeal against conviction of having wilfully, maliciously and mischievously broken down a wall. *Held*, that since appellant caused the wall to be destroyed in the knowledge that it was not his property, conviction should be upheld, although it was not clear to whom the wall belonged, the wall was of little value and the appellant claimed the destruction was to vindicate a right of way. But contrast: *Black v Laing* (1879) 4 Couper 276 Conviction quashed where removal of a fence which formed an obstruction to one of the entrances to the accused's property was not considered to warrant crime of malicious mischief, since in the circumstances the removal was justified as the gap was the only access to the garden and that question of rights was one to be determined by a civil court. *Clark v Syme* 1957 JC 1 Farmer shot and killed sheep which strayed from adjoining land under mistaken belief that he was legally entitled to do so. *Held*, on appeal by Crown, that wilful disregard of the property rights of another was sufficient to make the destruction of that property an act of malicious mischief.	
or result from deliberate disregard of another's property rights and therefore cannot be caused accidentally or unwillingly.	*Ward v Robertson* 1938 JC 32 Trespassers crossed an unfenced field of growing grass, on foot. Conviction of causing malicious mischief to the crop of grass quashed on appeal. It is essential that the accused had or should have had knowledge that he was likely to cause damage.	
Damage need not be physical.	*HMA v Wilson* 1983 SCCR 420 W activated emergency stop button of power station generator, causing loss of electricity costing £147,000 to replace. Sheriff held that the indictment of malicious mischief was irrelevant in the absence of an averment of physical damage. Overturned on appeal. *Held* that an element of physical injury is not necessary. Malicious mischief may be constituted by any patrimonial injury. Indictment held relevant. *Bett v Hamilton* 1997 SCCR 621 Appellant convicted of malicious mischief for moving position of bank's security cameras. *Held*, on appeal, malicious mischief requires intent to cause physical damage or patrimonial loss, and what was lost was benefit of security cameras performing proper function. This loss extended the concept of patrimonial too far: since there was no financial loss (because the cost of cameras running would have been incurred anyway), there was no patrimonial loss.	

COMMENTARY	CASE LAW	STATUTE LAW
Another's property A belief that the goods are one's own is also a good defence provided it is not held recklessly. Malicious mischief different from vandalism.	*Black v Allan* 1985 SCCR 11 Accused charged with vandalism contrary to s 78(1) of the Criminal Justice (Scotland) Act 1980: breaking window as result of horseplay. Court of appeal made it plain that this statutory offence differs from common-law crime of malicious mischief.	
		Criminal Law (Consolidation) (Scotland) Act 1995, s 51(1). Any person who without reasonable excuse wilfully or recklessly destroys or damages any property belonging to another shall be guilty of the offence of vandalism, but fire raising is excluded (s 52(2)).
	Opinion of the court: 'The statutory offence is an offence standing in its own language and is committed if the conduct in question resulting in damage to property is wilful or ... reckless.'	*Note:* Summary procedure is mandatory for vandalism, whereas malicious mischief can be taken on indictment.

References: Hume I, 122; Alison I, 448; Gordon, 711.

FIRE RAISING

Fire raising is the **wilful or reckless setting alight** of the **property of another.**

COMMENTARY	CASE LAW	STATUTE LAW
Wilful or reckless: If the fire is not started deliberately the *mens rea*—that it must be started intentionally—will be found if it is started with a high enough degree of recklessness. Recklessness in this context means that the actions of the accused must show a complete disregard for any of the dangers which may have resulted from what they were doing.	*HMA v Geo MacBean* 1847 Ark 262 MacB set fire to house by setting alight some straw and paper in a garret room with a lighted candle. Fire spread through his and neighbours' houses. *Held* that if fire is raised in such a state of reckless excitement, to show that the person raising it does not know or care what may result, the requisite degree is attained.	Criminal Law (Consolidation) (Scotland) Act 1995, s 52(2). It shall not be competent to charge acts which constitute the offence of wilful fire-raising as vandalism under this section.
But carelessness alone will not provide the necessary *mens rea*for culpable and reckless fire raising.	*Carr v HMA* 1994 SCCR 521 C setting fire to church hall into which he had broken. Sheriff directed the jury that if the fire was caused accidentally then the crime could not be wilful fire raising but could be culpable and reckless fire raising. Direction upheld on appeal in this regard but court said that in considering recklessness it was important to focus on whether C's actions showed complete disregard for any dangers which might result from what he was doing. *Thomson v HMA* 1995 SLT 827 Sheriff gave correct direction on recklessness, then mistakenly told jury that it would be reckless if a man lit his pipe and without thinking threw the match over his shoulder and it landed in a field and burned the crops. *Held*, the example was not a good one, but direction that recklessness involved a complete disregard of any potential danger which might result was correct, and appeal refused. Per LJ-C Ross: 'In a case of fire raising it is not the manner of doing an act which would otherwise be lawful which is in issue (as in reckless driving) but whether the accused had the necessary *mens rea* for the commission of the crime.' Dictum of LJ-G Hope in *Carr v HMA* 1994 SCCR 521 applied. *Byrne v HMA* 2000 SCCR 77. Per Lord Coulsfield at 163 'Mere negligence is not enough: the property must have been set on fire due to an act of the accused displaying a reckless disregard as to what the result of his act would be…'	
Setting alight The fire must have taken hold, no matter how minimally,	*John Arthur* (1836) 1 Swin 124 Chemist tried to set shop alight by igniting various chemicals. However, fire was discovered when only a part of the door was alight. *Held* to be sufficient to constitute fire raising, if proved. *Peter Grieve* (1866) 5 Irv 263 Door of the premises found to be charred. Jury question as to whether that implied fire had actually taken hold. Convicted. However, court observed that charring of a door did not necessarily mean that it had been *set* on fire.	

COMMENTARY	CASE LAW	STATUTE LAW
	Alexander Pollock (1869) 1 Couper 257 P set stock and materials alight. However, building itself did not seem to be on fire. Some time after extinction of the fire, smouldering joist discovered. Lord Ardmillan: 'To constitute fire raising, a portion of the fabric must actually have been on fire, through the act of the accused.'	
although it may not have been applied directly or initially to the property alight.	*Margaret Anderson* 1826 Hume I 130 Set fire to furniture in room from which the fire then spread through the house.	
	Janet Hamilton 1806 Hume I 129 H set fire to a cart-house adjoining a dwelling house which was subsequently burned down.	
Property The nature of the property does not now determine whether the fire raising is wilful or reckless, although certain property is protected by statute.	*Angus v HMA* (1905) 4 Adam 640 Conviction of wilful fire raising of a haystack upheld in the circumstances although haystack is not heritable property.	
	Blane v HMA 1991 SCCR 576 Hostel going on fire after the accused set fire to his bedding. Sheriff convicted, sufficient if the premises burnt as a result of the bedding being set on fire. Appeal. *Held* that there could be no transferred intent. Sheriff should have looked to the likely consequences, reckless indifference. Conviction for setting fire to bedding substituted.	
Of another It is not fire raising to set your own property alight but it may constitute the crime of 'fire raising with the intent to defraud insurers.'	*HMA v Paterson* (1890) 2 White 496 *Hannah McAtamney & Others* (1867) 5 Irv 363 McA set alight stock in her shop, intending to claim insurance. In both the above cases it was made clear that the crime was fire raising to defraud insurers.	
	HMA v Bell 1966 SLT (Notes) 61 B charged with setting his hotel alight with the intent to defraud his insurers. Despite Crown's failure to libel alleged intimation by B of claim to insurance company, charge held relevant, but proceedings later withdrawn and B found not guilty.	
Setting fire to moorland or land covered with heath except during specified period is an offence. (Specified period usually 16th April–30th September.)		Hill Farming Act 1946, s 25

References: Hume I, 122; Alison I, 429; Gordon, 719.

SENTENCING POLICY

Donaldson v HMA 1983 SCCR 216—D convicted of seven charges of fire raising. Had a bad record. Life sentence in young offenders' institution imposed. Appeal refused. Sentence not excessive. Indeterminate life sentence different from determinate sentence of preventive detention.

OFFENCES AGAINST THE PERSON

HOMICIDE

Homicide, the killing of another, is murder when the perpetrator **[wickedly] intends to take life** or is **wickedly reckless** as to the consequence of those actions which result in death. Homicide is **culpable homicide** where either the perpetrator intends to kill but there are **mitigating factors** relating to the act or where the perpetrator did not intend to kill but has been **criminally negligent** as to his actions.
Homicide will not be criminal when **casual** or **justifiable.**

COMMENTARY	CASE LAW	STATUTE LAW
Homicide The destruction of a human life other than one's own.	*HMA v Scott* (1892) 3 White 240 Accused strangled child immediately on birth. Evidence that the child breathed. *Held*, could be culpable homicide. Did not matter that child not fully born at the time.	
	Jean McCallum (1858) 3 Irv 187 LJ-C Inglis stating that child must have separate existence from its mother.	
Destruction of foetus not homicide.		Abortion Act 1961 Concealment of Birth (Scotland) Act 1809
	McCluskey v HMA 1989 SLT 175 Charge of causing death by reckless driving. Child in utero born but dying of injuries sustained in utero. *Held* on appeal, charge competent. Following Hume (I, 189) culpable homicide charge might be relevant in such circumstances.	
No time restriction exists between the time of death and the act(s) which caused it: proof of a causal link is what is required.	*Tess v HMA* 1994 SCCR 451 Victim dying 15 months after assault and three months after accused convicted of assault. Accused charged with culpable homicide. High Court upheld repelling of plea in bar of trial, since appellant was being charged with different crime. Observed, case of oppression could be made out if death occurred many years after the trial for assault.	
Premeditation is not necessary,	*HMA v Macdonald* 1867 5 Irv 525	
Nor is the *consent* of the victim a recognised defence.	*HMA v Rutherford* 1947 JC 1. '... Anyone who wilfully kills another person at the latter's request or command is guilty of murder...' per Lord Justice Clerk Cooper at p 6.	
Life must have been destroyed.	*Finlayson v HMA* 1978 SLT (notes) 60. No legal definition of how one determines when life has ended exists. It is instead a question of fact.	
[wickedly] Intends to kill: Murder and culpable homicide both have the same *actus reus* (destruction of life) and are thus only distinguishable by their respective *mens rea.*	*Drury v HMA* 2001 SLT 1013. Altered the Scots Law definition of murder by indicating that a 'wicked' intention was required, at least in cases where self-defence or provocation is at issue. The purpose of this important alteration was in distinguishing defendable murder charges from those which are not.	

COMMENTARY	CASE LAW	STATUTE LAW
Traditionally, Macdonald's classical definition of Homicide only necessitated an 'intention to kill' or a 'wicked recklessness as to whether the victim lives or dies' Macdonald p.89. The modern definition however is now qualified by the insertion of 'wicked' following the case of *Drury v HMA* 2001 SLT 1013.	'...just as the recklessness has to be wicked so also must the intention be wicked. Therefore, perhaps the most obvious way of completing the [classic] definition [of murder] is by saying that murder is constituted by any wilful act causing the destruction of life, by which the perpetrator either wickedly intends to kill or displays wicked recklessness as to whether the victim lives or dies...' (per Lord Justice-General Rodger at p 1016).	
Wickedly reckless: Constitutes a separate and distinct *mens rea* for murder as determined in *Cawthorne v HMA* 1968 JC 32.	*Cawthorne v HMA* 1968 JC 32. Attempted murder charge, C firing shots into a room containing four people. Per LJ-G Clyde: 'The *mens rea* which is essential to the establishment of such a common law crime may be established by satisfactory evidence of a deliberate intention to kill *or* by satisfactory evidence of such wicked recklessness as to imply a disposition depraved enough to be regardless of the con-sequences.'	
Intention to cause personal injury is a prerequisite of 'wicked recklessness'.	*HMA* v *Purcell* 2008 SLT 44. The Crown sought to charge Purcell with murder after he knocked down and killed a 10 year-old boy while speeding down the wrong side of the road. The court held that wicked recklessness necessitated an utter indifference to fatal consequences as well as an intention to cause personal injury. Lacking such an intention a charge of culpable homicide was appropriate. *Petto* v *HMA* 2011 HCJAC 80. In a bid to get rid of a dead body, Petto doused a first floor tenement building in petrol before setting it alight in which the resident of an adjoining flat died during the blaze. Petto originally pleaded guilty to the murder but subsequently appealed the decision on the basis that he did not intend to cause personal injury to the deceased as required by *Purcell*. *Held* on appeal '...Where a person starts a major fire on the ground floor of such a building, the inevitable conclusion is, in my view, that he does so in the certain knowledge that those who are in the building, and especially those in the upper floors, will be at a grave risk of being killed or seriously injured in consequence of the fire. While there may be no desiderative element in the mind of such a person, his appreciation of the virtual certainty that such a risk will eventuate and his deliberate acceptance of it should, in my opinion, be rightly equiparated with an intention that such consequences should occur.' per Lord Gill at para 13. See also: *Brennan v HMA* 1977 JC 38 Full bench. B killing father while in a state of self-induced intoxication. Murder conviction upheld. Intention to do serious injury sufficient for *mens rea*. *Halliday v HMA* 1998 SCCR 509 Murder. Deceased kicked by brothers, who left and returned to stamp on his head. They put him in recovery position and went home. They later returned and called ambulance. Convicted of murder. *Held*, on appeal, evidence of what happened once attack over could cast light on attitude of appellants during attack. They were wickedly indifferent to consequences of attack (by failing to call ambulance immediately after attack). Trial judge correct not to direct jury to leave these matters out of account. Appeal refused.	

COMMENTARY	CASE LAW	STATUTE LAW
Wicked recklessness *may* be shown by the use of weapons.	*HMA v McGuinness* 1937 JC 37 Victim killed by knife. *Held* 'People who use knives and pokers and hatchets against a fellow citizen are not entitled to say "we did not mean to kill" if death results. If people resort to the use of deadly weapons of this kind, they are guilty of murder, whether or not they intended to kill.' per Lord Justice Clerk Aitchison at p 41. Compare with: *Broadley v HMA* 1991 SLT 218. 'We would, however, stress that every case depends upon its own facts…in many cases where an accused has used a lethal weapon which has caused fatal injuries it will be for the jury to determine whether the proper verdict is one of murder or culpable homicide.' per Lord Justice Clerk Ross at pp 221–222.	
Homicide during the course of robbery.	*Miller and Denovan v HMA* (7 December 1960, unreported) CA Blow to the head of victim with block of wood during robbery causing death. *Held*, no room for culpable homicide. Homicide in course of robbery due to serious and reckless violence is murder.	
Culpable Homicide: Covers all unlawful killings in which the *mens rea* for homicide is absent, or where it is present but recognised mitigating factors can be established. Culpable Homicide can be further classified into three categories:	*Drury v HMA* 2001 SLT 1013. 'The crime of culpable homicide covers the killing of human beings in all circumstances, short of murder, where the criminal law attaches a relevant measure of blame to the person who kills.' at p 1017, para 13, per Lord Justice-General Rodger.	
(1) Voluntary Culpable Homicide – murder reduced to culpable homicide through the successful operation of a defence such as diminished responsibility or provocation.	*HMA v Hill* 1941 JC 59. Hill returned home from military duty in England to discover his wife with another man with whom she admitted having sexual relations with. Immediately after hearing such, Hill shot both his wife and her lover dead using his service revolver. *Held*, the discovery of sexual infidelity was enough to provoke and therefore reduce the charge from murder to that of (voluntary) culpable homicide. Provocation: See Special defences (Self-defence) p 89.	
(2) Involuntary Unlawful Culpable Homicide – arises where the accused causes someone's death during the commission of a crime.	*Mathieson v HMA* 1981 SCCR 196 Culpable homicide by culpable and reckless fireraising. *Held* that if the act causing death was unlawful, the appropriate conviction would be involuntary unlawful culpable homicide. See also: *Bird v HMA* 1952 JC 23 Accused assaulted a woman with a diseased heart who subsequently died from the emotional shock. *Held*, that death resulting from any assault no matter how minor would result in a conviction of culpable homicide. *Miller and Denovan v HMA* (7 December 1960, unreported) CA.	

COMMENTARY	CASE LAW	STATUTE LAW
(3) Involuntary Lawful Culpable Homicide – arises where the accused causes someone's death during the commission of a lawful act which has been undertaken recklessly.	*Paton v HMA* 1936 JC 19 Charge of culpable homicide by reckless driving. *Held* that a conviction of culpable homicide founded upon criminal negligence must amount to a 'gross, or wicked, or criminal negligence, something amounting or analogous to a criminal indifference to consequences' Per Lord Justice-Clerk Aitchison at p 23.	
	Sutherland v HMA (No 1) 1994 SCCR 80 A and B art and part in setting fire to A's house with intent to defraud insurers. B died in fire. *Held*, B's consent to fire raising no defence to charge of culpable homicide, and conviction upheld on appeal. See also:	
	Transco plc v *HMA* 2004 JC 29. Clarified the *Paton* model of recklessness detailed above by stating that it is *both* the behaviour and the state of mind of the accused which are to be assessed in determining whether or not their behaviour was reckless, introducing a subjective element to what was traditionally an objective test.	
Casual	*HMA v Rutherford* 1947 JC 1 Per LJ-C Cooper quoting with approval from Alison I, 139: 'It is casual homicide where a person kills unintentionally, when lawfully employed and neither meaning harm to any one nor having failed in the due degree of care and circumspection for preventing mischief to his neighbour.'	
Justifiable '... committed in the necessary prosecution of that which the killer is bound or hath a right to do.' Hume I, 195.		
Armed forces.	*HMA v Sheppard* 1941 JC 67 Soldier shooting a prisoner he was escorting who tried to escape. *Held* that if soldier acting in line of duty jury should acquit.	

References: Hume I, 179; Alison I, 1; Macdonald, 87; Gordon, 727; Gane, 479; Cubie, 168.

SENTENCING POLICY

LT v HMA 1990 SCCR 540—Mother setting fire to home killing two children. Mentally disturbed but no diminished responsibility. Ten years' imprisonment upheld on appeal. No need for life sentence: sentence reflecting public outrage and the need for treatment of the accused.

RJK v HMA 1991 SCCR 703—Twelve year-old convicted of culpable homicide of three year-old. Sentenced to be detained 'without limit of time'.
Held on appeal that it was competent under s 206 of the Criminal Procedure (Scotland) Act 1975 and appropriate here where the child needed psychiatric assessment over several years.

Casey v HMA 1993 SCCR 453—Murder in the course of a violent robbery. Trial judge under s 205A of the 1975 Act ordering minimum recommended sentence of 20 years. Appeal.
Held that recommendations may be made where crime particularly brutal or where accused a danger to the public. No recommendations of less than 12 years and normally will be 15 to 30 years. 15 years appropriate here.

Beddie v HMA 1993 SCCR 970—Culpable homicide. B killing victim by driving his car at him causing him to fall on the bonnet then braking so he fell on the road and fractured his skull. Four years' imprisonment. Appeal.
Held that the culpability was slight: six months substituted.

Baillie v HMA 1993 SCCR 1084—Culpable homicide. 22 year-old assaulting and killing 20 month-old child of cohabitee. Sentenced to life imprisonment to protect the public. Appeal.
Held that there was no evidence that public needed such protection; 15 years substituted.

McLaren v HMA 1994 SCCR 855—Attempted murder. Accessory sentenced to same period, 15 years, as person who fired gun. Upheld on appeal.

Sutherland v HMA (No 2) 1994 SCCR 350—Culpable homicide and setting fire with intent to defraud insurers.
Held, five years not excessive, since trial judge rightly modified sentence because appellant had no intention of killing friend and may himself have been killed in explosion.

McGuire v HMA 1995 SCCR 776—Appellant convicted of murder of victim he twice threw out of bedroom window of flat and later abandoned on waste ground in wheelie bin. Recommendation of 15 years.
Held, trial judge had discretion to make recommendations, but the effect in this case was to tie the hands of the parole board and the Secretary of State to a degree not justified by circumstances, and recommendations set aside.

Murphy v HMA 1995 SCCR 55—Murder by shooting. Accused had previous convictions for firearm offences.
Held, judge entitled in exercise of discretion to make recommendation of 15 years.

Houston v HMA 1996 SCCR 851—Culpable homicide. Fifteen-year sentence for placing objects on line derailing train, causing death of two persons.
Held, if punishment sole consideration there might have been room for leniency but not where court has duty to protect public and deter, and appeal refused.

Strathearn v HMA 1996 SCCR 100—Culpable homicide on grounds of diminished responsibility: appellant traumatised after deceased committed sexual offence against his son for which he received probation. Crown had deleted allegation of previous malice of appellant to deceased.
Held, judge should not have regard to deleted allegation and eight years excessive and seven years' imprisonment substituted.

Walker v HMA 1996 SCCR 818—Appellant convicted of culpable homicide of cohabitee who had abused her for two years. She stabbed deceased then went to kitchen and returned later with larger knife and killed deceased.
Held, considerable leniency already shown by reduction of charge to culpable homicide and trial judge entitled to strike balance with six-year sentence.

HMA v Gordon 1996 SCCR 274—Culpable homicide. Death caused by one blow at end of drunken brawl started by deceased.
Held, three years not unduly lenient in circumstances.

HMA v McC 1996 SCCR 842—15 and 16year-old males convicted of culpable homicide of 58year-old man after attack involving multiple punching and kicking.
Held, 18 months unduly lenient and trial judge failed, inter alia, to recognise public condemnation, and sentences of six years' detention imposed.

HMA v Spiers 1997 SCCR 479—Culpable homicide. Death caused by stabbing with broken bottle under provocation.
Held, except in exceptional circumstances a custodial sentence was only appropriate disposal and previous conviction highly relevant, and four years' imprisonment imposed.

Burns v HMA 1998 SCCR 281—Appellant pleaded guilty to culpable homicide. Blow delivered with little force and only landed on right ear because deceased, who was very drunk, moved away.
Held, result not in contemplation of anyone who witnessed blow, and given appellant's remorse and fact charge hanging over him for eight months, two years excessive and 240 hours' community service substituted.

HMA v Wheldon 1998 SCCR 710—Culpable homicide by stamping on deceased's head.
Held, four years' detention not unduly lenient. Trial judge had not erred on basis of medical evidence (minimum force), and attack was not pre-meditated (forming part of pattern of casual violence).

Davies v HMA 2000 G.W.D. 29-1134—The accused appealed against his sentence of three years' imprisonment for culpable homicide of the deceased, aged 71 and a local drunk who had been abusing the accused. The accused kicked the deceased in the stomach, resulting in his death 24 hours later.
Held, although a custodial sentence was appropriate, the trial judge had fettered his discretion by stating that he viewed three years as the lowest custodial sentence for culpable homicide. The accused was a first offender with an exemplary army and good work record, and had shown remorse and considered at low risk of reoffending. A sentence of 18 months was therefore substituted.

HMA v Jackson 2008 S.L.T. 709—Jackson was sentenced to 13 years' imprisonment after pleading guilty to a charge of culpable homicide after causing the death of a child and seriously injuring her mother, as a result of driving recklessly in a defective motor vehicle. The sentencing judge had selected a period of seven years to reflect the need to provide public protection, and then deducted that period from a starting point of 16 years before applying a discount of one third. On appeal it was held that his approach to the issue of discount was questionable, and the appropriate method was to apply a discount of 25 per cent to the whole figure of 16 years to reflect public protection. A sentence of 12 years was therefore substituted, *Weir (Robert) v HM Advocate* 2006 S.L.T. 353 being followed.

HMA v Simpson 2009 HCJAC 41—Simpson aged 16; pleaded guilty to culpable homicide after punching and kicking the deceased and repeatedly stamping on his head. A sentence of four years' detention, discounted from six years was imposed but was held to be unduly lenient as the trial judge placed insufficient weight on the level and nature of violence used.

Stewart v HMA and *Noble v HMA* 2012 HCJAC 103—Sentences of 10 years' imprisonment and eight years' detention imposed upon an adult and a boy aged 15 at the time of the offence following pleas of guilty to culpable homicide were excessive. Insufficient weight was placed upon the deceased's own conduct, the absence of the use of weapons, the age and developing maturity of the boy and the fact that the violence used could not have been anticipated to result in death were significant mitigatory elements.

ASSAULT

A **deliberate attack** on the person of another which may be **aggravated.** There may be **defences.**

COMMENTARY	CASE LAW	STATUTE LAW
Deliberate The *mens rea* of assault is the evil intention to injure. It is not a crime which can be committed through recklessness.	*David Keay* (1837) 1 Swin 543 K whipped and alarmed a pony which bolted and threw its rider. Per Lord Moncreiff: 'I cannot see what purpose the panel could have except to do him a direct injury or to put him in alarm ... if a person throws a stone out of a window into the street [causing injury] done without intention to hurt anybody he could not be charged with assault.' *John Roy* (1839) Bell's Notes 88 R maliciously broke glass which hit the eye of a girl whom he did not know to be in the vicinity. Acquitted of assault. *HMA v Phipps* (1905) 4 Adam 616 P, to frighten off salmon poachers, fired a sporting gun in their direction. Some of the shot lodged in the eye of one of them. Accused maintained this was accidental. Per Lord Ardwall: 'Evil intent is the essence of the charge.' Acquitted. *Note:* But could be convicted of reckless conduct. But see: *Connor v Jessop* 1988 SCCR 624 C charged with assaulting S by throwing tumbler at her. Tumbler thrown at someone with whom C fighting earlier, but had missed and hit S. C convicted. *Held* on appeal that circumstances were such that what happened was likely to occur as result of what appellant did and appeal refused. *Roberts v Hamilton* 1989 SCCR 240 R charged with assaulting C by striking him with a stick. C was attempting to separate two other men who were fighting, one of whom R had intended to strike. R convicted of assault and appealed on ground that she lacked the necessary mens rea to assault C. *Held* that where A intends to assault B and strikes C instead he is guilty of assaulting C; and appeal refused. *Lord Advocate's Reference (No 2 of 1992)* 1992 SCCR 960 Accused entering shop with imitation gun, telling shopkeeper to empty the till, then saying 'I'm only kidding'. Acquitted. *Held* that evil intention is the essence of assault which cannot be committed recklessly. Accused was acting deliberately with necessary intent, motive irrelevant. See also: *Quinn v Lees* 1994 SCCR 159. Dog owner was convicted of assault after setting his dog on a group of boys. *Gilmour v McGlennan* 1993 SCCR 837	
Attack Attack must be physical in character but need not result in physical injury.	*Stewart v PF Forfarshire* (1829) 2 SJ 32 S aimed a blow at someone but missed. Convicted.	

COMMENTARY	CASE LAW	STATUTE LAW
	Ewing v Earl of Mar (1851) 14 D 314 Accused rode horse at victim to alarm him. – Convicted.	
	Kay v Allan (1978) SCCR Supp 188 K set dog on two young boys in garden. Assault constituted by establishing intention to use dog to frighten person. Fact that dog caused injury is aggravation of that assault.	
Uttering threats is a separate crime.	*James Miller* (1862) 4 Irv 238 Per LJ-C Inglis: 'The use of threats is in certain well-known cases a crime in the eye of the law of Scotland.' See also: *Atkinson v HMA* 1987 SCCR 534 Atkinson and a co-accused robbed a petrol station where the co-accused held a knife to the cashier's neck whilst threatening him. Both men were found guilty of assault which 'may be constituted by threatening gestures sufficient to produce alarm' per LJ-C Ross at 535.	
The attack need not be direct *qui facit per alium facit per se*.	*David Keay* (1837) 1 Swin 543 *Quinn v Lees* 1994 SCCR 159	
Injury to the victim is unnecessary (Gordon, p 815).	*HMA v Jane Smith or Thom* (1876) 3 Couper 332	
Aggravated An assault may be aggravated by various factors, eg, by the nature of the injury caused.	*Kay v Allan* (1978) SCCR Supp 188	Criminal Procedure (Scotland) Act 1995, Sch 3 para 9(3) allows the Crown to obtain a conviction for assault if they are unable to provide evidence of the aggravating circumstances beyond reasonable doubt: 'Where any crime is charged in an indictment as having been committed ... with particular circumstances of aggravation it shall be lawful to convict of the crime without such ... aggravation.'
or by the identity of the person assaulted, eg officers of the law in the execution of their duty,	*Monk v Strathern* 1921 JC 4 M seriously injured a police constable returning home who prompted M and others to go home at a late hour of the night. The constable was in uniform. Conviction quashed on appeal on grounds that constable had left beat and was no longer on duty, although still in uniform. Accordingly, he was not assaulted in the execution of his duty.	Police (Scotland) Act 1967, s 41 See also: Criminal Procedure (Scotland) Act 1995, Sch 3, para 14. If the evidence demonstrates that the police officer was not in the execution of his duty there can be a conviction for assault at common law.
	Smith v Hawkes (1980) SCCR Supp 261 A police officer who has reasonable grounds for making proper inquiries is acting in the execution of his duty. *Annan v Tait* 1981 SCCR 326 Knowledge of fact that victim is a police officer is essential to the statutory charge.	

COMMENTARY	CASE LAW	STATUTE LAW
	Stocks v Hamilton 1990 SCCR 190 Assault on constable when accused attempting to leave a room in police station. *Held* on appeal that accused unlawfully detained, constable not in the exercise of his lawful duty so statutory charge not available.	
and by use of weapons,	*HMA v Fitchie* (1856) 2 Irv 485 By throwing acid on victim.	
	HMA v Morison (1842) 1 Broun 394 Assault, especially when committed by presenting a loaded firearm.	
although merely presenting a weapon at someone may or may not be an assault,	*Mackenzie v HMA* 1982 SCCR 499 Accused presented a knife onto which victim impaled himself in course of a scuffle. *Held* that the trial judge had misdirected the jury in withdrawing the defence of accident and verdict set aside but Crown given leave to raise fresh indictment. Per LJ-C Wheatley: 'I am not prepared to say that in every situation, irrespective of the facts, where a person presents a weapon at another with the intention of frightening him off from further violence, an assault is committed.'	
by circumstances of indecency,	*Sweeney v X* 1982 SCCR 509 Intercourse with drunken woman incapable of consent held to be an indecent assault.	
by intention, eg assault with intent to ravish,	*John Hosie* 1826 Alison I 186 Pursued woman into a pond where she had run to avoid his advances: assault with intent to ravish.	
	Robertson v HMA 1998 SCCR 390 Appellant was charged with attempted rape and convicted of assault with intent to ravish. *Held*, in absence of compelling reasons, court would not extend rule that assault with intent to ravish not competent on charge of rape to cases of attempted rape. Appeal refused.	
by the nature or seriousness of the injury caused.	*HMA v Jane Smith or Thom* (1876) 3 Couper 332 Assault to the danger of life. Charged with throwing a child out of a railway train. Although child uninjured, held relevant to libel that the assault had been to danger of life.	
	Kerr v HMA 1986 SCCR 91 K convicted of assault by stabbing to severe injury and the danger of life. Medical evidence that complainer's life had not in fact been endangered. K appealed on that ground against the retention of the aggravation of danger to life in the verdict. *Held*, following *HMA v Jane Smith or Thom* (1876) 3 Couper 332, that jury entitled to convict where the inference of danger to life had been drawn, even if the complainer's life was not in fact at risk.	
or by racial aggravation.	*Brown v HMA* 2000 SCCR 736. Accused seriously assaulted the victim in a takeaway restaurant. *Held*, attack was racially aggravated due to the racial abuse shouted before during and after the assault.	Section 50A of the Criminal Law (Consolidation) (Scotland) Act 1995 '(2) For the purposes of this section a course of conduct or an action is racially aggravated if—

COMMENTARY	CASE LAW	STATUTE LAW
		(a) immediately before, during or immediately after carrying out the course of conduct or action the offender evinces towards the person affected malice and ill-will based on that person's membership (or presumed membership) of a racial group; or (b) the course of conduct or action is motivated (wholly or partly) by malice and ill-will towards members of a racial group based on their membership of that group.'
Defences Generally where there is evil intent to injure, consent is not a defence to assault.	*Smart v HMA* 1975 SLT 65 Victim accepted challenge to a 'square go'. *Held* that state of mind of victim irrelevant and that consent was not a defence where there was an evil intent to inflict injury. Opinion of the court: 'It is in the public interest that it should be decided and made known that consent to a "square go" is *not* a defence to a charge of assault based on that agreed combat.'	
	C v HMA 1987 SCCR 104 C aged 14 charged with indecently assaulting girl aged 11. His defence was that she had consented, or at least that he believed she had so consented. *Held* that as an 11 year-old girl incapable in law of giving consent, C's state of mind as to conduct irrelevant.	
A physical attack may not be assault where it is so justified as to be protected by statute,	*Skinner v Robertson* 1980 SLT (Sh Ct) 43 Nurse in mental hospital charged with assaulting certain mentally handicapped children by throwing water over them, striking them on the face and head with his knuckles. *Held* that use of force reasonably required to control the children and in circumstances protected by s 107(1) of Mental Health (Scotland) Act 1960.	Mental Health (Scotland) Act 1960, s 107(1), now Mental Health (Scotland) Act 1984, s 122(1)
	Compare: *Norman v Smith* 1983 SCCR 100 Nurse at a mental hospital held to have exceeded the limits of reasonable restraint in relation to a patient.	
or where it constitutes *reasonable* chastisement,	*Stewart v Thain* 1981 SLT (Notes) 2 Headmaster held *not* to have exceeded the limits of proper chastisement of a 'difficult and fractious' pupil.	Standards in Scotland's Schools etc Act 2000, s 16: removes the right of teachers to chastise children.
	Peebles v McPhail 1989 SCCR 410 P charged with assaulting her two-year-old son by slapping him on the face. Child having a temper tantrum and P became angry. The force of the slap knocked him off balance and left red mark on face. *Held* that to slap child aged two on face, knocking him over, is an act as remote from reasonable chastisement as one could imagine and conviction upheld.	
	G v Templeton 1998 SCLR 180. 'the relevant issue is not the state of mind of the parent, but whether the punishment, viewed objectively, exceeded what was reasonable.' per Sheriff Principal Risk at p 184	Section 51 of the Criminal Justice (Scotland) Act 2003: now restricts and controls the physical punishment which a parent – or those with parental rights – may carry out on their child. In determining whether the chastisement of a child is justified, the court must have regard to the: nature, frequency, effect, age and personal characteristics of the child.

COMMENTARY	CASE LAW	STATUTE LAW
or carried out in *self-defence*,	See Special defences, p 89.	
or in exercise of citizen's right of arrest.	*Codona v Cardle* 1989 SCCR 287 Force used must not be excessive, and arrest by a private citizen only justifiable where the citizen has witnessed the crime or has 'information equivalent to personal observation'. *Bryans v Guild* 1989 SCCR 569 B chased group of youths who had been throwing things at his house. B mistakenly took hold of a youth who had not been part of the group and twisted his arm up his back, bruising his arm. B convicted of assault and admonished. On appeal *held* (1) B had not witnessed offence committed by complainer and had no right of citizen's arrest but (2) sentence quashed and absolute discharge substituted.	
Note: Recklessness. Culpable, reckless acts which may or do cause injury to others may incur criminal liability.	*RHW v HMA* 1982 SCCR 152 W charged with causing culpable and reckless injury by dropping a bottle from a fifteenth-floor flat. *Held* (1) mens rea required was total indifference to and disregard for public safety, and (2) appellant had shown recklessness so depraved as to be regardless of consequences. *MacPhail v Clark* 1982 SCCR 395 (Sh Ct) Culpably and recklessly endangering lieges. Farmer set fire to straw in field. Fire spread to verge of road. Smoke obscured visibility on road and collision resulted. *Held* that to allow the fire to spread demonstrated reckless indifference to the consequences for the public and road users. Convicted. *Khaliq v HMA* 1983 SCCR 483 Shopkeepers charged that they did culpably, recklessly and wilfully supply children with solvents in the knowledge of the intended use, that use being injurious to health and dangerous to lives. Convicted. On appeal, sentence reduced (see *Khaliq v HMA* 1984 SCCR 212). See also: *Normand v Morrison* 1993 SCCR 207 (Sh Ct) Accused charged with culpably and recklessly denying there was an unprotected needle in her handbag, permitting police officer to place his hand in the bag, exposing him to risk of infection. Plea to relevancy repelled. Accused has total disregard for health and safety of the officer. *Donaldson v Normand* 1997 SCCR 351 Culpably and recklessly endangering lieges. Accused failed to tell police of unguarded needle in sock prior to search, having forgotten it was there as a result of taking drugs. Conviction upheld, since self-induced intoxication was no defence to a charge involving criminal recklessness. *Brennan v HMA* 1977 JC 38 followed. *HMA v Harris* 1993 SCCR 559 Doorman pushing girl down stairs onto a road where she was struck by a car. Charged with assault or alternatively with culpably and recklessly causing injury. Plea to relevancy. *Held* on appeal (five-judge bench) that conduct can be criminally reckless either where there is danger to the lieges or reckless conduct causing actual injury. To be distinguished from assault which must be deliberate and cannot be committed recklessly.	

References: Macdonald, 115; Alison I, 175; Gordon, 815; Gane and Stoddart, 383.

SENTENCING POLICY

Brown v Normand 1988 SCCR 229—Assault resulting in permanent disfigurement. B sentenced to 240 hours of community service and ordered to pay £650 compensation. Appealed, submitting sentence excessive in light of fact that he was first offender and conduct of complainer. Appeal allowed: community service reduced to 100 hours, and as complainer's conduct would have prevented him from recovering compensation from CICB, compensation order quashed.

Stirling v Stewart 1988 SCCR 619—Appellants (aged 16) pleaded guilty to assaulting lone US serviceman at Dunoon pier. Sheriff imposed sentence of 30 days' detention as short, sharp shock and as deterrent to the frequency of such attacks.
Held that appeal court could not interfere with sheriff's sentence.

Mays v Brown 1988 SCCR 549—M convicted of assaulting water bailiff in course of his duty by throwing lamp at him. Fined £250. On appeal against sentence fine increased to £500.

Dick v Jessop 1989 SCCR 258—D convicted of assault by kicking A on head. D, aged 25, in good employment, had no previous custodial sentences and no previous convictions for crimes of violence. Sheriff imposed a two months' custodial sentence. On appeal *held* that although the assault was serious, careful weight should be given to the fact that D would lose job if imprisoned; and appeal allowed with hesitation and fine of £500 substituted.

McCardle v Douglas 1989 SCCR 262—Similar facts to *Dick v Jessop* 1989 SCCR 258. McC was 17 years old. Sentence of 30 days' detention quashed, compensation order of £200 substituted.

Ferguson v Lowe 1989 SCCR 281—F (aged 17, in employment, no previous convictions, but convicted of minor assault and two breaches of peace after offence in question) convicted of assaulting bus driver by knocking him down and repeatedly punching and kicking him. Sheriff sentenced to 60 days' detention. On appeal *held* that sheriff had exercised discretion properly. Appeal refused.

Pearson v HMA 1990 SCCR 125—P, a first offender, pleaded guilty to three assaults on his wife, the first two involving only punching and kicking. The third was an assault with knife to injury and permanent disfigurement. Fined on first two charges and sentenced to 15 months' imprisonment on third charge.
Held that as it was a domestic issue, parties were now divorced, assault out of character and P a first offender, appropriate disposal was probation for 18 months in place of imprisonment.

Murchie v McGlennan 1990 SCCR 533—Assault with cricket bat and meat tenderiser. Victim alleged to have used lewd practices towards appellant's children. Three years' imprisonment on the basis that court could not tolerate people taking law into their own hands.

Galloway v Mackenzie 1991 SCCR 548—Careers officer admonished on minor assault on youth scaring his children. Job exempt from Rehabilitation of Offenders Act 1974, admonition a conviction. On appeal *held* that an absolute discharge would be more appropriate.

Leslie v HMA 1992 SCCR 880—Punching glass into the face of victim to his severe injury. Eighteen months' imprisonment. Appeal. *Held* that custody appropriate but given accused's good background, no material previous convictions and six months served prior to appeal that sentence quashed. 240 hours' community service and £1,500 compensation order substituted.

McKay v HMA 1992 SCCR 584—Striking victim with glass to severe injury. Fifteen months' imprisonment *held* on appeal to be severe but not excessive. Alternatives looked to but not appropriate.

Modiak v HMA 1992 SCCR 572—Acid attack on wife to her permanent severe injury and loss of sight. Trial judge said it was hard to think of a more cowardly, wicked and premeditated crime. On appeal, no difficulty in upholding 20 years' imprisonment, devastating injuries.

Garrett v HMA 1993 SCCR 1044—G striking solicitor on face in the cells. 12 months' detention upheld on appeal. Officers of court must be able to carry out their duties free from violence at hands of clients.

Andrews v HMA 1994 SCCR 191—Indecent assault on 13 year-old boy by 27-year-old intellectually impaired stepbrother. On appeal *held*, custodial sentence inevitable, serious assault by person in position of trust but sentence too long. Two years' imprisonment reduced to nine months.

McGowan v HMA 1994 SCCR 217—M assaulting 63 year-old shopkeeper, threatening her with a needle and AIDS, pushing her to ground, breaking her hip. Seven years' imprisonment upheld on appeal. Serious injury and public anxiety about such matters.

HMA v Heron 1998 SCCR 449—Accused pleaded guilty to assault of estranged wife with knife to her severe injury. Psychiatric reports said custody less likely to reduce risk to complainer than statutory supervision. Sentence of three years' probation order with condition respondent did not approach complainer during that period.
On appeal *held*, sentence not unduly lenient.

HMA v O'Donnell 1995 SCCR 745—Assault to severe injury and danger of life by repeated punching and kicking and stamping on head.
Held, on appeal, trial judge took too narrow a view of aggravation and on basis of film evidence the whole attack constituted danger to life. Four years unduly lenient and seven years substituted.

Henderson v Carmichael 1995 SCCR 126—60 day sentence for an assault to severe injury which took place in a rugby match where appellant headbutted opponent, fracturing his nose.
Held on appeal, sentence not excessive.

Ferguson v Normand 1995 SCCR 770—Assault by professional footballer on another player during match.
Held, three months not excessive, since appellant on probation at time and was a public figure and assault in public before large number of spectators.

Sim v Lockhart 1994 SCCR 243—Criminal Justice (Scotland) Act 1975, s 290. Six months for second or subsequent offence inferring personal violence.
Held, sheriff wrong to take account of earlier conviction which postdated the current offence, and three months substituted.

Turner v Scott 1995 SCCR 516—Indecent assault by police officer against 20 year-old nieces.
Held, three months excessive given appellant's loss of employment, and 150 hours' community service substituted.

McNamee v HMA 1996 SCCR 423—19 year-old appellant pleaded guilty to assault to severe injury and permanent disfigurement. Struck complainer on face with tumbler. Only explanation was that he was affected by mother's death two months earlier. He was employed as apprentice and looked after siblings.
Held, in circumstances 12 months' detention quashed, and 240 hours' community service and £750 compensation substituted.

HMA v Jamieson 1996 SCCR 836—Assault to severe injury and danger of life. Unprovoked attack with hammer causing depressed fracture of skull.
Held, £3,000 compensation order and 240 hours' community service unduly lenient, but since £2,200 already paid the appropriate course was to refuse the appeal. Observed, not appropriate for complainer to be asked to consider whether he should return the money so that the respondent might receive a more severe sentence.

HMA v McColl 1996 SCCR 523—Respondent pleaded guilty to assault to severe injury and permanent impairment and disfigurement. Trial judge sentenced co-accused to five years, but deferred sentence on respondent for six months on condition he should attend clinic for medical treatment.
Held, respondent could attend outside clinic while detained, and sentence of three years' detention substituted.

Young v Hamilton 1996 SCCR 66—First offender aged 16 convicted of assault to injury sentenced to 60 days' detention. Upheld on appeal, given gravity of offence.

Marr v HMA 1996 SCCR 696—Indecent assault by taxi driver on passenger. Six months' imprisonment not held to be excessive.

HMA v Fallon 1996 SCCR 80—Indecent assault on stranger in street at night. Trial judge deferred sentence for six months with a view to dealing with the case by some form of community-based disposal.
Held, unduly lenient and nine months' imprisonment imposed.

Observed, normally longer sentence appropriate for such offence but for delay in bringing case and appellant's good behaviour.

HMA v Donaldson 1997 SCCR 738—Assault with attempt to rape an elderly woman by first offender under the influence of alcohol and suffering from stress.
On appeal, *held* two years' imprisonment not unduly lenient.

Hewitt v Vannet 1997 SCCR 530—Assault on hospital staff. First offender sentenced to 60 days' detention.
On appeal, *held* trial judge's approach was wrong. Community service does not indicate the offence is less serious than if a custodial sentence had been imposed. Sentence quashed and community service imposed.

Robertson v HMA 1997 SCCR 534—Assault and abduction of seven year-old girl with intent to commit sexual assault and to danger of her life. Accused described as danger to public.
Held, on appeal, life sentence with recommendation of minimum period of eight years not excessive, as appellant should be detained until doctors were satisfied he no longer presented a risk to young children and only appropriate that an indeterminate sentence be imposed.

HMA v Smith 1998 SCCR 637—Assault to danger of life and robbery of 83 year-old woman in home. Experts said non--custodial sentence to treat post traumatic stress disorder (from seeing friend commit suicide).
Held, not unduly lenient.

RAPE

Sexual Offences (Scotland) Act 2009:
Section 1 Rape:

(1) If a person ('A'), with A's penis—

(a) without another person ('B') **consenting**, and

(b) without any reasonable belief that B consents,

penetrates to any extent, either intending to do so or reckless as to whether there is penetration, the vagina, anus or mouth of B then A commits an offence, to be known as the offence of rape.

COMMENTARY	CASE LAW	STATUTE LAW
The Bill for this Act was passed by the Scottish Parliament on 10 June 2009, received Royal Assent on the 14 July 2009 and came into force on 1 December 2010. The Act codifies the law on sexual offences and abolishes the common law rules on: rape, clandestine injury to women, lewd indecent or libidinous behaviour and sodomy. All acts committed prior to the legislation's commencement however will still be prosecuted under the pre-existing common law.		Sexual Offences (Scotland) Act 2009, s 52(a): For all purposes not relating to offences committed before the coming into force of this section— (a) the common law offences of— (i) rape, (ii) clandestine injury to women, (iii) lewd, indecent or libidinous practice or behaviour, and (iv) sodomy, are abolished
Actus Reus= Penile penetration to any extent of the victim's vagina, mouth or anus without their consent. The accused therefore must be male; either by birth or through surgical reconstruction but the victim can either be male or female.		Sexual Offences (Scotland) Act 2009, s 1(4): In this Act— 'penis' includes a surgically constructed penis if it forms part of A, having been created in the course of surgical treatment, and 'vagina' includes— (a) the vulva, and (b) a surgically constructed vagina (together with any surgically constructed vulva), if it forms part of B,
Mens Rea= An intention to penetrate without any reasonable belief in the victim's consent *or* recklessness as to whether there is in fact penetration.		Sexual Offences (Scotland) Act 2009, s 1(1).
Consent= 'Free agreement' The Sexual Offences (Scotland) Act 2009, s 12 introduces a statutory definition of consent which is to be construed by the courts.		Sexual Offences (Scotland) Act 2009, s 1(1). In Parts 1 and 3, 'consent' means free agreement.

COMMENTARY	CASE LAW	STATUTE LAW
The Act also lists a set of six circumstances in which consent is automatically deemed to be absent.		Sexual Offences (Scotland) Act 2009, s 13(2) (a) where the conduct occurs at a time when B is incapable because of the effect of alcohol or any other substance of consenting to it, (b) where B agrees or submits to the conduct because of violence used against B or any other person, or because of threats of violence made against B or any other person, (c) where B agrees or submits to the conduct because B is unlawfully detained by A, (d) where B agrees or submits to the conduct because B is mistaken, as a result of deception by A, as to the nature or purpose of the conduct (cf *Hussain v Houston* 1995 SLT 1060), (e) where B agrees or submits to the conduct because A induces B to agree or submit to the conduct by impersonating a person known personally to B (f) where the only expression or indication of agreement to the conduct is from a person other than B.
Consent may be withdrawn at any time during the act.		Sexual Offences (Scotland) Act 2009, s 15(3)
An individual who is asleep, unconscious or suffers from an accepted mental abnormality is incapable of consenting.		Sexual Offences (Scotland) Act 2009, ss 14(2) and 17(2).
A lack of consent in fact may not render the accused behaviour criminal if reasonable grounds for his mistaken belief can be established.		Sexual Offences (Scotland) Act 2009, s 16: 'In determining whether a person's belief as to consent or knowledge was reasonable, regard is to be had to whether the [accused] took any steps to ascertain whether there was consent ... and if so, to what those steps were'.
Penetrate= A continuing act allowing for the withdrawal of consent at any time.		Sexual Offences (Scotland) Act 2009, s 1(2) and (3).

INCEST

Under the Criminal Law (Consolidation) (Scotland) Act 1995, a person who has sexual intercourse with a person of the opposite sex who falls within one of the **specified categories** is guilty of an offence unless he can establish a relevant **defence. Step relations** are also covered.

COMMENTARY	CASE LAW	STATUTE LAW
Specified categories	*KP v HMA* 2011 SCCR 36. Only applies to heterosexual penetrative intercourse which may be committed by male or female. The accused, a 27 year old woman who had been adopted as a baby pleaded guilty to incest after sleeping with her birth father on two separate occasions; the second of which occurring while they were on bail in respect of the first charge. *Held*, due to the exceptional circumstances of the case and the birth father's known vulnerability of the accused an identical punishment for the two was inappropriate. Thus, the father was sentenced to 16 months' imprisonment and on appeal the accused's prison sentence was substituted for a two-year probation period with a counselling condition.	Criminal Law (Consolidation) (Scotland) Act 1995 Section 1. Specified categories eg mother, sister, niece etc (or male equivalents if female charged). Half blood is treated as equivalent to full blood. Defences: accused did not know and had no reason to suspect the person was related to him/ her; did not consent to the sexual intercourse; married to the per-son within the specified category and the marriage is recognised as valid in Scotland.
Step relations	*McGregor v Haswell* 1983 SLT 626 'Member of same household' under the Social Work (Scotland) Act 1968 defined per LP Emslie as 'a group of persons held together by a particular kind of tie who normally live together ... akin to a family unit.' *McDade v HMA* 1998 SLT 68 Consent is not a relevant sentencing factor. Appellant convicted of committing incest with 18 year-old niece. Trial judge, sentencing to four years' imprisonment, said he was left in no doubt girl did not consent. *Held*, issue of consent not in issue, appeal allowed and 30 months' imprisonment substituted (ie if no consent then Crown should charge rape). *Note:* *R v HMA* 1988 SCCR 254 Any sexual relationship between a parent and child may also constitute public indecency following *Webster v Dominick* 2003 SLT 975.	Section 2. Offence for a step parent or former step parent to have intercourse with a step child or former step child if the child under the age of 21 or at any time before 18 years old the child lived in the parent's household and was treated as a child of the family. Defences: accused —did not know child was a step child; —had reasonable cause to believe the child was over 21 years old; —did not consent to the sexual intercourse; —was married to the child and the marriage was recognised as valid in Scotland.
Time bar for summary proceedings		Section 4(2). Provides a period of six months from when sufficient evidence in the opinion of the Lord Advocate becomes available. A certificate by him of that date is conclusive. Section 136(3) of the Criminal Procedure (Scotland) Act 1995 provides that proceedings are deemed to commence when a warrant to cite or apprehend the accused is granted where the warrant is executed without undue delay.

PUBLIC ORDER OFFENCES

BREACH OF THE PEACE

Breach of the peace is **conduct extreme enough** to **cause alarm** or **threaten serious disturbance**.

COMMENTARY	CASE LAW	STATUTE LAW
Definition.	*Smith (P) v Donnelly* 2001 SCCR 800.	
	Peace protestor challenge, as devolution issue, whether offence sufficiently defined to be compatible with European Convention on Human Rights; authorities and earlier cases reviewed. Held 'what was required was conduct severe enough to cause alarm to ordinary people and threaten serious disturbance to the community ... conduct generally alarming and disturbing to any reasonable person'.	
	Kinnaird v Higson 2001 SCCR 427.	
	Appeal: appellant's conviction quashed. Approached in the street by two constables, told there was outstanding arrest warrant. Replied (correctly) 'Fuck off I've nae warrant" Language, although offensive, did not nor was likely to cause alarm or distress. Gordon in commentary "... to be hoped ... that [constables] will accept being spoken to in everyday demotic ... just part of day's work'.	
	McDonald v Heywood 2002 SCCR 92.	
	Appeal: police called to locus of disturbance; on arrival no disturbance occurring but appellant, leaving with bleeding arm wrapped in towel, aggressive, threatening violence. Conviction upheld.	
	Grocan v Heywood 1999 SCCR 705.	
	Alarm or threat of serious disturbance reasonable expectation, not possibility appellant inside house shouting, swearing of police at door.	
	Biggins v Stott 1999 SCCR 590.	
	Appeal: 13 year old girl twice invited into appellant's house once from window then in street, offer of money, was 'terrified'. Conviction upheld.	
	McMillan v Higson 2003 SCCR 125 Appeal: appellant in access dispute over private road, blocking egress of neighbour's car, refusing to move at police request. Conviction quashed.	
	Refusal, even forceful or truculent to cooperate with police not sufficient to convict.	
	Allison v Higson 2004 SCCR 720.	
	Appeal: appellant ran onto football pitch, waving Union Jack flag, at international match. Conviction upheld "in highly charged atmosphere ever present and serious risk, of crowd trouble".	
	Jones v Carnegie	
	Barrett v Carnegie	
	Tallents v Gallacher	
	Carberry v Curkle	

COMMENTARY	CASE LAW	STATUTE LAW
	Park v France 2004 SCCR 361 (5 judge bench) Test is whether reasonable to conclude in absence of actual disturbance that serious disturbance and alarm would be caused.	
	Palazzo v Copeland 1976 JC 52. Shopkeeper discharging shotgun to scare off group of 'unsavoury and drunken youths' engaged in fracas 'Man may not commit one offence to stop another'.	
	Raffaelli v Yeatly 1949 JC 101. 'Peeping Tom' staring at women through chink in curtains late at night.	
	Bryce v Normand 1997 SLT 135. Video taken of neighbours 15 year old daughter getting undressed. Subsequently shown to another neighbour who was shocked.	
	Craig v Normand 1996 SCCR 823. Shouting and swearing by drunk removed from bus: conviction upheld.	
	Young v Heatly 1959 JC 66. School master making 'grossly improper remarks and suggestions' in interviews with adolescent pupils; convicted.	
Threaten serious disturbance	*Butcher v Jessop* 1989 SCCR 119. Professional footballers' aggression on pitch likely to lead to disturbance by fans. The *mens rea* therefore does not require an intention to cause a disturbance so long as it can be calculated that the behaviour undertaken could be objectively calculated to do so.	
Motive of conduct irrelevant	*Ralston v HMA* 1988 SCCR 590. Appeal: protest against prison conditions on prison roof; appeal refused, behaviour deliberate.	
Forming part of disorderly group	*Montgomery v Herron* 1976 SCCR (Supp) 131. Part of crowd preventing access to public meeting.	
	Tudhope v O'Neill 1983 SCCR 443. Not necessary to show individual's actions, once membership of crowd established.	

PUBLIC DISORDER

Meetings, street processions and **offences occasioned by procession or assembly** are the subject of statutory legislation.

COMMENTARY	CASE LAW	STATUTE LAW
Meetings Public parks, open spaces, etc, are invariably governed by local bye-laws or local legislation.	*Aldred v Miller* 1925 JC 21 Accused challenged bye-law requiring that permission be sought from local authority before holding meeting. Conviction upheld.	Civic Government (Scotland) Act 1982, s 53. Any person who, being on foot in any public place— (a) obstructs, along with another or others, the lawful passage of any other person and fails to desist on being required to do so by a constable in uniform, or (b) wilfully obstructs the lawful passage of any other person shall be guilty of an offence.
		Civic Government (Scotland) Act 1982, s 54. Playing instruments, singing, playing radios, etc (1) Any person who— (a) sounds or plays any musical instrument; (b) sings or performs; or (c) operates any radio or television receiver, record player, tape-recorder or other sound producing device so as to give any other person reasonable cause for annoyance and fails to desist on being required to do so by a constable in uniform, shall be guilty of an offence.
Streets and roads, too, are subject to local regulations.	*Aldred v Miller* 1924 JC 117 A began lecturing in a street, causing a large number of people to assemble, and thereby occa-sioning obstruction. A convicted under Glasgow Police Act 1866. Per LJ-G Clyde: 'If anybody causes an obstruction in a public street or hinders other members of the public in exercising the public right of free passage upon it—he selfishly engrosses the public right to himself, and his action is justly condemned.'	
Street processions No such prior sanction is required for a procession although powers exist to prohibit or regulate proposed march or to prevent march actually taking place.	*Loyal Orange Lodge v Roxburgh District Council* 1981 SLT 33 Power of district council to issue orders prohibiting or regulating processions is a wide one.	Civic Government (Scotland) Act 1982: s 62, requirement to give notice to regional council of a public procession; s 63, power of chief constable to pro-hibit and impose conditions; s 64, appeals against power granted by s 63.
Notice of intention to hold a procession is required.		
Offences occasioned by proces-sion or assembly		Civic Government (Scotland) Act 1982, s 65 sets out – penalties relating to offences committed by disregard of con-ditions laid down in ss 62 and 63 of the same Act.
	Deakin and Others v Milne (1882) 10 R (J) 22 Salvation Army parade. Officers convicted of committing a breach of the peace.	

COMMENTARY	CASE LAW	STATUTE LAW
	Marr v McArthur (1878) 5 R (J) 38 M and another convicted of statutory breach of the peace in that they played flutes in a public place. Tune played was of political nature. *Held*, on appeal, that the mere playing of such a tune, without further proven detail of actual breach of the peace, was insufficient and conviction quashed.	

References: Gordon, 971; J.L. Murdoch, 144.

Reference: Gordon, 971.

MOBBING

A mob is a **gathering,** intent on a **common purpose** to be effected illegally and to the alarm of the public, in which **mere presence** may be sufficient for guilt.

COMMENTARY	CASE LAW	STATUTE LAW
Gathering The number needed to constitute a mob is determined by their conduct and is not fixed.	*Sloan v Macmillan* 1922 JC 1 *Held*, three co-accused were charged with being part of a riotous mob. Per LJ-C Scott Dickson: 'The law is that the number of people required to constitute a mob depends on what these people do, the violence they show, the threats they use.'	
There need be no actual violence; force of numbers and/or intimidation will suffice	*Sloan v Macmillan* 1922 JC 1 Per LJ-C Scott Dickson: '... lied persistently ... in order to produce terror ... by saying that there were hundreds of desperate men outside. That seems to me to be enough to make the appellant constitute part of a riotous mob.'	
Common purpose Unless there is a common *criminal* purpose there is no mob.	*Daniel Blair and Ors* (1868) 1 Couper 168 Crowd assembled to pull down all gates. Per Lord Deas: 'The mere number of people, there may be thousands and thousands, does not constitute a mob. In order to constitute a mob there must be not merely a great number of people but a *common purpose*—and that common purpose must be illegal.' *Francis Docherty and Ors* (1841) 2 Swin 635 Per Lord Hope: 'Mobbing is not simply a breach of the peace by a number of persons; to constitute that crime it is absolutely necessary that there should be a common object.'	
But the purpose need not be antecedent to the formation of the mob,	*Alex Orr and Ors* (1856) 2 Irv 502 Accused attacked and burned a chapel. Also charged with mobbing and rioting. Per Lord Hope: 'If a mob take up a purpose, although it may not have been concerted beforehand, or may not at first have been known to the individuals at the bar; if the persons at the bar accompany that mob ... they are guilty of the out-rages committed by that mob.'	
and need have no motive other than to engage in disruptive behaviour.	*Michael Hart and Ors* (1854) 1 Irv 574 H was charged with forming part of a mob whose purpose was to attack Orangemen. There was insufficient evidence to support latter part of the libel but the jury were directed that they could nevertheless convict of mobbing and rioting.	
Evidence necessary to prove common purpose,	Convictions of mobbing quashed on appeal. Crown failed to prove accused intent on a common purpose, but only 'a series of unconnected and fortuitous events ... without any evidence of pre-knowledge or support or encouragement or countenance'. *Coleman v HMA* 1999 SLT 1261 *Held*, no member of a murderous mob can be convicted of murder purely on their membership of the mob. It must be shown that each member of the mob shared the same murderous purpose.	

COMMENTARY	CASE LAW	STATUTE LAW
but when proved, **mere presence** in a mob may be sufficient for guilt,	*HMA v Cairns and Ors* (1837) 1 Swin 597 Person can be guilty of mobbing by mere presence alone. But he may also be the very soul of the mob without doing much—a word, a nod may excite the mob and be the cause of all the mischief that follows.	
and where a mob arises there is a duty to quell or at least withdraw from it (Alison I, p 520).		
Macdonald (5th edn), p 135; also Hume I, 421. It is not necessary to infer guilt that the accused should have been present at the moment when a particular act was committed, or that he should have been personally present at all. The rule that the instigator be as guilty as the perpetrator applies with special force to the case of mobbing.		
'It is no defence that the mob's purpose was to prevent something being done by others which the mob thinks to be contrary to what the law allows' (Macdonald, p 132).		

References: Hume I, 416; Alison I, 509; Macdonald, 131; Gane and Stoddart, 691.

SENTENCING POLICY

Millsopp v HMA 1997 GWD 9-381—M (aged 21) and T (aged 25) were sentenced to three years' imprisonment for mobbing and rioting. They were part of a mob of 15 to 20 people which attacked two police officers. M's record included six offences of breach of the peace. T's record included seven offences of breach of the peace and one police assault.
High Court on appeal *Held*, sentence was excessive, mainly on grounds of comparative justice where co-accused X (aged 21) had similar sentence reduced to two years. Two years and two years respectively substituted.

HARASSMENT

A non-harassment order requires a person to refrain from such conduct towards the victim of the offence as may be specified in the order, for which period as specified. It can be made in addition to any other disposal which may be made. Such an order is a sentence for the purpose of an appeal. Harassment is defined as a course of conduct including causing alarm or distress on at least two occasions.

COMMENTARY	CASE LAW	STATUTE LAW
Non-harassment order		Criminal Procedure (Scotland) Act 1995, s 234A
On application of prosecutor.	*McGlennan v McKinnon* 1998 SCCR 285 Respondent convicted of breach of the peace for shouting at ex-girlfriend. Prosecutor sought a non-harassment order but was refused on grounds that there were no averments of conduct on two occasions. Prosecutor appealed arguing, inter alia, account could be taken of previous convictions for assaulting lady. *Held*: (1) harassment involves a course of conduct on at least two occasions; (2) the offence for which the accused has been convicted of when the order is sought which must itself involve a course of conduct, and it was not legitimate to look back over previous convictions to construct a course of conduct, and appeal refused. Observed, the exact scope of the dictum regarding not considering the details of previous convictions might require to be determined some day.	Section 234A. Where a person is convicted of an offence involving harassment, the prosecutor may apply for a non-harassment order against him. This will require him to refrain from such conduct to the victim of the offence as may be specified in the order, for such period (includes indeterminate period) as specified, in addition to any other disposal which may be made. Such an order is a sentence for the purposes of an appeal. For this section 'harassment' is defined, in s 8 of the Protection from Harassment Act 1997, as a course of conduct which amounts to harassment, includ-ing causing alarm or distress. A course of conduct must involve conduct on at least two occasions.
On the balance of probabilities.		Section 234A(2). The court may make a non-harassment order if satisfied on the balance of probabilities that it is appropriate to protect the victim from further harassment.
Penalties.		Section 234A(4). Breach of non-harassment order is an offence and penalties are: (a) on indictment, to imprisonment for a term not exceeding five years or fine, or both; (b) on summary, to imprisonment not exceeding six months or fine not exceeding statutory maximum, or both.

COMMENTARY	CASE LAW	STATUTE LAW
Revocation/variation of order.	*Robertson v Vannet* 1998 SCCR 668 Appellant subject to interim interdict by woman, C. Sheriff made non-harassment order for appellant not to approach or attempt to contact C or her father for five years. *Held*, refusing appeal, that s 8(5) of the Protection from Harassment Act 1997, which states court may not grant interim interdict and harassment order for same prohibition, applied only to civil proceedings and did not prevent criminal courts from making a non-harassment order. *Note*: father was a victim, because he knew of threats and was frightened. *Note*: Complainers can raise civil proceedings under the Protection from Harassment Act 1997.	Section 234A(6). The person against whom a non-harassment order is made, or the prosecutor at whose instance the order is made may apply to court to vary or revoke the order which it can do if appropriate on the balance of probabilities, but not so as to increase the period for which the order is to run.
Appeal.		Section 175(4) (as substituted by the Crime and Punishment (Scotland) Act 1997) entitles the prosecutor to appeal to the High Court against, inter alia, a decision not to make a non-harassment order. (For the procedure, see s 186.)
New offence of racially aggravated harassment.		**Racially aggravated harassment** Criminal Law (Consolidation) Scotland Act 1995, s 50A.
As from 30 September 1998.	*Anderson v Griffiths* 2005 1 J.C. 169; 2005 S.L.T. 86. X was charged with acting in a racially aggravated manner which caused or intended to cause alarm or distress at a football match, contrary to the Criminal Law (Consolidation) (Scotland) Act 1995, s 50A(1)(b), by continually making abusive remarks towards two football players. The remarks were not heard by the players. Thesheriff found *inter alia* that two spectators were upset and disgusted by the remarks and that X's conduct could reasonably be expected to have caused any observer to become alarmed or annoyed or to have provoked a disturbance. *Arthur v Brown* 2000 SCCR 94. A was sentenced to two months' imprisonment for challenging the staff of a fast food establishment to fight, shouting racial abuse, threatening violence and kicking the establishment's doors in.	Section 50A. Person guilty of racially aggravated harassment if he: (a) pursues a racially aggravated course of conduct which amounts to harassment of that person, and (i) it is intended to amount to harassment; or (ii) it occurs in circumstances where it appears to a reasonable person that it would amount to harassment of that person; or (b) acts in a manner which is racially aggravated and which causes, or is intended to cause, a person alarm or distress.
Definition of racially aggravated course of conduct.		Section 50A(2). A course of conduct is racially aggravated if: (a) immediately before, during or immediately after the course of conduct or action the offender evinces towards the person malice and ill-will based on that person's membership (or presumed membership) of a racial group; or (b) the course of conduct or action is motivated (wholly or partly) by malice or ill-will towards members of a racial group based on their membership of that group. Crime and Disorder Act 1998, s 96. Where an existing crime is proven to be racially aggravated the court shall take this into account in sentencing. See Sentencing below.

OFFENCES AGAINST THE COURT

CONTEMPT OF COURT

Contempt of court is conduct offending against the **dignity** or **authority** of a court **in or outwith its precincts**

COMMENTARY	CASE LAW	STATUTE LAW
Contempt of Court: *Actus reus*: Behaviour which challenges the dignity or authority of the court. *Mens rea*: Doing so wilfully.	*Robertson and Gough v McFadyen* 2008 SCCR 20. 'a sui generis offence committed against the court itself which is peculiarly within the province of the court to punish.' per Lord Justice-Clerk Gill at p 30.	
Disorderly conduct offending against the **dignity** of a court.	*John Allan* 1826 Shaw 172. Witness incapable of giving evidence because drunk.	
	Young v Lees 1998 SCCR 558 Y. Opened court door, shouted "you guppy" at sheriff: 60 days imprisonment.	
	Williams v Clarke 2001 SCCR 505. Accused, late for court, pled guilty, while in dock his mobile rang. Notices in court warned to switch off mobiles. Finding of contempt not wrong in principle (ie contempt may be commuted negligently) but conviction suspended because extraneous matters had influenced sheriff.	Criminal Procedure (Scotland) Act 1995, s 92(2): Misconduct making proper trial impossible – accused may be removed and trial with representation may proceed in absence.
	HMA v Dickie 312 SCCR. Amid great confusion, with cases being transferred from court to court and sitting to sitting there was a failure to provide advocate and solicitor representation by those instructed finding that conduct as consisent with 'sheer incompetence' and 'gross negligence' as deliberate challenge to court authority.	
Prevarication, refusal to answer, to take the oath or affirm challenges the **authority** of the court.	*Bacon* 1884 SCCR 389. Prevarication to avoid self incrimination by defence witness (no immunity from prosecution) not contempt.	Section 155(1): witness duly cited, failing – to attend – refusing to be sworn – refusing, after sworn, to answer – prevaricating may be punished forthwith for contempt.
	Dawes v Cardle 1987 SCCR 155 D. Refused to leave cell to appear in Court; visited in cell and warned by sheriff with court officials present; refused to tender plea when appearing thereafter in court.	Section 155(4) deals with failure to attend for Crown precognition or answer thereat s 291 deals with defence witnesses.
	HMA v Airs 1975 SLT 177. Journalist refusing to answer whether he had met one of accused: "Contempt of court not a crime within criminal law but offence sui generis which challenges ... affronts court or supremacy of law".	Contempt of Court Act 1981, s 10 Non Disclosure of source of information in publication only contempt if disclosure necessary in
	Urquhart v Hamilton 1996 SCCR 217. Failure to attend social work department for preparation of court report.	– interests of justice – national security – to prevent crime or disorder.
	Chappell v Friel 1997 SLT 1325. Witness failing to arrange childcare but not advising PP until 2 hours after due to appear.	Sections 1, 2 Strict liability if publication creates substantial risk to course to justice.
	McKinnon v Douglas 1982 SCCR 80. Late arrival because of wish to be properly dressed not contempt.	
Authority of court is impugned by publication of material prejudicial to administration of justice.	*Stirling v Associated Newspapers Ltd* 1960 SLT 5. Publication of photograph with article day after accused's initial detention.	

COMMENTARY	CASE LAW	STATUTE LAW
	Hall v Associated Newspapers Ltd 1978 SLT 241. Murder charge, accused in custody; publication of extensive reports on enquiry and accused from moment of arrest person concerned is under care and protection of the Court.	
	HMA v Caledonian Newspapers Ltd 1995 SCCR 330. Publication of photograph of escaped prisoner.	
	Muir v BBC 1996 SCCR 584. Petition to prevent publication of prison doctor's report granted to prison officers awaiting trial.	
	HMA v Express Newspapers plc 1998 SCCR 47. Proceedings deserted pro loco et tempore writer advised case still active and to contact publishers' lawyers who gave go ahead. Article conceded to be in contempt, risk of prejudice to prosecution.	
	HMA v Scottish Express Newspapers Ltd 1989 156 SCCR 156. Arrest on attempted murder charge: newspaper report described case as attempted political assassination of Yugoslav exile, giving impression of guilt.	Criminal Procedure (Scotland) Act 1995, s 47. Prohibition on identification of name, address, school or particulars of person under 16 in newspaper when person involved in court proceedings.
	HMA v Scottish Media Newspapers Ltd 1999 SCCR 599. Publication of report of arrest of actor on charge of deforcement of sheriff's officer contained extraneous reference to alcohol problems, unpaid bills, and neighbours' complaint. No serious risk of prejudice therefore no contempt because of probable ninemonth interval before trial.	
	Alan Scott McNeilage: Petitioner 1999 SCCR 471. Sheriff's report, as well as court minutes could be consulted. Sheriff found petitioner, Crown witness "changing his evidence as and when it suited him".	
	HMA v The Scotsman Publications Ltd. 1999 SCCR 163. Article reporting key witnesses in forthcoming trial of MP on fraud charges had asked for police protection "could hardly have been a more prejudicial suggestion".	
	Williams v Clark 2001 SCCR 505. Accused's mobile phone ringing while in dock – notices stating phones should be switched off. Contempt of court could be committed by negligent behaviour.	

SENTENCING POLICY

Hislop Petitioner 1986 SCCR 268.
Nine months' imprisonment for refusal by defence witness to name drug suppliers not excessive. Contempt of Court Act 1981, s 15(2).

Forrest v Wilson 1993 SCCR 631.
Prevarication – summary imprisonment. Restrictions on first imprisonment not applicable as court punishing, not sentencing.

Gallagher, petitioner 1996 SCCR 833.
Sentence of six months' imprisonment (reduced to three on appeal) for menacing stares at jurors after conviction of brother.

PERJURY

Perjury is **deliberate falsification** of **relevant and competent evidence** given **on oath** or **affirmation** in **judicial proceedings**

COMMENTARY	CASE LAW	STATUTE LAW
Deliberate falsification	*HMA v Cairns* 1967 JC 37.	Criminal Law (Consolidation) (Scotland) Act 1995, ss 44–46.
Express denial.	C gave evidence at own trial, on oath, that he did not stab deceased, acquitted. Later tried for perjury.	Perjury is statement on oath known to be false or not believed to be true (s 44(1)).
Express assertion.	*Simpson v Tudhope* 1987 SCCR 348. S, police officer, gave evidence he was accompanied by other officer, knowing he did not know whether this was correct or not.	Extends to eg statutory declaration (s 44(21) [Aider and abetter prosecuted as principal time limits for prosecution (s 46).
Relevant and competent	*Hall v HMA* 1968 SLT. 275.	Form of oath immaterial (s 46(1)(a)) Affirmation equivalent (s 46(1)(b)).
	Denial of making statement to police relevant to credibility.	
	Aitchison v Simon 1976 SLT (Sh. Ct) 73.	
	Evidence is denied.	
	Statement to police material in original trial, fact that statement might not have been competent of no bearing on its relevance to accused's credibility.	
	Lord Advocate's Reference 1986 SCCR 329.	
	Per LJG Emslie "All that is required ... is that perjury charge [will be] if allegedly false evidence was competent and relevant at earlier trial" quoad proof or credibility.	
Sentencing.	Policy.	
	Hagen v HMA 1983 SCCR 245. *Gordon v Hamilton* 1987 SCCR 146 *HMA v McKinlay* SCCR 1998. These cases varied sentences downwards but sustained convictions, in any event not appealed.	

MISCELLANEOUS

ROAD TRAFFIC

Road Traffic Act 1988, ss 185–192, provides a series of definitions of important terms.

COMMENTARY	CASE LAW	STATUTE LAW
Driver Includes separate person engaged in steering the vehicle as well as another person engaged in controlling the vehicle.		Road Traffic Act 1988 Section 192(1): General Interpretation of the Act.
	Tyler v Whatmore [1976] RTR 83 One person controlling the steering of the car from passenger seat, while person in driver's seat controlled propulsion. Both held to be driving. *Langman v Valentine* [1952] 2 All ER 803 Learner driver and instructor in dual-control car. Both held to be drivers. *Evans v Walkden* [1956] 3 All ER 64 Qualified driver simply sat beside learner driver. Although able to reach brake and steering wheel did not do so. *Held* not to be in control, thus not driving. *Ames v MacLeod* 1969 JC 1 A car ran out of petrol. Pushed car down straight incline while walking alongside it with one hand on the wheel to steer. *Held* to be driving, because 'in a substantial sense controlling the movement and direction'. *Hoy v McFadyen* 2000 SCCR 873 Appellant in driving seat of car on hill with engine running; defective handbrake. Driver – the correct test is to look at what the appellant was doing, and not necessarily the result. But see: *R v MacDonagh* [1974] RTR 372 States differing English approach. In *McArthur v Valentine* 1989 SCCR 704 a five-judge appeal court held that the test applied in *Ames v MacLeod* is to be preferred to the English test in *R v MacDonagh*. M had been drinking and arranged for S to drive him home. In course of helping S to start car by jump starting, M pushed car with one hand on steering wheel. *Held* to be driving.	
Mechanically propelled vehicle Test of mechanical propulsion—will be regarded as mechanically propelled, even if broken down, unless there is no reasonable prospect of the vehicle ever being made mobile again.	*Newberry v Simmonds* [1961] 2 QB 345; [1961] 2 All ER 318 Engine removed from car. Evidence showed that it might be replaced shortly and power restored. *Held* still to be a mechanically propelled vehicle. *Smart v Allan* [1962] 3 All ER 893; [1963] 1 QB 291 Vehicle had no gearbox and engine in such bad repair that future mobility was not possible. *Held* not to be mechanically propelled.	Road Traffic Act 1988 Section 185(1): Meaning of 'Motor Vehicle'.

COMMENTARY	CASE LAW	STATUTE LAW
	Tudhope v Every 1977 SLT 2 Car had clutch slipping. Gear box stuck in second gear. *Held* that this car was a motor vehicle and ought only to be released from that classification when it reached such a state of structural or mechanical decrepitude that it would offend common sense to call it a 'mechanically propelled vehicle'. It was also held that the vehicle required to be insured although only parked.	
Intended or adapted for use on roads		
	Nichol v Leach [1972] RTR 476 Car rebuilt solely for auto-cross racing. *Held* still to be for use on road, although owner did not intend to use it for such.	Section 185(1)
Test is objective.	*Woodward v Young* 1958 SLT 289 Agricultural tractor may be a vehicle intended or adapted for use on roads.	
	Childs v Coghlan (1968) 112 SJ 175 *Held* that a machine whose primary use was not on roads, which regularly went on roads from one site to another, was intended for use on roads.	
	Holliday v Henry [1974] RTR 101 Roller skates placed under each wheel of a vehicle so that it was not actually 'on' the road. *Held* still to be on the road for purposes of s 8, Vehicles (Excise) Act 1971.	
Roads Any highway and any other road to which the public has access.		Roads (Scotland) Act 1984, s 151(1); Road Traffic Act 1988, s 192(2)
Public access may be a matter of fact or circumstance.	*Harrison v Hill* 1932 JC 13; 1931 SLT 598 Any road may be regarded as a road to which the public have access where members of the public are to be found who have not obtained access either by overcoming a physical obstruction or in defiance of prohibition express or implied.	
'Private' notes are not conclusive proof that the road is not public.	*Hogg v Nicholson* 1968 SLT 265 Road marked 'Private'. However, used by police cars and delivery vans, and also for access to post office. *Held* to be a road.	
Public access to, eg, car parks and forecourts does not render them roads per se, unless they could be naturally and ordinarily described as such.	See: *Purves v Muir* 1948 JC 122; 1948 SLT 529 *Henderson v Bernard* 1955 SLT (Sh Ct) 27	
	Griffin v Squires [1958] 3 All ER 468 Car park held not to be a road simply because public had access. 'Nobody ... would think of a car park as a road.'	
	But see:	
	Paterson v Ogilvy 1957 JC 42 *Held* that a private field being temporarily used as a car park was a 'public place'.	
	Vannet v Burns 1998 SCCR 414 *Held*, car park was no less a public place because frequented by a special section of public (patrons), and case of driving with excess alcohol remitted to sheriff to proceed as accords.	

COMMENTARY	CASE LAW	STATUTE LAW
	Brown v Braid 1984 SCCR 286 *Held* that garage forecourt is a public place if there is a high probability of the presence of pedestrians on it. *Beattie v Scott* 1992 SCCR 435 *Young v Carmichael* 1992 SCCR 332 *Dick v Walkingshaw* 1995 SCCR 307 Appellant convicted of driving without insurance on the car deck of a ferry at a time when the deck was connected to a ramp on the deck and the cars were disembarking. Upheld on appeal: since public had access, albeit restricted, car deck was road at time ramp in place. *Rodger v Normand* 1994 SCCR 861 Conviction of careless driving. Upheld on appeal: playground was a public place, since used outside school hours by public as leisure park, and persons not trespassers as this use tolerated by owners.	

Dangerous and careless driving

Road Traffic Act 1988, as amended by Road Traffic Act 1991:
Section 1: Causing death by dangerous driving = 'A person who **causes** the death of **another** person by driving a mechanically propelled vehicle **dangerously** on a road or other public place is guilty of an offence.'
Section 2: Dangerous driving = 'A person who drives a mechanically propelled vehicle **dangerously** on a road or other public place is guilty of an offence.'
Section 3: Careless and inconsiderate driving = 'If a person drives a mechanically propelled vehicle on a road or other public place **without due care and attention,** or **without reasonable consideration for other persons using the road** or place, he is guilty of an offence.'

COMMENTARY	CASE LAW	STATUTE LAW
Causes Accused's driving need not be a substantial cause of the accident, only a material cause.	*R v Hennigan* [1971] 3 All ER 133 H drove dangerously fast but other motorist he killed was also blameworthy. Per Lord Parker CJ: 'so long as the dangerous driving is a cause and more than de minimis the statute operates.' *Watson v HMA* [1978] SCCR Supp 192 Jury directed by trial judge that W could only be acquitted if other party 'wholly to blame'. *Held* that this was a misdirection and conviction quashed.	
Another Can be a passenger in same car.	*R v Klein* (1960) Times, 3 April K's passenger died as a consequence of K's reckless driving. *Davidson v HMA* 1996 SCCR 736 D convicted of causing death by dangerous driv-ing. He was taking friend to work and took bend too fast. *McCluskey v HMA* 1989 SLT 175 Driver who caused injuries to unborn child which died as a result, convicted under this section.	
Dangerous	*Abbas v Houston* 1993 SCCR 136 A driving at 108 mph on motorway in good road conditions. Conviction upheld on appeal. Such a conviction possible under RTA 1988, s 2A when accused driving at a grossly excessive speed.	Road Traffic Act 1988, s 2A(1). Person driving dangerously if (a) driving far below that expected of a competent and careful driver and (b) it would be obvious to such a driver that such driving would be dangerous.
	Mitchell v Lockhart 1993 SCCR 1070 Dangerously driving. M driving 61 mph on 15 mph esplanade. Esplanade empty at the time. Con-victed. Upheld on appeal. Under RTA 1988, s 2A a driver must have regard to potential dangers, in this case of pedestrians walking onto the esplanade. Observed that RTA 1988, s 2A based on the language in *Allan v Patterson* 1980 JC 37.	
	Brown v Orr 1994 SCCR 668 Conviction of dangerous driving for doing 104 mph on A9 where limit 60 mph quashed and conviction for speeding substituted as road conditions good.	

COMMENTARY	CASE LAW	STATUTE LAW
	Trippick v Orr 1995 SCCR 736 Conviction of dangerous driving upheld on appeal, where driver doing 114mph in 70mph limit. Only car on road and good road conditions. *Held*, potential risks combined with grossly excessive speed created danger. *Brown v Orr* 1994 SCCR 668 distinguished. See also: *McQueen v Buchanan* 1996 SCCR 826. *Service v Baldrup* SCCR 2005 693.	
Note: Alternative verdicts If accused charged with RTA 1988, s 1 and the evidence showed he did not cause the death, he can still be convicted under RTA 1988, s 2.		Road Traffic Act 1991, s 24. Various alternative verdicts open eg conviction for careless driving competent in a charge of dangerous driving.
It can be a defence to a charge of dangerous driving that the driver without fault of his own was deprived of control of the vehicle by a mechanical defect which he did not know about or could not with reasonable diligence have discovered.	*R v Spurge* [1961] 2 All ER 688 Driver convicted—knew of defect but continued to drive.	
It is unclear whether there can be a defence of necessity.	*McNab v Guild* 1989 SCCR 138 *Held* that if defence of necessity is available, it could only be made out if immediate danger to life or of serious injury at the material time, which was not the case here.	
Court cannot assume without evidence that vehicle must have developed defects.	*Rabjohns v Burgar* [1972] Crim LR 46 B's car hit bridge wall on dry road on a clear day. Two skid marks behind car. B gave no explanation for collision. Prosecution did not have to prove that there was no steering defect.	
Without due care and attention Standard of due care and attention is an objective one, inferred from the circumstances and is therefore a question of fact.	*Jarvis v Williams* [1979] RTR 497 Solitary car damaged in accident. Unexplained accident not attributable to road surface, weather or defect in vehicle. *Held*, on appeal that the inference was that the defendant was not driving with due care and attention.	RTA 1988, s 3
Careless driving.	*Sigournay v Douglas* 1981 SCCR 302 Careless driving. Driver hit pedestrian who ran in front of her on dual carriageway. Convicted. Appealed. *Held* that the appellant had reasonable grounds for believing that the risk of pedestrian crossing road had passed and had no reason to anticipate pedestrian's actions; there was no evidence to support the suggestion that a swerve could have avoided the accident. Conviction quashed. *MacPhail v Haddow* 1990 SCCR 339 H using a hand-held telephone while driving. No evidence of lack of control or danger to others. Convicted. On appeal *held* that although such driving is contrary to the Highway Code, unless there is actual or potential danger demonstrated it is not an offence in itself.	RTA 1988, s 3

COMMENTARY	CASE LAW	STATUTE LAW
Inexperience or error of judgment is not an excuse to this offence.	See also: *Rae v Friel* 1992 SCCR 688 *Stock v Carmichael* 1993 SCCR 136 *McCrone v Riding* [1938] 1 All ER 157 Learner driver found guilty of offence under s 3. *Held* irrelevant that carelessness was due to inexperience.	
	Simpson v Peat [1952] 1 All ER 447 If a driver does not exercise that degree of care and attention which a reasonable and prudent man would exercise in the circumstances, he is guilty, whether or not committing an error of judgment.	
Knowledge of the carelessness not an essential element of careless driving.	*Hampson v Powell* [1970] 1 All ER 929 Lorry driver who was not aware he had hit a stationary vehicle was held to be rightly convicted of careless driving.	
	Farquar v McKinnon 1986 SCCR 524 Driver of large articulated vehicle reversed slowly along road without assistance, using only mirrors, in area where he was aware children were playing. Ran over child and found guilty of careless driving because he had reversed without clear vision to rear, notwithstanding that lorry showing hazard light.	
	Brunton v Lees 1993 SCCR 98 Speeding, 60 mph in 40 mph zone. Speed held to be excessive but not grossly so. Conviction upheld on appeal. Speed in itself sufficient for careless driving.	
No exemption from prosecution exists for emergency services.	*Wood v Richards* [1977] Crim LR 295 Police officer convicted of careless driving. *Held* that there is no special exception or standard to be applied to emergency services.	
	Husband v Russell 1997 SCCR 592 Appellant pleaded guilty to dangerous driving. He was driving fire engine on emergency and struck vehicle trying to overtake. Fined £100 and endorsed three points. *Held*, on appeal, minor degree of want of care and absolute discharge appropriate.	
Without reasonable consideration	*Dilkes v Bowman-Shaw* [1981] RTR 4 DC Motorway with two-lane carriageway. Accused moved into left-hand lane and overtook. No inconvenience caused to other driver. *Held* that although the manoeuvre was in contravention of the Highway Code, no one was actually endangered or inconvenienced. No conviction and appeal court upheld decision of lower court and rejected Crown appeal.	
	But see Wheatley, p 57. This authority might not be followed in Scotland.	
Other persons using the road Includes passengers in the vehicle being driven by the accused.	*Pawley v Wharldall* [1966] 1 QB 373 Driver of double-decker bus. Five passengers gave evidence that accused's driving caused panic and alarm to them. No evidence that anyone else outside the bus was treated without reasonable consideration. Convicted.	
Proof by road marks.	*Ryrie v Campbell* 1964 JC 33 Tyre impression on wrong side of road and matching paint on lamp-post and at collision were enough to convict despite no eye-witnesses.	

COMMENTARY	CASE LAW	STATUTE LAW
No offence of 'causing death by careless driving'.	*McCallum v Hamilton* 1985 SCCR 368 Careless driving. McC drove car in such manner that it collided with another car causing the latter to mount pavement thereby injuring two pedestrians and killing another. Details of these consequences in complaint objected to as irrelevant. Sheriff repelled objection. *Held*, on appeal, that the consequential injuries were relevantly detailed in complaint. However, the word 'fatal' was irrelevant and must be deleted. To do otherwise would effectively create by the back door offence of causing death by careless driving a crime unknown to statute. Per LJ-C Ross: '... the complaint reads as though it were libelling an offence of causing death by careless driving. There is no such offence under the Road Traffic Acts....' *Sharp v HMA* 1987 SCCR 179 *Held* that it was wrong for sheriff to take into account the fatal consequences of a piece of careless driving in considering sentence.	
		Note: practitioners should ascertain which provisions of the Road Safety Act 2006 have been brought into force.

SENTENCING POLICY

HMA v Noche 2011 HCJAC 108.

A sentence of community service for causing death and injury by dangerous driving was unduly lenient where it fell outwith the range of sentences that a sentencing judge, applying her mind to all the relevant factors, could reasonably have imposed. N's dangerous driving had not been limited to the point of the collision and the injuries of the victim were not taken properly into account. The community service order was duly quashed and a sentence of 12 months' imprisonment substituted.

Drink-related offences

Road Traffic Act 1988 section 3A: makes it an offence to cause death by careless driving while unfit through drink or drugs, or with excess alcohol, or fail within 18 hours to provide a specimen.
Road Traffic Act 1988, s 4.
Section 4(1). **Driving** or **attempting to drive** a motor vehicle while **unfit to drive** through **drink or drugs**.
Section 4(2). **Being in charge of** a motor vehicle while **unfit to drive** through **drink or drugs.**
Section 4(3). It is a defence to a charge under s 4(2) that there is **no likelihood of driving** while unfit through drink or drugs.
Road Traffic Offenders Act 1988.
Section 15(3) provides a defence of **post-incident drinking** if the prosecution relies on analysis of breath, blood or urine specimen.

COMMENTARY	CASE LAW	STATUTE LAW
Driving When motor vehicle moving subject to one's control and direction.	*R v Kitson* (1955) 39 Cr App R 66 K was a passenger in car and awoke to find car moving with no one in driving seat and no key in ignition. K steered car onto grass verge. *Held* that K was driving.	Road Traffic Act 1988 Section 4(1)
	Ames v MacLeod 1969 JC 1 A walking beside car. Car engine not running. Guided car downhill by use of steering wheel. *Held* driving.	
Attempting to drive Intention may be inferred from the circumstances.	*R v Cook* [1964] Crim LR 56 C found in front seat of car fiddling with dashboard which was lit up. Later admitted would have driven away if not caught. *Held* attempting to drive.	
	Guthrie v Friel 1992 SCCR 932 G found in car asleep with engine and lights on. Convicted. *Held* on appeal that the facts showed that G may have been preparing to drive but not actually attempting ie would need handbrake to be off.	
but there must be de facto control.	*Harman v Wardrop* [1971] RTR 127 Motorist effectively prevented from driving at time of breath test as his keys had been taken by another person. *Held* not driving.	
Driving as result of coercion or necessity may prove a valid defence.	*Tudhope v Grubb* 1983 SCCR 350 (Sh Ct) G locked himself in car to avoid violent attack by several persons. Drove off to escape further injury to car and self. *Held* attempted to drive to avoid further injury following unprovoked assault. Acquitted.	
	But see *MacLeod v MacDougall* 1988 SCCR 519 Driving must cease as soon as necessity is over.	
	Moss v Howdle 1997 SCCR 215 (see Coercion). *Roxton v Lang* 1998 SCCR 1 (Sh Ct) (see Coercion).	

COMMENTARY	CASE LAW	STATUTE LAW
Driving in an emergency.	*Watson v Hamilton* 1988 SCCR 13 Court must be satisfied that no other reasonable alternative has been ignored. Pregnant guest in W's house awoke bleeding heavily and fearing miscarriage. W attempted to find phone and get help but at 2 am set off to hospital. It was *held* that it was not reasonable to have expected W to rouse his neighbours at 2 am.	
Unfit to drive High alcohol content in blood may not indicate unfitness.	*MacNeill v Fletcher* 1966 JC 18 *Held* that although urine sample showed high alcohol content, doctor was entitled not to certify accused as unfit to drive.	Road Traffic Act 1988 Section 4(5) '...a person shall be taken to be unfit to drive if his ability to drive properly is for the time being impaired.'
Normal driving does not raise presumption of fitness.	*Murray v Muir* 1949 JC 127; 1950 SLT 41 *Held* that fact that accused drove 200 yards in proper manner did not create presumption of sobriety which medical evidence could not disprove. See *McEwan v Higson* 2001 SCCR 579	
Drink	*Armstrong v Clark* [1957] 2 QB 391 Diabetic took dose of insulin and became incapable of driving properly. Charged under section similar to present RTA 1988, s 4(1). *Observed* that 'drink' probably means alcoholic drink.	
or drugs	*Armstrong v Clark* [1957] 2 QB 391 'Drug' means any medicine given to cure, alleviate or assist an ailing body, and includes insulin.	RTA 1988, s 11(2), as amended by Road Traffic Act 1991, Sch 4, para 44, states that drug includes any 'intoxicant other than alcohol', ie wider definition than that given by Lord Goddard CJ in *Armstrong v Clark*.
Solvents having drugging effect.	*Duffy v Tudhope* 1983 SCCR 440; 1984 SLT 107 *Held* that driver whose capacity to drive is impaired because he has been inhaling solvents cannot claim that such solvents are not drugs, if they have a drugging effect.	
Being in charge of motor vehicle.	*Macdonald v Crawford* 1952 SLT (Sh Ct) 92 Taxi driver sitting in taxi which had broken down, waiting for tow. *Held* in charge. *Lees v Lowrie* 1993 SCCR 1 Accused supervising 'L' driver, not a lesson. Evidence led that he would not have taken over driving. *Held* that the accused was in charge of the vehicle but no likelihood of driving.	RTA 1988, s 4(2)
Not in charge.	*Adair v McKenna* 1951 SLT (Sh Ct) 40 *Held* that motor mechanic engaged in repairing fault in vehicle by roadside not in charge. *Crichton v Burrell* 1951 JC 107; 1951 SLT 365 Car owner waiting for another person with duplicate keys to drive him home. *Held* not in charge of vehicle, as not in de facto control. *Dean v Wishart* 1952 JC 9; 1952 SLT 86 *Held* that person insensible in back of vehicle which had been immobilised by removal of rotor arm not in charge. *Winter v Morrison* 1954 JC 7 Car owner in front passenger seat. Wife in driving seat with engine running. Wife's provisional licence expired. *Held* that car owner not in charge.	

COMMENTARY	CASE LAW	STATUTE LAW
No likelihood of driving Defence to s 4(2) charge.	*Neish v Stevenson* 1969 SLT 229 *Held* that burden of proof, on a balance of probabilities, is on accused. *Morton v Confer* [1963] 2 All ER 765 *Held* that court must be satisfied that, on balance of probabilities, there was no likelihood that intention not to drive would be departed from. *Northfield v Pinder* [1969] 2 QB 7 Driver found near his car so drunk as to be incapable of driving, finding car, or walking to it. *Held* no defence; no evidence that driver would not have driven when worst effects had worn off.	Road Traffic Act 1988 Section 4(3)
Post-incident drinking Defence to section 4(1) and (2) as well as section 5(1)(a) and (b).	*Neish v Stevenson* 1969 SLT 229 Standard of proof as in this case. *Hassan v Scott* 1989 SCCR 49 Accused may not have to prove exact amount of ale subsequently consumed. If defence evidence demonstrates that there is a reasonable doubt about Crown case, accused entitled to acquittal.	Road Traffic Offenders Act 1988 Section 15(3)
Causing death	*R v Ash* 1999 RTR. 347. A drove with a blood alcohol concentration well in excess of the legal limit. He collided with another vehicle, killing its driver. A was ultimately convicted of causing death by dangerous driving under s 1 of the RTA 1988 and sentenced to four years' imprisonment, five years' disqualification and having to take a driving test thereafter, On appeal, A submitted that due to the seriousness of his own injuries which resulted in only one forensic blood sample being taken rather than the two required by the Road Traffic Offenders Act 1988, s 15 – the blood sample ought not to be admitted in evidence as well as his sentence being unduly excessive. *Held*, dismissing the appeal that it could not be said that the use of the sample was unfair if open to the jury to conclude that it was such as to affect the quality of the defendant's driving, and that the sentence was not manifestly excessive notwithstanding A's injuries and previous good character due to the circumstances of the case. See also: *Ross v HMA* 2003 SCCR 1	RTA 1988, s 3A(1). If a person causes the death of another person by driving a mechanically propelled vehicle on a road or other public place without due care and attention or without reasonable consideration for other persons using the road or place, and (a) he is, at the time when he is driving, unfit to drive through drink or drugs; or (b) he has consumed so much alcohol that the proportion of it in his breath, blood or urine at that time exceeds the prescribed limit; or (c) within 18 hours of that time, he is required to provide a specimen in pursuance of s 7 of this Act, but without reasonable excuse fails to provide it, he is guilty of an offence. Section 3A(2). For the purposes of this section a person shall be taken to be unfit to drive at any time when his ability to drive properly is impaired. Section 3A(3). Subsection 1(b) and (c) shall not apply in relation to a person driving a mechanically propelled vehicle other than a motor vehicle.

SENTENCING POLICY

Ross v HMA 2003 SCCR 1

R appealed against a sentence of three years' imprisonment following a conviction for causing death by careless driving, in terms of the Road Traffic Act 1988, s 3A(1). *Held*, refusing the appeal, that, although the degree of carelessness could be a mitigating factor to a conviction under s 3A(1), the fact that R had been driving at excessive speed, had been drinking and had refused to provide a specimen of blood to enable the level of alcohol in his blood to be measured, and that the car had left the carriageway for no apparent reason, all pointed to a degree of carelessness which was sufficiently serious to justify the sentence of three years.

Alcohol concentration above prescribed limit

Road Traffic Act 1988, s 5.
Section 5(1)(a). Driving or attempting to drive motor vehicle or
(b) in charge of motor vehicle
after consuming so much alcohol that **proportion in breath, blood or urine exceeds prescribed limit.**
Section 5(2). Defence to s 6(1)(b)) that **no likelihood of driving** vehicle while proportion of alcohol in breath, blood or urine remained likely to exceed prescribed limit.
Road Traffic Offenders Act 1988.
Section 15(3). Defence of post-incident drinking.

COMMENTARY	CASE LAW	STATUTE LAW
Proportion in breath, blood or urine	*Jordan v Russell* 1995 SCCR 423 Appellant charged with driving with excess alcohol in his blood. Crown evidence of duplicate test carried out under quality checks gave average of 93 µg from which safety factor of six deducted. Defence test by single analyst gave reading of 80 µg. Conviction upheld: it was all right to reject defence evidence and accept Crown's, which had confirmatory tests and quality checks.	Road Traffic Act 1988 Section 11(2). Prescribed limits are: (a) 35 microgrammes of alcohol in 100 millilitres of breath, or (b) 80 milligrammes of alcohol in 100 millilitres of blood, or (c) 107 milligrammes of alcohol in 100 millilitres of urine, or such other proportion as may be prescribed by the Secretary of State.
Court may discount evidence if, for example, specimen obtained illegally by deception or under duress.	*R v Fox* [1985] RTR 337 Per Lord Fraser: 'If the appellant had been lured to the police station by some trick or deception, or if the police officers had behaved oppressively towards the appellant, the justice's jurisdiction to exclude otherwise admissible evidence ... might come into play.'	Road Traffic Offenders Act 1988 Section 15(2). All readings, no matter how they were obtained, must be considered. Section 15(4). Specimen of blood will be disregarded unless taken from accused, with consent, by medical practitioner.
Exceeds prescribed limit	*R v Coomaraswamy* [1976] RTR 21 *Held* that if driver's specimen discloses an excess over prescribed limit, it is not necessary to prove a particular degree of excess. *Lockhart v Deighan* 1985 SCCR 204; 1985 SLT 549 It was made clear in this case that because of a letter from the Crown Agent to the Law Society of Scotland, published in the September issue of JLSS, the Crown has effectively barred itself from prosecuting where the breath alcohol level is less than 40 microgrammes. This delimitation was strictly construed in this case and held not to extend to blood alcohol levels. *McConnachie v Scott* 1988 SCCR 176 Motorist provided two specimens of breath of less than 40 milligrammes. *Held* to be incompetent for police officer to require motorist to provide specimen of blood or urine in these circumstances.	
No likelihood of driving Defence to s 5(1)(b) charge.	See: *Neish v Stevenson* 1969 SLT 229 *Northfield v Pinder* [1969] 2 QB 7	

Preliminary tests

Road Traffic Act 1988, s 6.
Section 6(1): Constable may require a driver to co-operate with any one or more **preliminary tests** administered to the person by that constable or another constable if he **reasonably suspects** that the person:
Section 6(2):
(a) is driving, is attempting to drive or is in charge of a motor vehicle on a road or other **public place**, and
(b) has alcohol or a drug in his body or is under the influence of a drug.
Section 6(3):
(a) has been driving, attempting to drive or in charge of a motor vehicle on a road or other public place while having alcohol or a drug in his body or while unfit to drive because of a drug, and
(b) still has alcohol or a drug in his body or is still under the influence of a drug.
Section 6(4):
(a) is or has been driving, attempting to drive or in charge of a motor vehicle on a road or other public place, and
(b) has committed a traffic offence while the vehicle was in motion.
Section 6(6): A person commits an offence if **without reasonable excuse** he fails to co-operate with a preliminary test in pursuance of a requirement imposed under this section.

COMMENTARY	CASE LAW	STATUTE LAW
Preliminary Tests: s 6A – Preliminary breath test s 6B – Preliminary impairment test s 6C – Preliminary drug test		Road Traffic Act 1988, s 6(8): 'In this section – a reference to a preliminary test is to any of the tests described in sections 6A to 6C...'
Reasonably suspects	*Copeland v Macpherson* 1970 SLT 87 Suspicion arose out of information given to constable by another officer. *Held* to be reasonable. *Topping v Scott* 1979 SLT (Notes) 21. Police received anonymous phone call informing them that white van involved in accident with blue car. Police found white van with traces of blue paint parked outside accused's house. Accused gave positive breath test. *Held* that sheriff entitled to convict. Police had knowledge of accident although they had not witnessed it. *MacKenzie v Hingston* 1995 SCCR 386. Appellant drove to harbour and left vehicle and ran into his boat. Constables followed him on and detected smell of alcohol and required specimen. He refused and was convicted. *Held*, prior view of police that road traffic offence committed (as distinct from view he had alcohol on his body) entitled police to require specimen and pursue appellant onto boat as a matter of urgency.	Road Traffic Act 1988, s 6(1)

COMMENTARY	CASE LAW	STATUTE LAW
Wide powers to stop vehicles, but these must not be exercised oppressively.	*Chief Constable of Gwent v Dash* [1985] Crim L R 674 Constable may stop a motorist with sole intention of seeing whether or not he has been drinking.	Road Traffic Offenders Act 1988 Section 15(2). All readings, no matter how they were obtained, must be considered. Section 15(4). Specimen of blood will be disregarded unless taken from accused, with consent, by medical practitioner.
Public place	*Alston v O'Brien* 1992 SCCR 238 Breath test, 'public place', car on farm drive. *Held* on appeal that the public were not expected to be there so not a public place. See also: *Thomson v MacPhail* 1992 SCCR 513	
Failure to provide specimen **without reasonable excuse.**	*R v Lennard* [1973] RTR 252 Per Laxton LJ: '[N]o excuse can be adjudged a reasonable one unless the person from whom the specimen is required is physically or mentally unable to provide it, or the provision of the specimen would entail a substantial risk to his health'.	RTA 1988 Section 6(6)
Once issue of reasonable excuse sufficiently raised, it is for prosecution to rebut it.	*Earnshaw v HMA* 1982 JC 11.	
Reasonable excuse relates to taking of test only.	*McNicol v Peters* 1969 SLT 261 Not a reasonable excuse for driver to maintain he had not consumed alcohol. *McGrath v Vipas* [1984] RTR 58 Not a reasonable excuse that accused not driver at material time. *McLaren v MacLeod* 1994 SCCR 478 Constable requiring a specimen does not require to ask the person if there are medical reasons why blood should not be taken although the suspect should be told that not giving the specimen without reasonable excuse is an offence.	
Constable must be in uniform		RTA 1988 Section 6(7): 'A constable may administer a preliminary test by virtue of any of subsections (2) to (4) only if he is in uniform.'

Provision of specimens for analysis

Road Traffic Act 1988, ss 7, 8.
Section 7(1). Constable may require person suspected of offence under s 3A, s 4 or s 5
(a) to provide two specimens of breath for **analysis by means of a device of type approved by Secretary of State** or
(b) to provide a specimen of blood or urine for a laboratory test.
Section 7(2). Requirement to provide specimens of breath under s 7(1)(a) can only be made at a police station, hospital, or at or near a place where a relevant breath test has been administered to the person concerned or would have been so administered but for his failure to co-operate with it.
Section 7(3). Requirement to provide specimen of **blood or urine** under s 7(1)(b) can only be made at police station or hospital, and cannot be made at police station unless
(a) constable has reasonable cause to believe that for **medical reasons** breath-specimen cannot be provided or should not be required, or
(b) **no device or reliable device available**, or
(c) suspected offence is under s 3A or 4 and medical advice suggests conditions may be due to drugs.
Section 7(4). If specimen other than breath required, constable decides whether blood or urine is required, unless medical practitioner advises blood cannot or should not be taken.
Section 7(5). Specimen of urine shall be provided within one hour of its requirement, and after provision of previous specimen.
Section 7(6). Failure to provide specimen, without **reasonable excuse**, is an offence.
Section 7(7). Constable must warn that failure to provide specimen may lead to prosecution.
Section 8(1). Where two breath specimens have been provided in pursuance of section 7, the one with the lower proportion of alcohol in the breath shall be used, and the other disregarded.
Section 8(2). If the specimen with the lower proportion of alcohol contains no more than 50 mg of alcohol in 100 ml of breath, the person who provided it may elect to replace it with a specimen of blood or urine, under s 7(4).

COMMENTARY	CASE LAW	STATUTE LAW
Requirement to provide specimen must be corroborated.	*Carmichael v Gillooly* 1982 SCCR 119.	
Analysis by means of a device of type approved by Secretary of State.	*Knox v Lockhart* 1984 SCCR 463 Crown failed to present in evidence at trial that device used was of type approved by Secretary of State. *Held*, on appeal, Crown must prove in evidence that device used is of approved type. See also: *Pickard v Carmichael* 1995 SCCR 76 Proof required that device approved.	
Specimen of blood.		Road Traffic Act 1988, s 11(4). Person must consent to blood being taken by medical practitioner.
Only one breath specimen provided.	*Reid v Tudhope* 1985 SCCR 268 Conviction upheld where R in attempt to frustrate procedure failed to provide second specimen. But compare:	Section 7(1)(a)

COMMENTARY	CASE LAW	STATUTE LAW
	Douglas v Stevenson 1986 SCCR 519 Accused gave one specimen. After genuine failure to provide second specimen, he was refused opportunity to try again. *Held* that police had not given him fair opportunity for provision of second specimen.	
Medical reasons.	*Dempsey v Catton* [1986] RTR 194 Decision of constable is subjective, and he is not required to obtain medical advice. Defendant refused to give specimen claiming he suffered from agoraphobia, and phobia of machines. Constable accepted the latter and required blood specimen.	Section 7(3)(a)
No device or reliable device available.	*Gilligan v Tudhope* 1985 SCCR 434 G charged with driving with excess alcohol on basis of blood sample. He had earlier provided two breath specimens. Readings on the visual display showed that it was in working order, but device then produced printout giving nonsensical dates and times. *Held* that analytical function of device working and no justification for requiring blood test. Conviction quashed. See also: *Walker v Walkingshaw* 1991 SCCR 358 *Ramage v Walkingshaw* 1992 SCCR 82 *Carson v Orr* 1992 SCCR 260	
Test is subjective.	*Burnett v Smith* 1989 SCCR 628 B had provided two breath specimens but police concluded device unreliable and required blood specimen. On appeal *held* that proper test is subjective and police entitled to require blood specimen if they concluded on reasonable grounds that device unreliable, even if it was reliable, and appeal refused.	
Blood or urine: constable decides.	*Bain v Tudhope* 1985 SCCR 412 B gave positive breath specimen and elected to exercise right to provide alternative specimen. Required to provide urine, but failed, and convicted on breath specimen. *Held* that decision to require blood or urine was to be left wholly to discretion of constable. See also: *MacLeod v MacFarlane* 1992 SCCR 178 *Simpson v McClory* 1993 SCCR 402	Section 7(4)
Failure to provide specimen without **reasonable excuse.**	See p 53 *McLeod v Murray* 1986 SCCR 369 M, lorry driver, gave evidence that he had been assaulted by police officers who required specimens, and he refused to give specimens because he did not trust officers not to tamper with them. *Held* (1) that accused's evidence, if believed, would constitute reasonable excuse; and (2) onus of proof that there was no reasonable excuse lay on the Crown, and accused had raised reasonable doubt on the matter: accused acquitted. See also: *McIntosh v Lowe* 1991 SCCR 154	Section 7(6)

COMMENTARY	CASE LAW	STATUTE LAW
Accused must raise reasonable excuse at time of requirement if asked why he cannot provide specimen,	*Singh v McLeod* 1986 SCCR 656 At trial S claimed that asthmatic attack prevented him from providing breath specimen. S's doctor gave evidence that any asthmatic attack would have been obvious to anyone. S had not mentioned asthma at time of requirement to provide specimen. *Held* to be sufficient evidence of no reasonable excuse.	
but if not asked no obligation to volunteer information.	*Pringle v Annan* 1988 SCCR 423 P unable to provide breath specimen as result of injuries suffered. *Held* that physical inability constituted reasonable excuse, and there is no general duty on motorist to inform police of the reason for his inability to provide specimen.	
	McClory v Owen-Thomas 1989 SCCR 402 O-T required to give specimen of blood and refused to do so saying 'There's no way I want to give blood. I tend to get faint ...'. At trial evidence led of O-T's suffering from phobic fear of needles. Sheriff acquitted. On appeal *held* onus of establishing absence of reasonable excuse lies on Crown; no onus on motorist to disclose anything to police; appeal refused.	
	But compare: *Milne v Westwater* 1990 SCCR 46 M gave evidence that because of earlier amputations he was terrified of doctor putting needles in his arm. Sheriff disbelieved him and convicted. On appeal *held* that onus of proving absence of reasonable excuse was on Crown, but that as sheriff disbelieved him and no rational explanation provided, no merit in appeal.	
	Manual v Steward 1986 SCCR 121 It is not a reasonable excuse to refuse to give specimen until solicitor arrives.	
Accused must **unequivocally** agree to provide specimen,	*Beveridge v Allan* 1986 SCCR 542 On being required to provide specimen, B replied 'Yes, I refuse'. Officer asked him why and B said 'Oh well, I'll blow the thing'. Officer did not allow him to give specimen, but charged B with failure to provide breath. *Held* that sheriff entitled to treat B's initial response as a refusal. Not open to B to change his mind.	
and cannot specify part of body from which sample to be taken.	*Salesbury v Pugh* [1969] 2 All ER 1171 Driver insisted on samples being taken from big toe. Convicted of failure to provide.	
	Friel v Dickson 1992 SCCR 513 Blood specimen, RTA 1988, s 11(4). Accused under the influ-ence of medication. Sheriff said that the Crown had failed to show consent and exclude the possibility of less than complete consciousness. Appeal. *Held* that the Crown must show consent which it had not but need not exclude the possibility of less than complete consciousness. Not convinced here that T knew what was being asked of him.	
Police must not exert pressure on driver to provide blood or urine,	*Green v Lockhart* 1985 SCCR 257	

COMMENTARY	CASE LAW	STATUTE LAW
and must inform driver fully of his rights.	*Pelosi v Jessop* 1990 SCCR 175 Police told P that he could give specimen of blood, without mentioning urine. *Held* proper procedure not carried through and conviction quashed.	
Police decide whether to require blood or urine.	*Bain v Tudhope* 1985 SCCR 412.	
Timeous objections.	*Macaulay v Wilson* 1995 SCCR 133 Appellant charged with driving with excess alcohol in urine. Solicitor never objected to Crown evidence, and sheriff never allowed him to lead evidence to contradict the execution of service. *Held*, analyst's certificate was sufficient in absence of timeous objection and appeal refused.	

See further, Wheatley *Road Traffic Law in Scotland* (4 ed).

Mitigating circumstances; special reasons

Mitigating circumstances may avoid disqualification which normally results from the 'totting up' of a total of twelve penalty points incurred over a period of three years.
Special reasons for not ordering obligatory endorsement or disqualification.

COMMENTARY	CASE LAW	STATUTE LAW
Mitigating circumstances: all the circumstances both in relation to the offence and the offender, including all previous offences.		Road Traffic Offenders Act 1988 Section 35. Where a driver has incurred twelve points within a three-year period, he must be disqualified for at least six months unless the court is satisfied, having regard to all the circumstances, that there are grounds for mitigation and thinks fit to order a shorter period of disqualification or none at all.
	Smith v Craddock 1979 JC 66 Speeding. Driver by trade and would lose employment if disqualified. Wife and children relied totally on accused for income. Sheriff refrained from disqualification and imposed a fine. *Held*, on appeal by Crown, that sheriff entitled to take such factors into consideration in his exercise of discretion.	RTOA 1988, s 35(4). The court, in considering whether such mitigating circumstances exist, may not take account of (a) triviality of the offence; (b) hardship, other than exceptio-nal hardship; (c) circumstances pre-viously taken into account by any court within the previous three years.
Exceptional hardship—loss of licence involving loss of employment and house.	*Stephens v Gibb* 1984 SCCR 195 S convicted of offence involving discretionary disqualification. S's driving licence contained endorsements showing that the number of penalty points to be taken into account was such as to involve disqualification. Appealed. *Held* that '... by reason of a combination of factors special and peculiar to this particular appellant, disqualification would result in exceptional hardship...' Appeal allowed; disqualification quashed. But compare: *Holden v McPhail* 1988 SCCR 486 Observed that court should examine very carefully any suggestion of exceptional hardship and hold it established only on clearest possible evidence. *Stephens v Gibb* was a very special case and was not authority for proposition that in every case loss of job and inability to pay mortgage constituted exceptional hardship. *Mowbray v Guild* 1989 SCCR 535 *Held* to be exceptional hardship in that loss of licence would lead to loss of business, affect M and his wife's health, and interfere with child's education. *Howdle v Davidson* 1994 SCCR 751 Exceptional hardship. Accused stood to lose, inter alia, business and income to support family. Crown appealed sheriff's failure to disqualify and relied on *Ewen v Orr* 1993 SCCR 1015 as laying down a rule that exceptional hardship required that persons other than accused's immediate family would suffer. *Held*, no such rule and sheriff entitled to view hardship in case was exceptional and appeal refused. See also cases under Sentencing, Totting Up, below.	RTOA 1988, s 28 provides for award of penalty points on conviction of contraventions of Road Traffic Act 1988. RTOA 1988, s 35(4): 'No account is to be taken under subsection (1) of ... (b) hardship, other than exceptional hardship.'

COMMENTARY	CASE LAW	STATUTE LAW
Special reasons Question of whether a special reason exists is one of law.	*Muir v Sutherland* 1940 JC 66 Speeding charge. *Held* that question whether a special reason existed was one of law and not of discretion.	RTOA 1988, s 34 and Sch 2. Certain offences carry obligatory disqualification. In all these instances disqualification can only be avoided if offending motorist successfully pleads special reasons for not being disqualified.
Special reasons for reducing period of disqualification or ordering not to be disqualified.	*Orttewell v Allan* 1984 SCCR 208 Disqualified driver pushed broken down car off busy main street and then got into driving seat and was pushed into car park where it collided with another vehicle. *Held* to be sufficient grounds to reduce period of disqualification from three years to one year.	
Reason must be special to the facts of the *offence* and not to the peculiar circumstances of the offender.	*Adair v Munn* 1940 JC 69 Drunk driving charge. *Held* that considerations of hardship and similar mitigating circumstances personal to the convicted person were not 'special reasons' entitling the court to reduce or remit the sentence. *Carnegie v Clark* 1947 JC 74 Charge of driving while disqualified. Fact that sentence might lead to expulsion from university not a special reason. *Muir v M'Pherson* 1953 SLT 307 Charge of drunk in charge of a motor vehicle under Road Traffic Act 1930, s 15(2). Accused was a taxi driver. Fact that disqualification would cause considerable personal hardship held not to constitute a special reason. *Robertson v M'Ginn* 1955 JC 57 Insurance. Submitted as special reasons that offender was a 'man of substance' and required to drive for business as a farmer and for local government affairs. *Held*, no special reason. *Norman v Cameron* 1992 SCCR 390 RTOA 1988, s 5(1)(a) disqualification. Accused said that he had waited some three and a half hours after consuming a small amount of alcohol, believing he was thus fit to drive. Accepted by sheriff as a special reason. Overturned on appeal, special reasons must relate to the facts which constitute the offence not the circumstances or beliefs of the accused. See also: *McClelland v Whitelaw* 1993 SCCR 1113	
Medical condition.	*Scott v Hamilton* 1988 SCCR 262 Lady motorist pled guilty to failure to provide specimen but claimed she had been suffering from pre-menstrual tension, and was not amenable to reason. *Held* that this was not special reason for not disqualifying.	
Accused's mistaken belief.	*Robertson v McNaughtan* 1993 SCCR 226 Driving while disqualified, special reasons. R thought his disqualification was suspended pending an appeal but it had revived when his solicitor failed to lodge the appeal timeously. Sheriff imposing penalty points but not disqualifying on the grounds that there were special reasons. Appeal. *Held* that there were special reasons and licence should not even have been endorsed.	

COMMENTARY	CASE LAW	STATUTE LAW
	Scott v Ross 1994 SCCR 538 Appellant not disqualified. Sheriff held there were mitigating circumstances, because appellant parked at locus he wrongly thought was not a road. *Held*, by a full bench, allowing appeal: sheriff to consider first whether there are special reasons why the respondent's licence should not be endorsed with penalty points before he decides whether the respondent must be ordered to be disqualified under RTOA 1988, s 35(1).	
	See also: *Carmichael v Shelvin* 1991 SCCR 247 *Norman v Cameron* 1992 SCCR 390.	
	Watson v Adam 1996 SCCR 382 Driver realised that he had drunk alcoholic beer and not non-alcoholic beer as first thought, but decided to drive anyway. *Held*, he took risk and one-year disqualification upheld and sheriff wrong to suggest special reasons require corroboration.	
	Marshall v McLeod 1998 SCCR 317 Appellant convicted of driving another person's vehicle without insurance. *Held*, on appeal, overturning sheriff, that special reasons were established where owner told him that he was covered by owner's insurance and no reason to disbelieve owner.	
The safety of the public in their use of the roads must be viewed as the vital consideration.	*Adair v Munn* 1940 JC 69 Considerations tending to show that the safety of the public on the roads would not be prejudiced by a reduction or remission were special reasons.	
	Fairlie v Hill 1944 JC 53 Insurance contravention under Road Traffic Act 1930, s 35(2). *Held* that in considering a remission or reduction in relation to disqualification the protection of the public is the chief criterion. If reasons adduced by offender tend to show public protection will not be prejudiced, the court has a discretion and may have regard to personal hardship.	
	Lowe v Mulligan 1991 SCCR 551 Driving with excess alcohol. M had moved car a short distance to prevent it being a hazard. The road on which he had originally parked prior to going into the pub was due to become one-way in the morning due to road works. *Held* that it was a special reason.	
Performance of public duties cannot in itself be a special reason. Exceptions made to this rule during wartime.	*Murray v Macmillan* 1942 JC 10 Insurance contravention under s 35(2) of Road Traffic Act 1930. Convicted person was a doctor with a number of emergency posts in relation to colliery and aerodrome for which a car was essential.	
	Compare with:	
	M'Fadyean v Burton 1954 JC 18 Charge of drunk driving. Officer in Territorial Army used car for related duties. *Held* did not constitute special reason.	
Triviality of the circumstances of the offence not a special reason.	*Tudhope v Birbeck* 1979 SLT (Notes) 47 Pedestrian crossing. Fact that circumstances of offence trivial and that no danger caused to anyone did not constitute a special reason.	

COMMENTARY	CASE LAW	STATUTE LAW
Circumstances held to have established special reasons include emergencies: *accused* must prove there was a genuine emergency	*Graham v Annan* 1980 SLT 28 Driving while disqualified and without insurance. Pregnant woman who was driving car became ill and husband, who was disqualified, took over. *Held*, on appeal, that circumstances disclosed a special reason for not ordering further disqualification or endorsement.	
and offence must have been committed out of circumstances of real necessity.	*Copeland v Sweeney* 1977 SLT (Sh Ct) 28 Drunk driving charge. Daughter who suffered from unusual medical condition was stung by wasp. Father drove to his daughter collecting medicine on the way. *Held* no special reason. 'Must show not only that the circumstances amounted to a medical emergency but also that the driver had a compelling reason and no alternative in the circumstances but to drive.' But see: *Norman v Logue* 1996 SCCR 797 (Sh Ct) Special reasons established where disabled woman drove car 10 ft in distraught state to remove it from broken glass from break-in in her street. Car only mode of transport for her and 90 year-old mum. No public interest in disqualifying her. *Lees v Macdonald* 1997 SCCR 189 (Sh Ct) Special reasons where warden of elderly home left flat for fear of assault and drove to friends. *Held*, since no record, and concern not to wake residents, it was appropriate not to disqualify her. *Dolan v McLeod* 1998 SCCR 653 *Held*, purpose of driving was to observe ex-boyfriend's gang, not to escape apprehended violence. Convicted and disqualified. Upheld on appeal.	
Where driver breaks the law only because he is ordered to do a certain act by a police officer.	*Farrell v Moir* 1974 SLT (Sh Ct) 89 Refusal to give sample. Convicted. Argued that he should not be disqualified in that he had driven only because police had ordered him to move his car. On appeal, disqualification quashed and admonition substituted.	
Onus lies on *accused* to establish special reasons,	*McLeod v Scoular* 1974 SLT (Notes) 44 Drugs and driving. Observations made by Lord Justice-Clerk on proper procedure for determining whether special reasons have been established. Onus on accused to satisfy the court that there are special reasons and prosecution should have opportunity to contradict or qualify that evidence.	
although such reasons may be established without specific reference to their 'special' quality.	*Keane v Perrie* 1982 SCCR 377 Careless driving. Plea of guilty by letter. No reference in letter to special reasons as such but referred to certain mitigating factors and his driving record. *Held*, on appeal by Crown, that sheriff entitled to refrain from ordering endorsement and not necessary for circumstances to be expressly described as special reasons in the letter. See also: *Trotter v Burnet* 1947 JC 151 Plea of guilty by letter. Where reasons purporting to prejudice the public interest are raised, the court should be slow to pronounce sentence in accused's absence.	

COMMENTARY	CASE LAW	STATUTE LAW
	Herron v Sharif 1974 SLT (Notes) 63 Small excess of alcohol in blood. Not a special reason. See also Sentencing Policy, Totting Up, below.	

MISUSE OF DRUGS

Production, supply and possession of controlled drugs

Misuse of Drugs Act 1971, ss 4, 5.
Section 4(1)(a). It is an offence for a person **to produce** a **controlled drug**.
Section 4(1)(b). It is an offence to **supply** or offer to supply a controlled drug to another.
Section 5(1). It is an offence for a person to have a controlled drug in his **possession**.
Section 5(3). It is an offence for a person to have a controlled drug in his **possession**, whether lawfully or not, **with intent to supply** it to another unlawfully.

COMMENTARY	CASE LAW	STATUTE LAW
Produce	*R v Farr* [1982] Crim LR 745 CA F allowed C and A to use F's kitchen knowing that C and A were producing pink heroin there. *Held*, allowing F's appeal against conviction of producing a controlled drug contrary to MDA 1971, s 4(2), that there had to be some identifiable participation in the process of producing a controlled drug before a conviction under s 4(2) could be sustained. Appropriate charge should have been under MDA 1971, s 8, allowing premises to be used for production of the drug. F had made no prior arrangements with C and A, and the evidence showed only passive presence. *R v Russell* (1992) 94 Cr App R 351 Court of Appeal upheld that converting cocaine hydrochloride into free base cocaine (crack) amounts to producing class A drug 'by other means', and even though they shared generic term cocaine they had different properties. *Attorney General's Reference (No. 93 of 2005)* [2005] EWCA Crim 3186. During the course of a police search, 307 cultivated cannabis plants with a street value of £42,000 were found at the residence of the accused who was duly convicted of producing cannabis contrary to s 4(2)(a) of MDA 1971. Also convicted of supplying the drug contrary to s 4(3)(a) of MDA 1971.	Misuse of Drugs Act 1971 Sections 4(2) 'it is an offence for a person – (a) to produce a controlled drug in contravention of subsection (1) above' and 37(1): produce 'by manufacture, cultivation or any other method'.
Controlled drug	*Doherty v Brown* 1996 SCCR 136 Full bench. Conviction under MDA 1971, s 5(3) upheld. Accused mistakenly believed tablets contained ecstasy. *Held*, factual impossibility does not preclude Crown charging an attempt. Where accused knows of impossibility there can be no attempt. *HMA v Anderson* 1928 JC 1 disapproved. See Attempts. *McCallum v McKay* 1997 SCCR 558 Appellant convicted of supplying cannabis. No evidence of analysis of material but those supplied said material was cannabis resin and they had involvement in drugs. Conviction upheld on appeal: evidence was sufficient.	Section 2(1): Any controlled drug, ie, substance or product specified in Sch 2.
Supply	*R v Mills* [1963] 1 QB 522 Per Lord Parker CJ: '... "supply" must denote the parting of possession from one person to another ...'	Section 4(3): '... it is an offence for a person—(a) to supply ... a controlled drug to another... .'

COMMENTARY | **CASE LAW** | **STATUTE LAW**

R v Harris (Janet) [1968] 1 WLR 769
Held that the administration of a controlled drug to another who is already in possession of it does not constitute supplying of the drug by the person administering it.

Kerr (DA) v HMA 1986 SCCR 81
The offence of being concerned in the supplying of a controlled drug to another, contrary to MDA 1971, s 4(3)(b), may be established even though there has been no actual supply to another person.
Per Lord Hunter: 'I consider that section 4(3)(b) was purposely enacted in the widest terms ... to cover a great variety of activities both at the centre and on the fringes of dealing in controlled drugs. It would include ... the activities of financiers, couriers and other go-betweens, lookouts, advertisers, agents and many links in the chain of distribution.'

Douglas v Boyd 1996 SCCR 44
MDA 1971, s 4(3)(b). Respondent not present when father sold drugs, but she asked for payment a fortnight later. Sheriff held no case to answer.
Held, on appeal, supply not at an end when payment requested, and appeal allowed.

Morrison v Normand 1997 SCCR 469
Appellant convicted of supply and possession with intent to supply. Police officers offered 'hash or jellies' and appellant found in possession of cannabis. Upheld on appeal, since offer was entirely different to fact of possession.

Dickson v HMA 1994 SCCR 478
Observed, bulk buying and separating is covered by MDA 1971, s 5(3) (possession with intent to supply), and involvement before and after date of possession in transactions is covered by MDA 1971, s 4(3)(b) (supply), and jury should be directed to distinctions between sections.

Clark v HMA and Beattie v HMA 2002 SCCR. 675.
C and B made periodical trips from Glasgow to Manchester and London with the intention of supplying diamorphine. Each was convicted of a contravention of the Misuse of Drugs Act 1971, s 4(3)(b) and sentenced to 11 years' imprisonment. Appeals refused.

Aggravation of offence to supply of a controlled drug:

Can only result if:
(1) The offence is committed on or in the vicinity of school premises at a relevant time and;
(2) During the commission of the offence the offender used a courier who, at the time the offence was committed, was under the age of 18.

MDA 1971
Section 4A:
(1) This section applies if–
(a) a court is considering the seriousness of an offence under section 4(3) of this Act, and
(b) at the time the offence was committed the offender had attained the age of 18.
(2) If either of the following conditions is met the court–
(a) must treat the fact that the condition is met as an aggravating factor (that is to say, a factor that increases the seriousness of the offence), and
(b) must state in open court that the offence is so aggravated.

COMMENTARY	CASE LAW	STATUTE LAW
Possession Possession requires more than mere control, ie knowledge.	*Lockyer v Gibb* [1966] 2 All ER 653; [1967] 2 QB 243 Per Lord Parker CJ: 'It is quite clear that a person cannot be said to be in possession of some article which he or she does not realise is, or may be, in her handbag, or in her room, or in some other place over which she has control. It is necessary to show that the appellant knew that she had the article which turned out to be a drug.'	
	Warner v Metropolitan Police Commissioner [1969] 2 AC 256 Defendant found with a parcel containing a controlled drug and convicted. *Held*, on appeal to the House of Lords, that though there was a very strong inference of fact that a man who possesses a package also possesses its contents, he is entitled to be acquitted if he can show that he genuinely believed the parcel to contain an innocent substance and that he had no reasonable opportunity of examining its contents.	
	Gill v Lockhart 1987 SCCR 599 Cannabis resin found in accused's golf bag. Accused claimed he had placed it there two years ago and forgotten it. Convicted. *Held* on appeal that once a person knowingly has possession of a drug, his possession persists even if he forgets its presence. Appeal refused.	
	Hughes v Guild 1990 SCCR 527 Possession, drugs found in the living room of flat occupied by two persons. *Held* on appeal that drugs lying in the open in room enough for inference of knowledge and control.	
	Feeney v Jessop 1990 SCCR 565 Possession. Drugs found in F's towel in cell. *Held* on appeal that F must have known of them and had control over them.	
	Davidson v HMA 1990 SCCR 699 Possession. Drugs found in co-accused's room next to scales bought by D. *Held* on appeal that given D tried to escape when police raided house there was just sufficient evidence for knowledge and control.	
	Murray v MacPhail 1991 SCCR 245 Possession. Accused allowing a friend to hide drugs in his room. Convicted. Upheld on appeal, sufficient knowledge and control.	
	White v HMA 1991 SCCR 555 Possession. Drugs found in W's flat to which others had access, made statement 'I'm saying nothing about it.' Conviction quashed on appeal, statement not special knowledge.	
	McTurk v HMA 1997 SCCR 1 Lost purse handed in to nightclub management. Drugs found next to undisturbed credit cards. Conviction under MDA 1971, s 5(3) upheld: no absolute rule that evidence of possession insufficient if more than one party had access.	
	Bath v HMA 1995 SCCR 323 Drugs found in engine of car in garage rented by appellant and father. Convicted but quashed on appeal: where accused and one other has access, some other evidence is required that accused knew of presence and impossible for jury to say which of them put drugs in engine.	

COMMENTARY	CASE LAW	STATUTE LAW
	McAllan v HMA 1996 SCCR 899 Drugs found in cigarette packet in compound six days after accident. Conviction under MDA 1971, s 4(3)(b) upheld on appeal: fanciful that drugs planted. Observed: dictum in *Bath v HMA* 1995 SCCR 323 at 325 not intended as statement of general application, ie each case of possession where access to accused and others must be decided on facts. See Evidence.	
Possession while in the custody of another.	*Amato v Walkingshaw* 1989 SCCR 564 A, a seaman employed on ship plying between Larne and Cairnryan. Posted envelope containing drugs to himself at Larne. Purser kept it for him but became suspicious and handed it to authorities in Cairnryan. Convicted. *Held* that A must have known that purser would hold envelope on his behalf, element of knowledge and control present and appeal refused. See also:	Misuse of Drugs Act 1971, s 37(3): 'For the purpose of this Act the things which a person has in his possession shall be taken to include any thing subject to his control which is in the custody of another.'
Onus.	*R v Marriott* [1971] 1 All ER 595 *McKenzie v Skeen* 1983 SLT 121 *R v Cugullere* [1961] 1 WLR 258; [1961] 2 All ER 343 The onus remains throughout on the Crown to prove knowledge. See also:	
Inferences.	*Warner v Metropolitan Police Commissioner* [1969] 2 AC 256 *DPP v Brooks* [1974] 2 All ER 840 *Held*, that running away may justify the inference.	
Although no provisions as to quantity, important in cases re minute quantities of drugs.	*R v Worsell* [1970] 1 WLR 111; [1969] 2 All ER 1183 W charged with unlawful possession of a tube containing droplets of heroin. *Held* that as the tube was in reality empty (ie the droplets were invisible to the human eye and could only be discerned under a microscope and could not be measured or poured out), it was impossible to hold that there was any evidence that the tube contained a drug. However: *Bocking v Roberts* [1973] 3 All ER 962 Per Lord Widgery CJ: 'When dealing with a charge of possessing a dangerous drug without authority the ordinary maximum of de minimis is not to be applied.'	
The quantities of drug found may be small but must be capable of being weighed, measured and identified to sustain prosecution.	*R v Frederick* 53 Cr App R 455 CA; [1970] 1 WLR 107; [1969] 3 All ER 804 Direction that if the jury thought the defendant was in possession of traces they should find him guilty because one must not have any dangerous drug in one's possession, no matter how small the quantity. Upheld. See also: *R v Graham* [1969] 2 All ER 1181 CA; [1970] 1 WLR 113 Scrapings in defendants' pockets sufficient to be measured. *R v Colyer* [1974] Crim LR 243 Traces measurable in the sense that they represented the minimum weight capable of being detected.	

COMMENTARY	CASE LAW	STATUTE LAW
	R v Marriott [1971] 1 All ER 595 Traces of drug found on penknife; although it was also necessary to show that the defendant had reason to know there was foreign matter on the knife. *Hambleton v Callinan* [1968] 2 QB 427; [1968] 2 All ER 943 *Held* that when a drug is consumed, it changes its character and it cannot be said that the drug is then in a person's possession, although traces of it are found in his urine. *Keane v Gallacher* 1980 JC 77; 1980 SLT 144 Police discovered on top of sideboard a small quantity of resinous material which was visible and could be measured. Argued by defence that the quantity was not 'useable'. Sheriff acquitted. G convicted on appeal. 'It is possession of the drug which is an offence, not its potential use.' *Murdo McKay v Hogg* (1973) SCCR Supp 40; 1973, Crown Office Circular 1224 Appellant asleep naked on couch. Search of his clothes on the chair disclosed nothing. After he had dressed, 16 tablets of LSD were found on seat cover. No one had anything to do with the chair except the appellant. He must have had the tablets for a second or two. *Held* that such fleeting contact was not enough to justify possession in terms of MDA 1971.	
Defence to 'possession' offence		MDA 1971, s 5(4)(a): It is a defence to prove that the accused 'took possession [of the drug] for the purpose of preventing another from committing ... an offence ... and that as soon as possible ... he took all such steps as were reasonably open to him to destroy the drug or to deliver it into the custody of a person lawfully entitled to take custody of it; or (b) that ... he took possession of it for the purpose of delivering it into the custody of a person lawfully entitled to take custody of it ... '
Possession for valid medical reason must be proved by defendant.	*Wood v Allan* 1988 SCCR 115.	Regulation 10(2) of Misuse of Drugs Regulations 1985, SI 1985/2066.
Possession with intent to supply	*Morrison v Smith* 1983 SCCR 171 M admitted unlawful possession of a controlled drug, but denied knowledge of a large amount of other drugs found in house. Convicted. *Held*, in absence of an explanation for possession, that the sheriff was entitled to infer intention to supply from the value, quantity and diversity of the drugs. *Haq v HMA* 1987 SCCR 433 H convicted of possessing cannabis resin with intent to supply. H in possession of large block of the drug weighing 91 g. No evidence of intent to supply other than size of block and evidence from one police officer that block too large for personal use. Appeal against conviction refused. *Held* to be sufficient evidence to infer intent.	MDA 1971, s 5(3): '... it is an offence for a person to have a controlled drug in his possession, whether lawfully or not, with intent to supply it to another in contravention of section 4(1) ...'

COMMENTARY	CASE LAW	STATUTE LAW
	Donnelly (Mary) v HMA 1984 SCCR 419 Heroin. Possession with intent to supply. D occupier of house where 'considerable quantity' of diamor-phine found in separate envelopes with street value of £10 or £20 each. Appeal against conviction refused. Per Lord Dunpark: '...where a large quantity of controlled drugs, separately packaged in quantities normally sold in the streets, are found in the possession of a person, it is open to a jury to infer that that person intended to supply them to another. If the appellant ... did no more than allow [S] to uplift drugs in her physical possession, she was thereby supplying them to another, namely, [S].' *Sim v HMA* 1996 SCCR 77 Appellant convicted of possession with intent to supply. Search of house found opaque grocery bag containing 16 bags with 100 temazepam capsules. Trial judge directed Crown required to prove bag and contents in accused's physical control and he knew general character of contents but not that they were particular drugs. *Held*, direction correct and conviction upheld. *McKenzie v Skeen* 1983 SLT 121 followed.	

References: Gordon, 1000; Bovey, 6, 7; 20-39; 55-85.

SENTENCING POLICY

Clark v HMA and Beattie v HMA 2002 SCCR 675.
C and B made periodical trips from Glasgow to Manchester and London with the intention of supplying diamorphine. Each was convicted of a contravention of the MDA 1971, s 4(3)(b) and sentenced to 11 years' imprisonment.

Crichton v HMA 2007 SCCR 339
C supplied a small amount of cocaine to undercover police officers contrary to the MDA 1971, s 4(3)(b). C pleaded guilty to the charge at the diet trial and was subsequently sentenced to three years imprisonment with the addition of another three months due to his bail aggravation. On appeal, it was held that this sentence was excessive and a greater regard ought to have been given to C's early guilty plea. The sentence of three years imprisonment was quashed and substituted by a sentence of 18 months imprisonment which was to be backdated to the date upon which C was remanded in custody.

OFFENSIVE WEAPONS

The **carrying** of an **offensive** weapon or a weapon **intended for use** as such, in a **public place** without lawful authority or **reasonable excuse** is a criminal offence**.** It is also an offence to carry a knife in a public place.
The law is now to be found in the Criminal Law (Consolidation) (Scotland) Act 1995, ss 47–50.

COMMENTARY	CASE LAW	STATUTE LAW
The offence is the carrying, not the use, of a weapon.	*Bates v Bulman* [1979] 3 All ER 170 Nature of offence under Prevention of Crime Act 1953, s 1(1) is the carrying and not the use of a weapon. Person who borrowed a clasp knife, not offensive per se, with the immediate intention of using it as an offensive weapon is not guilty of an offence under this Act (in England at least).	Criminal Law (Consolidation) (Scotland) Act 1995. Section 47(1). Any person who has with him in any public place any offensive weapon shall be guilty of an offence, and shall be liable – (a) on summary conviction, to imprisonment for a term not exceeding six months or a fine not exceeding the statutory maximum, or both; (b) on conviction on indictment, to imprisonment for a term not exceeding [four years] or a fine, or both.
	See also:	Section 47(2). Where person is convicted of offence under sub-section (1) the court may order forfeiture or disposal of weapon.
	R v Jura [1954] 1 QB 503 Airgun held not to be offensive weapon.	
'has with him'	*Smith v Vannet* 1998 SCCR 410 Appellant had with him offensive weapon and knife. Weapons six feet away in car and he had keys in pocket. Conviction upheld on appeal: 'with him' purposively interpreted as meaning readily available to him, albeit not on his person. *McVey v Friel* 1996 SCCR 768 distinguished because that case was under the Firearms Act 1968, and accused was in bedroom and separated from car containing the weapon by greater distance.	Section 47(3). A constable may arrest without warrant any person whom he has reasonable cause to believe to have committed or to be committing an offence under subsection (1) above.,
Offensive (1) Offensive per se, eg swords, daggers, coshes, knuckledusters	*Tudhope v O'Neill* 1982 SCCR 45 *Held*, a flick knife is an offensive weapon intended for use for causing injury and was therefore an offensive weapon per se. *Woods v Heywood* 1988 SCCR 434 W charged with possessing machete. Sheriff held that machete offensive weapon per se. *Held* on appeal that machete had twofold purpose, ie as a weapon and as a tool, and could not be described as an offensive weapon per se, and conviction quashed. *McGlennan v Clark* 1993 SCCR 334 Shuriken Chinese throwing star is an offensive weapon per se. Only purpose was for causing personal injury.	Section 47(4): '"offensive weapon" means any article made or adapted for use for causing injury to the person or intended by the person having it with him for such use by him.' or by some other person.

COMMENTARY	CASE LAW	STATUTE LAW
	McKee v MacDonald 1995 SCCR 513 Prevention of Crime Act 1953, s 1(4). Souvenir in shape of police truncheon. Accused convicted on basis article made for causing personal injury. *Held*, on appeal, article made from light wood and could not be compared to truncheon. Sentence quashed.	
(2) Adapted for use for causing injury, eg bicycle chain with razor-blade attached, or broken bottle.		
(3) Not offensive per se but intended for use for causing personal injury.	*R v Petrie* [1961] 1 WLR 358 *Held* that an ordinary razor was not an offensive weapon per se but would be offensive under Prevention of Crime Act 1953, s 1(4) if intention proved. *Glendinning v Guild* 1987 SCCR 304 Flail not per se offensive. Waving it in the air does not render it offensive. *Coull v Guild* 1985 SCCR 421 Sheath knife not per se an offensive weapon. *Houston v Snape* 1993 SCCR 995 Seven-inch dagger still an offensive weapon per se, even when contained in a protective sheath.	
Intended for use		
	R v Petrie [1961] 1 WLR 358 If not per se an offensive weapon the Crown must prove the intent to use to cause injury.	
Statutory question of intention to use is one to be drawn from all the circumstances.	*Lopez v MacNab* 1978 JC 41 Accused convicted of possession of a kitchen knife in a public place. Argued, Crown failed to prove intention to use it offensively. *Held* that intention was to be inferred from the facts and circumstances of the case. *Normand v Matthews* 1993 SCCR 856 Accused said he had clasp knife for 'protection'. On appeal *held* that this statement corroborated by two witnesses was sufficient evidence of accused's intention. *Ralson v Lockhart* 1986 SCCR 400 R charged with having an offensive weapon, ie a modelling knife, with intention to use it for causing personal injury. R was driving stolen car and when stopped by police, ran off. Sheriff inferred from these facts that he intended to use knife as offensive weapon. *Held* on appeal that it could not be inferred from his flight from the car that he intended to use knife and sheriff had inverted onus of proof which lay on prosecution to prove R had necessary intention. Conviction quashed. *Lopez v McNab* 1978 JC 41 distinguished.	

COMMENTARY	CASE LAW	STATUTE LAW
	Cunningham v Thomson 2011 SCCR 127. C found with 16 inch wooden baton in the style of an old police truncheon within his car during a routine police search. At first instance it was held the baton was an offensive weapon because it had been 'made or adapted for use for causing injury to the person'. On appeal however the conviction was quashed as the sheriff failed to give proper consideration to the decorative markings and true purpose of the baton which was red in colour, made with a lightwood and bore the emblem and markings of Liverpool Football Club rendering it a souvenir.	
Intention must be to cause injury.	*R v Rapier* (1979) 70 Cr App R 17 CA Rapier convicted of possession of carrying knife, having threatened a doorman with it. *Held*, on appeal, that intimidation was not enough unless the person intended to cause injury to the person (in England at least).	
	Farrell v Rennicks 1959 SLT (Sh Ct) 71 Knife found on accused who pleaded guilty to a house-breaking charge. Accused explained in evidence that knife was to be used as a housebreaking tool. *Held* that knife not in accused's possession for the purpose of causing personal injury. Acquitted of offensive weapons charge.	
Public place		
	Philips v Orr 1997 GWD 226 Prevention of Crime Act 1953, s 1(4). Pool cue in a car. Car was in a public place and Parliament had proceeded on the basis that its interior and all its contents were also deemed to be in a public place. Conviction upheld on appeal.	CL(C)(S)A 1995, s 47(4): '"public place" means any place other than — (a) domestic premises, (b) school premises (within the meaning of section 49A(6)), (c) a prison (within the meaning of section 49C(7)), "domestic premises" means premises occupied as a private dwelling (including any stair, passage, garden, yard, garage, outhouse or other appurtenance of such premises which is not used in common by the occupants of more than one such dwelling).
	Normand v Donnelly 1993 SCCR 639 Treatment cubicle in a casualty department necessarily private but conviction upheld on the inference that the accused walked through a public place to get there.	
	R v Theodoulou [1963] Crim LR 573 T convicted of carrying an offensive weapon, namely, an open razor in a public place, namely, a coffee bar. The trial judge assumed this was a public place rather than leaving it to the jury and because of this the conviction reluctantly quashed on appeal.	
	Owens v Crowe 1994 SCCR 310 Prevention of Crime Act 1953, s 1(1). Possession of lock knife in disco. *Held*, sheriff entitled to draw inference of intention to injure.	

COMMENTARY	CASE LAW	STATUTE LAW
	Wallace v Ruxton 1998 SCCR 701; 1999 SLT 447 *Held*, offensive weapon in 'public place' as not suggested appellant accessed neighbour's garden other than from public path and not suggested he was handed spanner in garden.	
Reasonable excuse		
	Grieve v MacLeod 1967 JC 32 Taxi driver carried a piece of rubber hose tipped with metal. Argued that it was for defensive purposes, taxi drivers often being subject to attack. *Held* that he had contravened the Prevention of Crime Act 1953. Per LJ-C Grant: 'One object of the Act is to ensure that ordinary citizens do not, unless in exceptional and justifiable circumstances, take the law into their own hands.'	
	Donaldson v Brown 1998 J.C. 31; 1998 SLT 1007; 1997 SCCR 689. A was charged with possession of a knife in a public place contrary to the CL(C)(S)A 1995, s 49(1). A unsuccessfully argued that he had not threatened anyone nor had he displayed any intent to injure and that the knife was exclusively for the purpose of self-defence.	
	Frame v Kennedy [2008] HCJAC 25; 2008 SLT 517; 2008 SCCR 382. A male stripper had been approached by two police officers outside premises where he had been booked to perform. The man had been dressed as a police officer and had been carrying a side handled baton, a friction lock baton and a spray, for possession of which he was charged under the CL(C)(S)A 1995, s 47(1). The sheriff acquitted the accused concluding that the weapons, although dangerous per se, were not intended to cause harm or injury to others but instead used as props within the strippers employment.	
Concealment. The offence under CL(C)(S)A 1995 is obstruction of, or concealment from, a PC who is exercising his powers of search for an offensive weapon under the Act.	*Burke v MacKinnon* 1983 SCCR 23 The offence of concealment of an offensive weapon under Criminal Justice (Scotland) Act 1980, s 4(2)(b) can only be established where it is shown that active steps were taken to conceal the weapon; thus failure to reveal possession would not likely lead to a conviction under the section. Sheriff Gordon in his commentary at p 25 states that whether or not a carrier will be prosecuted under this section, as well as, or instead of, under the Prevention of Crime Act 1953 will depend on the policy of the prosecutor.	Criminal Law (Consolidation) (Scotland) Act 1995, s 48. It is an offence to obstruct a PC or conceal an offensive weapon from him in the exercise of his powers of search.

COMMENTARY	CASE LAW	STATUTE LAW
Knife or other sharply pointed article	*Normand v Walker* 1994 SCCR 875 Clerk of Court lent a ruler to two policemen to measure blade and officers gave evidence that blade exceeded three inches. Sheriff upheld no case to answer in absence of evidence as to accuracy of ruler. *Held*, on appeal, sufficient evidence and appeal allowed. Observed, that evidence of use of everyday object like ruler is admissible without further evidence ofruler's accuracy. *Lister v Lees* 1994 SCCR 548 L carrying metal spike in railway station, said he had forgotten to throw it away after opening the tin of glue he was sniffing. *Held* on appeal that the question was whether at the time of his arrest L had a 'good reason'. Explanation not sufficient here. 'Good reason' different from 'reasonable excuse' under the Prevention of Crime Act 1953 but will still depend on the facts and circumstances of each case. *Brown v Farrell* 1997 SCCR 356 Carrying of Knives etc (Scotland) Act 1993, s 1(4). *Held*, using a knife to cut cans in preparing heroin for injection was not a 'good reason' for carrying knife. *Donaldson v Vannet* 1997 SCCR 689 Appellant charged under s 49 of Criminal Law (Consolidation) (Scotland) Act 1995, and offered to plead guilty as not charged under s 47. Presumably Crown accepted he never threatened anyone with knife. Appellant was reindicted under s 47. On appeal he argued his reply that knife for self-defence irrelevant to a charge under s 49. *Held*, reply would have been admissible to counter any defence of permissible reasons under CL(C)(S)A 1995, s 49(5), and no oppression, and appeal refused. Observed, Crown will frustrate Criminal Procedure (Scotland) Act 1995, s 258 (agree uncontroversial evidence) if re-indict following discussions with accused. *Stewart v Friel* 1995 SCCR 492 Carrying of Knives etc (Scotland) Act 1993, s 1(3). Folding pocketknife was lockable and this additional feature not mentioned in subsection. Conviction upheld on appeal.	CL(C)(S)A 1995 Section 49(1)–(3). Carrying of knife or other sharply pointed article is an offence and liable: (a) on summary conviction, to imprisonment for a term not exceeding twelve months or a fine not exceeding the statutory maximum or both; and (b) on conviction on indictment, to imprisonment for a term not exceeding four years or a fine or both. This does not apply to a folding pocket-knife with a blade of less than three inches (7.62 cms). Section 49(4). Defence that the person had 'good reason' or lawful authority for having the article. Section 49(5). Examples of potential 'good reasons', ie religious reasons, part of national costume, for use at work. Section 49A. Any person who has article to which s 49 and offensive weapon to which s 47 applies with him on school premises shall be guilty of an offence. Section 49B. A constable may enter school premises and search for article or offensive weapon if reasonable grounds for suspecting offence under s 49A being committed. (Section 50 is similar to s 48: it is an offence to obstruct a police constable or conceal an offensive weapon from him in exercise of his powers of search under s 50). The Knives Act 1997 deals with the marketing of 'combat knives' and is designed to control efforts to advertise and sell knives in a way which portrays them as suitable for violent use.

Reference: Gordon, 861-865.

SENTENCING POLICY

Jacobs v Wilson 1989 SCCR 9—J, first offender, pleaded guilty to having butcher's knife with ten-inch blade in street at 4 am. He stated he had been chased by two youths and had entered his house and come out with the knife, by which time the two youths had gone. Sheriff sentenced J to three months' imprisonment following the sentence in *Smith v Wilson* 1987 SCCR 191.
Held on appeal (1) that sheriff must not be seen to be fettering his discretion, and had come close to suggesting that all offensive weapons should be dealt with by a custodial sentence and (2) that *Smith v Wilson* was distinguishable because weapon not per se offensive. Sentence quashed and order for 120 hours' community service substituted.

Mir v Normand 1993 SCCR 654—Second conviction for possessing a knife. Sentenced to six months' imprisonment and deportation order recommended. Upheld on appeal.

Noble v Lees 1993 SCCR 967—Sixteen-year-old convicted of possessing a knife. Had armed himself to 'settle the score' after an earlier assault. Sentenced to three months' detention. Appeal.

Held that not enough account taken of N's good background. 180 hours' community service substituted.

Prior v Normand 1993 SCCR 118—Possession of lock knife in centre of Glasgow. P telling police he would use it on them. Three months' imprisonment increased to six months' imprisonment on appeal. Carrying knives '... always been a problem in Glasgow'.

Reid v Normand 1994 SCCR 475—Breach of the peace, vandalism and offensive weapon charge regarding a baseball bat. Six months' imprisonment on weapon charge upheld on appeal.

Hamilton v Hamilton 1996 SCCR 652—Possession of offensive weapon by 16-year-old who said he was carrying it for protection from creditors looking for payment for drugs.
Held, on appeal, six months' detention not excessive.
Observed, per Lord Sutherland, that custodial sentence not inappropriate for 16-year-old first offender, since it was people of this age who carried and were liable to use knives.

Keaney v Vannet 1997 GWD 19-885—Three months' detention for assault by brandishing knife and six months concurrent for possessing knife.
Held, excessive since K, aged 17, trying to free girlfriend detained in house, K had no previous convictions and recurrence unlikely. 240 hours' community service substituted.

Ross v Reith 1997 GWD 33-1681—R had 12 to 16-inch metal chain with taped handle for protection.
Held, two months' detention for R, a first offender, in employment was appropriate and not excessive.

Miller v Vannet 1997 GWD 16-732—*Held*, three months' detention for first offender for possession of knife (three-to-four-inch sharpened blade) not excessive given dangers of such actions.

McFarlane v Spiers 1997 GWD 20-968—Three months' detention for 16-year-old first offender for carrying knife 'for protection' (M in employment and lived with parents and had stable background).
Held, not excessive.

Reilly v Heywood 1997 GWD 21-1030—Three months' imprisonment for carrying two knives. R in bed and breakfast accommodation and subject to bad influences. Social enquiry report recommended probation to help R move forward.
Held, sentence excessive. One year's probation and 100 hours' community service substituted.

Larkin v Friel 1997 GWD 22-1080—60 days' detention for first offender carrying knife in public place 'for protection'.
Held, sentence excessive, since L saving money to go to university, had spent seven days in custody and of good behaviour. Community service substituted.

McIlraith v Vannet 1998 GWD 3-121—Four months for possessing knife in public place. M had analogous conviction in 1991.
Held, sentence excessive, since M had changed lifestyle and was drug-free, in employment and had been given police nomination for helping save a life. Community service substituted.

Arthur v Carnegie 1998 GWD 23-1168—One accused challenged person to a fight and asked other accused to hand him knife with which he threatened to stab person.
Held, 60 days' detention for 16 year-old first offenders excessive and 200 hours' community service and two years' probation substituted.

Boyle v Vannet 1998 GWD 25-1257—Three months for 16-year-old first offender possessing butcher knife with 8-inch blade. He took it to 14 year-old pregnant girlfriend's house because frightened of father. Boy and girl now lived together, and B was in employment.
Held, with hesitation, that sentence excessive, and 240 hours' community service substituted.

PRINCIPLES

ART AND PART GUILT

All persons who **participate** in the commission of a crime **together** are **equally liable for the outcome** of that act irrespective of the particular role played by each individual in its commission.

COMMENTARY	CASE LAW	STATUTE LAW
Participate Before a person may be held so responsible, he must have actually participated in the crime. Mere presence at, or failure to prevent, the commission of an offence will not, in the absence of any 'special duty', impose guilt for that offence.	*HMA v Kerr and Ors* (1871) 2 Couper 334 Three accused charged with assault with intent to ravish. One of the accused, Donald, had taken no direct part in the attack but had only stood at the other side of a hedge watching the attack. Had not spoken to his friends or the girl during the attack. *Held* no art and part liability.	Criminal Procedure (Scotland) Act 1995, s 293(1) applies the concept of art and part guilt to all statutory offences.
	Mitchell v HMA 1994 SCCR 440 No averment that accused acted along with another person. *Held*, Crown entitled to rely on Criminal Procedure (Scotland) Act 1975, s 45. Observed, per Lord Clyde, that where the Crown intend to submit accused guilty with others who can be named and identified, the preferable course is for that to be made specific in the indictment.	
	HMA v Meikleham 1998 SCCR 621. *Held*, an averment of art and part guilt still implied in all indictments.	
Presence and profiting is also insufficient	*Lawler v Neizer* 1993 SCCR 299. A co-accused had bought a round of drinks with a counterfeit banknote before passing the £54 change to the accused. On appeal, it was held that the accused's presence and possession of money was not enough to establish art and part guilt.	
Dissociation must be explicit and can only result during the planning of the crime. Once the crime has actually commenced, it is impossible for the accused to escape art and part liability.	*MacNeil v HMA* 1986 SCCR 288Per L J-G Emslie: 'A person who is an instigator of a contemplated crime or a participator in preparation for it, may successfully dissociate himself from criminal responsibility in the crime, if it is committed by others, if he clearly intimates to them that he is withdrawing and seeks to discourage them from proceeding. ... In such circumstances he cannot be guilty of the crime if it is nevertheless committed.'	
Special duty	*Bonar v McLeod* 1983 SCCR 161 Two police officers. One assaulted prisoner. Senior officer did nothing. *Held* art and part guilty as did not dissociate himself from actions; thus even stronger than position of official standing by and allowing offence; placed in active position as part of escort.	
	Spiers v HMA 1980 JC 36 All accused charged with murder and attempted murder. S was not proven present at attack. Appeal court held S could only be liable art and part if he instigated the attack, this being antecedent concert. Conviction quashed.	

COMMENTARY	CASE LAW	STATUTE LAW
A person may be held to have so parti-cipated and thus invoke art and part guilt by several methods.		
(1) Instigation: by 'serious, earnest and pointed' instigation or advice whose effect is to induce the commission of a crime (Hume I, 278).	*Meikleham and Parker v HMA* 1998 SCCR 621. Instigation occurs where one person procures another to commit a crime. Where A hires B to kill C, both A and B will be guilty, art and part, of murder.	
'The instigation must be to such an act as was likely to result in the crime charged.' (Macdonald, p 4).	*Martin v Hamilton* 1989 SCCR 292. Mere advice in itself is not enough to constitute art and part liability. Some evidence of actual involvement either in the planning or commissioning of the crime is required.	
'The connection between the instigation or assistance and the act must continue to the last. If the instigator repent, he is not guilty if he genuinely attempts to dissuade the person whom he instigated... .' (Macdonald, pp 5–6).	See *MacNeil v HMA* 1986 SCCR 288 above.	
(2) Common Plan: A pre-arranged criminal purpose or objective. May be express or implied. Is to be determined by the court using an objective approach.	*McKinnon v HMA* 2003 SLT 281. Leading authority. Four co-accused plotted to commit a house robbery. Prior to its commission, one of the co-accused obtained a set of kitchen knives. On arrival, this co-accused attacked the occupants of the flat seriously injuring two and killing the third. Despite it being forensically determined that only one person had inflicted the injuries, each co-accused was convicted of both the assaults and murder, on the basis of art and part liability. *On appeal*, it was held that by taking an objective approach in determining the common plan of the co-accused, it ought to have been clear to each that using knives during the commission of their robbery brought with it a serious risk of taking life, thus upholding the decision at first instance. Only in cases where there is a question as to whether the common plan has been exceeded shall it be competent for the court to look subjectively at each of the individual co-accused.	
The *mens rea* for art and part murder is therefore fundamentally altered.	*Poole* v *HM Advocate* 2009 SCCR 577. 'The question is not ... whether there was evidence from which it could be said that the appellant had the *mens rea* necessary for murder [proper]. The question, following *McKinnon v HMA*, comes to be whether there was evidence entitling the jury to find that it was *objectively foreseeable* to the appellant that such violence was liable to be used as carried an obvious risk of life being taken.' (per Lord Kingarth at para 11).	
Common plan must be proven by the prosecution amongst each of the co-accused. If not, each co-accused may be prosecuted individually.	*Johnston and Woolard v HMA* 2009 SLT 535. Each co-accused was successfully convicted of murder as the prosecution were unable to prove the existence of a murderous common plan.	
(3) Provision of material assistance: By supplying material assistance prior to the commission of the crime, eg supplying a car for a bank robbery where the supplier knows of the imminent plot to commit the crime, or	*HMA v Semple* 1937 JC 41; 1937 SLT 48 Charge of attempting to procure an abortion through instigation and supply of powders to a pregnant woman held relevant.	

COMMENTARY	CASE LAW	STATUTE LAW
(4) Participation: By actual participation in the commission of the crime itself whether in pre-concert or spontaneous.	*Gallacher v HMA* 1951 JC 38; 1951 SLT 158 One of accused started a fight with the deceased and a number of men joined in. All stood round the victim and kicked him to death. Per Lord Keith: 'If the accused were in a kicking crowd animated by a common purpose, joining in the attack, assisting and encouraging, each and all are responsible for the consequences.' Three of the accused convicted of murder.	
	Melvin v HMA 1984 SCCR 113 *Held* that a jury are entitled, in the absence of intent to kill or any antecedent concerted intention to carry out an assault and robbery, to assess the degree of recklessness displayed by each participant, and to return verdicts of murder or culpable homicide in accordance with that assessment.	
	Malone v HMA 1988 SCCR 498 Two appellants charged with murdering B after repeated kicks and blows to his face. First appellant found guilty of murder, second appellant who desisted from assault shortly before first appellant found guilty of culpable homicide. Convictions upheld but observed by LJ-G Emslie: 'If a distinction is to be made in a case involving a joint assault causing deaths it could normally only be justified if there were striking differences in the relevant conduct of each of the assailants.'	
Where accused knew or should have known that a weapon was used by the co-accused.	*Walker v HMA* 1985 SCCR 150 W and R involved in fight with deceased in discothèque. R's conviction of murdering victim by stabbing him upheld on appeal. W convicted art and part on the basis that he knew or should have known of knife attack but still continued with his own assault. Conviction against W quashed on appeal.	
	Mathieson v HMA 1996 SCCR 388 Appellants C and W M took part in attack with other men. S produced knife and stabbed victim while appellants continued to kick victim. *Held*, they had witnessed use of knife and were art and part liable of culpable homicide (S convicted of murder). Per LJ-G Hope: '... the knife wounds had already been inflicted during the period when the deceased was still being assaulted by the appellants.'	
or if weapon used sufficiently similar to those contemplated.	*O'Connell v HMA* 1987 SCCR 459 O and three others charged with murder, formed common plan to assault deceased with sticks, one of which was three or four feet long. Deceased killed by blow from his own hammer no evidence which accused had wielded it: where the weapons used were of a broadly similar nature it was for jury to decide whether the assailants should have anticipated the use of a broadly similar weapon.	
Art and part guilt applies even where a person could not be convicted as the principal.	*Vaughan v HMA* 1979 SLT 49 V accused that, acting along with the mother of a small boy, he forced the boy to have intercourse with the mother, contrary to Incest Act 1567. The accused was not related to either the mother or the son and argued that he could not be found guilty since not within the forbidden degrees. *Held*, on appeal, that Act did not exclude its application to those art and part in commission of offence. Convicted.	Criminal Procedure (Scotland) Act 1995, s 293(2): '... any person who aids, abets, counsels, procures or incites any other person to commit an offence against the provisions of any enactment shall be guilty of an offence ...'

COMMENTARY	CASE LAW	STATUTE LAW
	HMA v Lappen 1956 SLT 109 L charged along with five others with assault and robbery. Convicted. Per Lord Patrick: 'If a number of men form a common plan whereby some are to commit the actual seizure of the property and some, according to the plan, are to keep watch and some, according to the plan, are to help carry away the loot ... then, every one is guilty of common plan to commit the robbery.	
Together: It is only the common criminal purpose which has to be equal. The actions or roles of the co-accused may vary.	*HMA v Lappen* 1956 SLT 109 L charged along with five others with assault and robbery. Convicted. Per Lord Patrick: 'If a number of men form a common plan whereby some are to commit the actual seizure of the property and some, according to the plan, are to keep watch and some, according to the plan, are to help carry away the loot ... then, everyone is guilty of common plan to commit the robbery.'	
	Vogan V HMA 2003 SCCR 564 Attempted murder appellant with two others forced entry to complainer's flat. No participation in actual attack, but art and part guilty as 'part of attacking group'.	
A party cannot dissociate himself from the crime once it has been perpetrated.	*MacNeil v HMA* 1986 SCCR 288 Appellant (S) and seven others charged with importing cannabis into UK. S engaged as engineer on vessel which sailed from Oban to West Africa and helped to store cannabis in fuel tank. *Held* no defence of dissociation.	
Equally liable for the outcome: Where the common plan or purpose is proved, the accused will be held responsible for any foreseeable consequences of the crime whether or not they were intended, but not for any action which goes unforeseeably out with the common plan or purpose.	*Docherty v HMA* 1945 SC 89; 1945 SLT 247 *Boyne v HMA* 1980 JC 47; 1980 SLT 56 Three men convicted of murder during assault and robbery. Conviction of murder against two accused quashed since there was no evidence to show that they either knew or had reason to anticipate the use of a knife, or that they continued the attack once the knife was produced. *Brown v HMA* 1993 SCCR 382 Homicide. Two accused attacking victim with knife and iron bar, both denied inflicting the fatal wound. Culpable homicide withdrawn, convicted of murder. Appeal. *Held* that for murder both accused would require the necessary degree of wicked recklessness, if either of their intentions was only to inflict serious injury the culpable homicide open. Culpable homicide convictions substituted.	

CONSPIRACY

Conspiracy is complete as soon as two or more persons **have agreed** together to commit a **crime**.

COMMENTARY	CASE LAW	STATUTE LAW
Conspiracy '... process is properly brought under this generic name, for any sort of conspiracy or machination, directed against the fame, safety, or state of another, and meant to be accomplished by the aid of subdolous and deceitful contrivances, to the disguise or suppression of the truth ...' (Hume I, 170).	*Crofter Hand-Woven Harris Tweed Co v Veitch* 1942 SC (HL) 1 Per Viscount Simon LC: 'Conspiracy ... is the agreement of two or more persons to effect any unlawful purpose whether as their ultimate aim or only as a means to it, and the crime is complete if there is such agreement even though nothing is done in pursuance of it.'	
Gordon refers to three possible categories of conspiracy:	*HMA v Wilson, Latta and Rooney* (1968, unreported), High Court—see Gordon, 200 Charge of conspiring to have false evidence led and thus defeat the ends of justice. Viscount Simon's statement adopted by LJ-C Grant.	
(1) Conspiracy where a specific crime has been carried out in pursuance of that conspiracy.	*HMA v Wilson, Latta and Rooney* (1968, unreported), High Court—see Gordon, 200) Charge was a conspiracy to pervert the course of justice and the commission of subornation and attempted subornation in pursuance thereof. LJ-C Grant directed jury that they could acquit in the conspiracy and convict on the subornation.	
However, a conspiracy to do something by criminal means is not a crime unless the criminal means are proved.	*Sayers v HMA* 1982 SLT 220 Charged with conspiring to aid the UVF by criminal means and by contravention of Prevention of Terrorism (Temporary Provisions) Act 1976. Jury found accused guilty of conspiracy but deleted specification of criminal means libelled. Appeal against conviction allowed; charge was irrelevant because of lack of specification and was not a crime known to the law of Scotland.	
(2) Conspiracy where no specified crime is charged in pursuance of the conspiracy, where charge does not set out specified crime by which conspiracy to be effected.	*HMA v Walsh and Ors* 1922 JC 82—see Gordon, 204 Conspiracy to further the purposes of the IRA by the unlawful use of force and violence by the use of explosive substances to be used to endanger the lives and persons and property of the lieges.	
(3) Conspiracy may often be charged as a substitute for attempt. There is an attempt where the person involved goes beyond the stage of preparation for the crime into perpetration. Thus there may be a conspiracy charge where accused person does not move into perpetration but has agreed with another to commit the crime.	*West v HMA* 1985 SCCR 248 W and another charged with conspiracy to assault and rob persons employed in named premises. They loitered suspiciously outside these premises and were in possession of blade from pair of scissors and open razor, respectively. Conviction for conspiracy upheld on appeal. Per LJ-G Emslie: 'Taking all the evidence together ... we are of the opinion that there was sufficient... .'	
Have agreed As soon as two or more persons have agreed to commit a crime they are guilty of a complete crime of conspiracy. The mens rea of the offence is the intention to commit the crime libelled.	*Smith and Ors* (1975, unreported), High Court—see Gordon, 198 Lord Keith directed the jury that to 'find a conspiracy they would have to be satisfied that matters went beyond the putting forward by one man of his ideas to another with a view to the matter being discussed and possibly agreed upon at another date. There must be actual agreement.'	

COMMENTARY	CASE LAW	STATUTE LAW
Crime Only conspiracies to do what would be criminal if done by one person are criminal conspiracies (Macdonald, p 185).	Ibid, supra.	
Factual impossibility of achievement of the ultimate object of the conspiracy does not act as a defence to the charge.	*Maxwell v HMA* 1980 JC 40; 1980 SLT 241 Three accused convicted of conspiracy to bribe licensing board to approve transfer of gaming licences. At dates of offence, board did not have legal power to approve transfer since the matter of the issue of the licence was at the time under appeal to sheriff. Conviction sustained on appeal. It is the criminality of *purpose* and which makes the crime a criminal conspiracy.	
Incitement to murder	*Baxter v HMA* 1997 SCCR 437 Incitement to murder. Convicted but appealed as no settled plan to kill the victim in a particular way. Appeal refused. Per LJ-G Rodger: 'A person can incite another to commit a crime without actually instructing him to do so. Depending on the circumstances it may be enough if, for example, he encourages or requests him to do so.'	

ATTEMPT

A person may be convicted of **attempting a** crime where he has taken an overt step in pursuance of his criminal intention and has passed from the stage of **preparation** to the stage of **perpetration**, but has not completed the crime.

COMMENTARY	CASE LAW	STATUTE LAW
Under statute any person charged with a crime may also be convicted of attempt. To this extent, the attempt to commit a crime is as criminal as the completed act itself.		Criminal Procedure (Scotland) Act 1995. Section 294(1). Attempt to commit any indictable crime is itself an indictable crime. Section 294(2). Attempt to commit any offence punishable on complaint shall itself be an offence punishable on complaint.
The **mens rea** for an attempted crime is the same as for the com-pleted crime.	*Cawthorne v HMA* 1968 JC 32; 1968 SLT 330 *Held* that attempted murder may be committed either intentionally or recklessly.	
Mere **preparation** not enough. An attempted crime is where the accused failed to complete the crime but had actually taken overt steps in the **perpetration** of it.	*HMA v Mackenzie* 1913 SC(J) 107; 1913, 2 SLT 48 'The law does not strike at preparation to commit a crime ... the overt act ... is essential to a conviction.' Per LJ-C Macdonald: '... the preparation of a fraudulent document, or a document intended to be fraudulently used is not in itself a punishable crime ... it requires an overt act of use to constitute an indictable offence.'	
'But the vicious will is not sufficient, unless it is coupled to a wrongful act. And here the question arises, how far must the culprit have proceeded in the prosecution of his wicked purpose, to make him answerable in the tribunals of this world?' (Hume I, 26).	*HMA v Camerons* (1911) 6 Adam 456Where deciding whether what accused had done amounted to attempted fraud, Lord Dunedin charged the jury that 'the root of the whole matter' was 'to discover where preparation ends and where perpetration begins. In other words, it is a question of degree, it is a jury question'. Case involved an accused who had faked a robbery but was subsequently apprehended before they could fraudulently claim their insurance.	
The fact that it was impossible for the accused to complete the crime is no defence against attempt.	*Lamont v Strathern* 1933 JC 33; 1933 SLT 118 Attempted to steal from an empty pocket. *Doherty v Brown* 1996 SCCR 136 (Full Bench) Appellant charged with and convicted of contravention of Misuse of Drugs Act 1971, s 5(3) and s 19. He possessed tablets he believed contained ecstasy but in fact did not. He thus attempted to have said controlled drug in his possession with intent to supply it to another. Fact that impossible to commit complete crime does not preclude Crown from charging an attempt.	
A criminal act may be charged with intent to commit a further crime. Where murder or culpable homicide is charged and it is not proved that death resulted from the assault, convictions may be assault with intention to murder or kill. Similarly, in assault to danger of life, where it is not proved life was endangered the conviction may be for assault with intent to endanger life.	*Strachan v HMA* 1994 SCCR 341 Attempted murder. Charge libelled he had brandished knife at officers, threatened them and made to strike them and struggled with them, and repeatedly did strike them. Neither officer could say if actually struck and conviction under deletion of part of charge referring to striking. Conviction upheld on appeal.	

SENTENCING POLICY

Moore v HMA 1984 SCCR 25. Attempted robbery by threats. Attempt to rob a post office by handing employees a note asking for money and adopting a menacing attitude to them. Four years' imprisonment. Appeal dismissed.
Per LJ-G Emslie: '… one could hardly have quarrelled with a longer sentence.'

PROCEDURE

BAIL

Admission to bail is competent for all crimes and offences. There are **standard conditions** and there may be **special conditions**. **Bail** may be allowed where **reports** are **called for**.

COMMENTARY	CASE LAW	STATUTE LAW
Admission to bail		
	G v Spiers SCCR 1988 517 If unopposed by Crown cannot be refused by judge *ex proprio motu.*	Criminal Procedure (Scotland) Act 1995, ss 22A–33.
	Maxwell v McGlennan SCCR 1989 117 If the Crown does not oppose bail will be granted.	Bail Applications. Section 23(1). Accused person entitled to apply for bail on any occasion when brought before sheriff prior to his committal until liberated in due course of law. Prosecutor may object.
	Normand v B 1995 SCCR 128 Misuse of Drugs Act 1971. Crown opposed bail because making further inquiries which would be impeded if bail granted. *Held*, per Lord McCluskey: 'If PF makes a motion to commit ... the court should not seek to go behind that statement.' Sheriff had misdirected himself.	
	Normand v JL 1995 SCCR 130 Bail granted. Upheld on appeal. Crown not seeking to detain accused for further inquiries bearing on charge in petition but rather investigating accused's link to offences in England.	Section 23(2). Discretionary judicial power to refuse application until committal stage.
	Mayo v Neizer 1994 SLT 931 Bail order continues for so long as accused at liberty.	Section 23(4). Application, if refused, may be renewed at committal stage.
		Section 23(5). Grant or refusal of bail within sheriff's discretion.
	Lau, Petr 1986 SCCR 140 Per Lord Justice-Clerk: 'Presentation can only occur when the application has been transmitted to the sheriff.'	Section 23(7). Application to be dealt with within 24 hours of its presentation to the sheriff, failing which liberation forthwith.
	Gibbons, Petr 1988 SCCR 270 Petitioner fully committed for trial on 18.4.88 at 11.30 am and immediately applied for bail. Sheriff adjourned application till 9.45 am the next day. Case not heard till 11.50 am owing to delay in bringing peititioner from prison. Sheriff refused bail and petitioner appealed to High Court. *Held* that requirement of Criminal Procedure (Scotland) Act 1975, s 28(2) was mandatory and petitioner entitled to be liberated.	Bail, Judicial Appointments etc (Scotland) Act 2000
Entitlement to Bail		CP(S)A 1995, s 23B(1) – Bail is to be granted to an accused person: (a) except where: (i) by reference to section 23C of this Act; and (ii) having regard to the public interest, there is good reason for refusing bail; (b) subject to section 23D of this Act.

COMMENTARY	CASE LAW	STATUTE LAW
Relevant Grounds: Considering Bail Applications		CP(S)A 1995, s 23C(1) – In any proceedings in which a person is accused of an offence, the following are grounds on which it may be determined that there is good reason for refusing bail: (a) any substantial risk that the person might if granted bail: (i) abscond; or (ii) fail to appear at a diet of the court as required; (b) any substantial risk of the person committing further offences if granted bail; (c) any substantial risk that the person might if granted bail: (i) interfere with witnesses; or (ii) otherwise obstruct the course of justice, in relation to himself or any other person; (d) any other substantial factor which appears to the court to justify keeping the person in custody…
Restriction on Bail: Solemn cases		CP(S)A 1995, s 23D(1) – Where subsection (2) or (3) below applies, a person is to be granted bail in solemn proceedings only if there are exceptional circumstances justifying bail. (2) This subsection applies where the person: (a) is accused in the proceedings of a violent or sexual offence; and (b) has a previous conviction on indictment for a violent or sexual offence. (3) This subsection applies where the person: (a) is accused in the proceedings of a drug trafficking offence; and (b) has a previous conviction on indictment for a drug trafficking offence.
Standard conditions	*MacNeill v Milne* 1984 SCCR 427 M pled guilty to some, not guilty to other, charges on summary complaint. Bail allowed on sole condition that M attend all subsequent diets. Appeal by prosecutor against omission of other standard conditions upheld. *Held* mandatory to impose standard conditions. Per LJ-C Wheatley's interlocutor: '… finds that the sheriff was wrong in forming the view that the imposition of the standard conditions or any of them was a matter for his discretion.'	Bail and bail conditions. Section 24(1). All crimes and offences except murder and treason are bailable. Section 24(2). Nothing in this Act shall affect the right of the Lord Advocate or the High Court to admit to bail any person charged with any crime or offence. Section 24(4). In granting bail the court shall impose on the accused: (a) the standard conditions; and (b) such further conditions as necessary to secure standard conditions observed and that accused available for ID parade or to have print/sample taken from him.

COMMENTARY	CASE LAW	STATUTE LAW
		Section 24(5). The standard conditions are that the accused (a) appears at diets in case; (b) does not commit offence on bail; (c) does not interfere with witnesses, nor obstruct course of justice; (ca) does not behave in a manner which causes, or is likely to cause, alarm or distress to witnesses; (cb) whenever reasonably instructed by a constable to do so— (i) participates in an identification parade or other identification procedure; and (ii) allows any print, impression or sample to be taken from the accused; (d) makes himself available for inquiries/report to assist court; (e) where the (or an) offence in respect of which he is admitted to bail is one to which section 288C of this Act applies, does not seek to obtain, otherwise than by way of a solicitor, any precognition of or statement by the complainer in relation to the subject matter of the offence. Section 24(6). Money bail. Court or Lord Advocate may impose requirement that accused or cautioner deposits sum of money in court where satisfied such condition is appropriate to special circumstances of the case.
	Reilly v HMA 1995 SLT 45. Accused admitted to bail. At judicial examination gave different address to that in bail order. Did not appear at diet. *Held*, address in order remained domicile of citation. (Under CP(S)A 1995, s 25(2), accused can apply in writing to alter domicile of citation.)	Section 25(1). Court shall specify in order granting bail, copy of which shall be given to accused: (a) conditions imposed; (b) domicile of citation.
	Lockhart v Stokes 1981 SLT (Sh Ct) 71 Assault. S, on petition, granted bail under Bail etc (Scotland) Act 1980. Address given was a fairground site. Attempts to serve indictment unsuccessful because site not in use. Warrant to arrest granted. Per Sheriff Gow: '... a showground which is occupied on a seasonal basis only, and is simply a piece of waste ground at a time when citation is to be effected, is not a "proper domicile of citation" under the Bail Act.'	Section 25(2). Accused may apply in writing to change domicile of citation. Section 24 provides for monitoring.
Reports called for		Section 27. Committing an offence while on bail. Section 27(3)–(5). Now treated as aggravation of subsequent offence and sentencing court shall have regard to: (a) fact offence committed on bail, number of bail orders at time of offence; (b) any previous conviction for breach of bail condition;

COMMENTARY	CASE LAW	STATUTE LAW
		(c) the proportion of sentence for previous conviction attributed to aggravation. Where maximum penalty for subsequent offence specified by enactment this maximum shall be increased to fine up to level 3 in all courts, and up to 60 days' imprisonment in JPCourt and up to six months in other courts. Section 27(4A). Bail is a special capacity. Section 27(6). Court should state extent and reasons where sentence different due to aggravation.

JUDICIAL EXAMINATION

When an accused appears on **petition** he may intimate his wish either to emit or not emit a **declaration**. Whether he does so or not, the prosecutor may then **examine** the accused with a view to eliciting any denial, admission, explanation or justification. The prosecutor may also question the accused on any alleged **confession**.

COMMENTARY	CASE LAW	STATUTE LAW
Must be entirely the composition of the accused.	*Carmichael v Armitage* 1982 SCCR 475 Accused read a declaration prepared by his solicitor on his instructions. *Held* that declaration was inadmissible, as being more of the nature of a precognition altering the declaration's true sense and character.	Judicial examinations is held in terms of Criminal Procedure (Scotland) Act 1995, ss 35–39 and Chapter 5of the Act of Adjournal (Criminal Procedure Rules) 1996, SI 1996/513.
The accused is entitled to a private interview with his solicitor prior to the judicial examination.	*HMA v Goodall (1888)* 2 White 1 A failure by the court to alert the accused of his right to a private meeting with his counsel may vitiate any admissions made during the declaration despite such meetings not being obligatory.	CP(S)A 1995, s 17(2)
	The accused's solicitor is entitled to be present;	Section 35(1)
	to allow his attendance the sheriff may delay the examination;	Section 35(2)Section 35(3)
	if the accused does not desire to emit a declaration it need not be taken at first appearance;	Section 35(4)
	but may be made later;	Section 35(4A)
	in sexual offences the accused has to be informed that legal representation will be requisite;	
	the accused can be brought again before the court for examination quoad an extra-judicial confession.	Section 35(5)
Examine The prosecutor may put certain questions to the accused, i.e. to elicit any admission, denial, explanation, justification or comment.		Criminal Procedure (Scotland) Act 1995.
Any proceedings before the sheriff during an examination or further examination shall be conducted in private chambers and out-with the presence of any co-accused. CP(S) A 1995, s 35(7)		Section 36(1). ...an accused on being brought before the sheriff for examination on any charge...may be questioned by the prosecutor in so far as such questioning is directed towards eliciting any admission, denial, explanation, justification or comment which the accused may have as regards anything to which subsections (2) to (4) below apply.
		Section 36(5). Questions put by the prosecutor should not be designed to challenge the truth of anything said by the accused; there should be no reiteration of a question which the accused has refused to answer; and there should be no leading questions. The sheriff has the duty to ensure that questions are fairly put to and understood by the accused.

COMMENTARY	CASE LAW	STATUTE LAW
Where the accused declines to answer a question put to him in the examination, his having so declined may be commented on by the prosecutor, judge or any co-accused at subsequent trial even if he declines to answer on the advice of his solicitor.	*McEwan v HMA* 1990 SCCR 401 M giving no response to questions at examination on the advice of his solicitor, gave evidence of an alibi at trial. *Held* on appeal that the judge was allowed to comment on M's silence notwithstanding the legal advice. *Dempsey v HMA* 1995 SCCR 431 *Held*, as appellant had not given evidence it was not open to sheriff to pass any comment on silence at judicial examination.	Section 36(8). Where the accused declines to answer a question put to him in examination, his having so declined may be commented on by the prosecutor, judge or any co-accused at any subsequent trial, only where accused (or witness called on his behalf) in evidence avers something which could have been stated appropriately in answer to that question, even if he declines to answer on advice of solicitor.
	McGhee v HMA 1991 SCCR 510 Murder. At examination M not answering questions regarding an admission he was alleged to have made to the police, on legal advice. Judge commenting that such advice would have been extraordinary if lawyer had known of the proposed alibi defence. *Held* that the judge had gone too far, making comment as to his view of the facts and not relating to the jury M's explanation for not answering.	Rule 5.5(4) of Act of Adjournal (Criminal Procedure Rules) 1996, SI 1996/513: 'Trial judge ... may in determining whether having so declined may be commented on have regard to the terms of the charge to which the questions related.' *Note*: Section 32 of the Criminal Justice (Scotland) Act 1995 repealed s 14(1)(b) of the Criminal Procedure (Scotland) Act 1975. So prosecutor can now comment on accused's failure to lead evidence. Section 36(6). Warning by sheriff: inform accused he has right to consult solicitor before answering any questions; and if answers disclose an ostensible defence the prosecutor shall be under a duty to investigate it to such an extent as reasonably practicable. Section 36(7) With sheriff's permission, the solicitor for the accused may ask the accused any questions in order to clarify any ambiguity in an answer given by the accused to the prosecutor or to give him an opportunity to answer a question which he has previously refused to answer.
Confession A statement clearly susceptible of being regarded as incriminating.	*McKenzie v HMA* 1982 SCCR 545 *Held* that the statement 'Just my luck, I knew I'd be picked out' was clearly a statement susceptible of being regarded as incriminating and thus constituted a 'confession' within the terms of CP(S)A 1975. *Robertson v HMA* 1995 SCCR 152; 1996 SCCR 243 Two separate reports dealing with aspects of same case. Failure to comply with provisions for recording declaration. *Held* (LJ-C dissenting): this did not render subsequent indictment incompetent, and if accused claimed he suffered grave prejudice he could raise matter by preliminary plea of oppression or during trial.	Section 36(10), (11). Ostensible defence disclosed: prosecutor under duty to investigate to such extent as reasonably practicable.

STATUTORY TIME LIMITS

The limits' objectives are to **prevent undue delay** in the commencement of trials.

COMMENTARY	CASE LAW	STATUTE LAW
		The principal statutory provision is the Criminal Procedure (Scotland) Act 1995 ss 65 (solemn procedure) and ss136 (summary procedure). As amended by: Crime and Punishment (Scotland) Act 1997. Criminal Procedure and Investigations Act 1996. Criminal Procedure (Amendment) (Scotland) Act 2004. Solemn procedure: Section 65. High Court proceedings require: a preliminary hearing within 11 months; commencement of trial Elsewhere: within 12 months of first appearance on petition, save where accused has been subject of non-appearance warrant, provisions for extensions are found in and for bail admissions after varying periods in section. The corresponding provisions for summary procedure are found in s 136. As amended.

SPECIAL DEFENCES

GENERAL

The special defences of **alibi**, **impeachment** or **incrimination**, **mental disorder**, **self-defence**, **automatism**, **necessity** and **coercion** are those which, if established in relation to a relevant charge, are a complete answer to that charge.

COMMENTARY	CASE LAW	STATUTE LAW
Proof of special defences generally.	*Adam v McNeill* 1971 SLT (Notes) 80 The effect of such a defence, if successful is to secure the acquittal of the accused.	Criminal Procedure (Scotland) Act 1995
	Lambie v HMA 1973 JC 53; SLT 219. Per LJ-G Emslie: 'The only purpose of the special defence is to give fair notice to the Crown ... When a special defence is pleaded ... the jury should be charged in the appropriate language and all that requires to be said of the special defence ... is that if the evidence is believed or creates in the minds of the jury reasonable doubt as to the guilt of, the accused ... they must acquit'.	Solemn procedure s 78 noted *supra* General Section 78. Plea of special defence to be lodged in a High Court case with the clerk of justiciary and intimated to Crown Agent and to any accused not less than seven clear days before the preliminary hearing; in a sheriff court case with sheriff clerk and intimated to the procurator fiscal and to any co-accused or his solicitor at or before the first diet (unless in any case the court, on cause shown, otherwise directs). Section 78 applies to alibi, incrimination, insanity, self-defence, automatism and coercion.
	O'Connell v HMA 1996 SCCR 614 (see Competent Evidence) *Held*, in terms of s 307(1) of CP(S)A 1995, first diet in s 78 included any continuation thereof, and since substitute special defence in proper form and duly lodged in terms of s 78(3) it ought to have been received, and cause did not require to be shown.	
Burden of Proof: The onus of proof remains with the Crown in all cases except in relation to the special defence of insanity to which the burden of proof shifts to the accused on the balance of probabilities.	*See:* *Lambie* v *HMA* 1973 SLT 219, *Lindsay v HMA* 1996 SCCR 370 *Lilburn* v *HMA* 2011 SCCR 326	Note: The Criminal Justice and Licensing (Scotland) Act 2010 reforms and replaces common law insanity; both as a special defence and a plea in bar of trial. Please see section on 'Insanity'

COMMENTARY	CASE LAW	STATUTE LAW
Consent: Consent is a special defence to certain sex offences under Sexual Offences (Procedure and Evidence) Scotland Act 2002, s 6.		Sexual Offences (Procedure and Evidence) Scotland Act 2002, s 6: (1) In section 78 (which provides for, amongst other things, prior notice of special defences in proceedings on indictment) of the 1995 Act— (a) in subsection (2), for "or coercion" there is substituted ",coercion or, in a prosecution for an offence to which section 288C of this Act applies, consent"; (b) after that subsection there is inserted— "(2A) In subsection (2) above, the reference to a defence of consent is a reference to the defence which is stated by reference to the complainer's consent to the act which is the subject matter of the charge or the accused's belief as to that consent. (2B) In subsection (2A) above, "complainer" has the same meaning as in section 274 of this Act."

ALIBI

This **special defence** is that at the time of the alleged offence the accused was **not at the locus libelled but at some other specified place**.

COMMENTARY	CASE LAW	STATUTE LAW
A **special defence** intimates that the defence evidence will be of a certain specific nature: the burden of proof is unaltered.	*HMA v Hayes* 1973 SLT 202 Posting packet containing explosives. Special defences of alibi and incrimination. Per Lord Cameron: 'The purpose of a special defence in Scots law is to give to the prosecution proper notice of a particular line which the defence of an accused person may take ... there is no obligation on an accused person to establish that special defence under a penalty that if he fails to do so then conviction would follow.'	Criminal Procedure (Scotland) Act 1995 Solemn procedure s 78 noted, *supra* General
	Fraser v HMA 1982 SCCR 458 Assault and robbery. Special defence that F was in public house at time of crimes. Convicted. On appeal conviction sustained. Opinion of the court: '... we disagree with the inherent proposition that a judge is bound to give proper and clear direction with regard to the nature, purport and effect of the special defence of alibi. The simple reason is that the special defence has played all the part it has to play in the trial when it has given notice to the Crown of a possible line of evidence which will or may be held on behalf of an accused person.'	**Summary procedure:** Section 149. Notice of intention to lead alibi evidence to be given to prosecutor before first witness is sworn. Notice to be given with particulars as to time and place and of the witnesses by whom it is proposed to prove it. The prosecutor is entitled to an adjournment.
At the time of the alleged offence the accused was **not at the locus libelled but at some other specified place**.	*Gilmour v HMA* 1982 SCCR 590 Murder and rape. Special defence that accused was at home alone. Convicted. Per trial judge, Lord Dunpark: 'Now, before I turn to the charge in this case let me just dismiss this so-called special defence of alibi which was read to you at the outset. It is miscalled a special defence because there is no onus on the accused, and I think you should ignore the alibi so-called special defence in this case, because if you believe the evidence of the accused that he was alone in his house between two and four o'clock on 4th -November 1981, you would acquit him; and if you were left with a reasonable doubt about that you would also acquit him.' Appeal against conviction dismissed. Per LJ-C Wheatley: 'That direction was in line with current practice, and, rather than constituting prejudice to the appellant, it was to his advantage. We need say no more on that, and in the result we reject both branches of this ground of appeal.'	
	Balsillie v HMA 1993 SCCR 760 Theft by housebreaking. Sheriff not allowing B's explanation as to his whereabouts at the relevant time because no notice of special defence lodged. *Held* on appeal that notice not required where B was saying he was at the locus but did not go into the house. Only where accused saying he was at a specified other place was notice required.	

IMPEACHMENT OR INCRIMINATION

This **special defence** is that the offence was committed not by the accused but by another person, named if known. It is **competent** to call a **co-accused** as a witness.

COMMENTARY	CASE LAW	STATUTE LAW
A **special defence** intimates that the defence evidence will be of a certain, specific nature; the burden of proof is unaltered.	*Lambie v HMA* 1973 JC 53; 1973 SLT 219 Theft. Others named as responsible for crime. Per LJ-G Emslie: 'The only purpose of the special defence is to give fair notice to the Crown. ... When a special defence is pleaded ... the jury should be charged in the appropriate language, and all that requires to be said of the special defence, where ... evidence in support of it has been given is that if that evidence ... is believed, or creates in the minds of the jury reasonable doubt as to the guilt of the accused ... they must acquit.'	
Specific reference to the special defence by the judge is unneces-sary if the significance of all the evidence, including the special defence, is brought to the jury's attention.	*Mullen v HMA* 1978 SLT (Notes) 33 Rape. Defence claim that crime committed by principal Crown witness. Convicted. Appeal on misdirection refused. Per LJ-C Wheatley: 'It does not follow that failure by the trial judge to make specific reference in terms to such a special defence necessarily amounts to a misdirection such as to vitiate a conviction.'	
Co-accused's evidence is **compe-tent**.	*HMA v Ferrie* 1983 SCCR 1 Murder and serious assaults. One of the accused, Y, pled guilty to one of the assault charges. Subsequently the prosecution called Y as a witness against his co-accused. Per trial judge, Lord Stewart: '... the advocate-depute may call the witness subject only to any representations about delay in such call to enable the taking of defence precognitions ... the conclusion reached [is] the witness may be called.'	Criminal Procedure (Scotland) Act 1995. Co-accused compellable only when giving evidence or pleading guilty: s 266(9), (10). If co-accused gives evidence, an accused may cross-examine and if co-accused pleads guilty (sentenced or not) prosecutor or defence may call him as a witness without notice.
	McQuade v HMA 1996 SCCR 347 *Held*, on appeal, a notice of incrimination not necessary, since evidence could not have secured the appellant's acquittal (see Competent evidence for facts).	Section 266(1), (2). Accused a competent defence witness whether on trial alone or with co-accused but only upon own application.
There is no onus to prove a special defence of incrimination.	*Lambie v HMA* 1973 JC 53; 1973 SLT 219 Per LJ-G Emslie: '... we have come to be of opinion that the references in [earlier cases] of *Len-nie* and *Owens* to there being an onus upon the defence were unsound. It follows that [this] can now be regarded as an accurate statement of the law only in the case of the plea of insanity at the time.'	

MENTAL DISORDER

This **special defence** is that the accused suffered a **Mental Disorder** at the time of commission of the offence or at the time of trial.

Criminal Justice and Licensing (Scotland) Act 2010 s 168
Before section 52 of the Criminal Procedure (Scotland) Act 1995 insert—

51A Criminal responsibility of persons with mental disorder:

(1) A person is not criminally responsible for conduct constituting an offence, and is to be acquitted of the offence, if the person was at the time of the conduct unable by reason of mental disorder to appreciate the nature or wrongfulness of the conduct.

(2) But a person does not lack criminal responsibility for such conduct if the mental disorder in question consists only of a personality disorder which is characterised solely or principally by abnormally aggressive or seriously irresponsible conduct.

(3) The defence set out in subsection (1) is a special defence.

(4) The special defence may be stated only by the person charged with the offence and it is for that person to establish it on the balance of probabilities.

(5) In this section, "conduct" includes acts and omissions.

Mental Disorder at the time of the trial

Criminal Justice and Licensing (Scotland) Act 2010, s 170
After section 53E of the Criminal Procedure (Scotland) Act 1995 insert—

53F Unfitness for trial:

(1) A person is unfit for trial if it is established on the balance of probabilities that the person is incapable, by reason of a mental or physical condition, of participating effectively in a trial.

(2) In determining whether a person is unfit for trial the court is to have regard to—

(a) the ability of the person to—

(i) understand the nature of the charge,

(ii) understand the requirement to tender a plea to the charge and the effect of such a plea,

(iii) understand the purpose of, and follow the course of, the trial,

(iv) understand the evidence that may be given against the person,

(v) instruct and otherwise communicate with the person's legal representative, and

(b) any other factor which the court considers relevant.

(3) The court is not to find that a person is unfit for trial by reason only of the person being unable to recall whether the event which forms the basis of the charge occurred in the manner described in the charge.

(4) In this section "the court" means—

(a) as regards a person charged on indictment, the High Court or the sheriff court,

(b) as regards a person charged summarily, the sheriff court.

COMMENTARY	CASE LAW	STATUTE LAW
Traditional legal definition and construction of 'insanity' was repealed and replaced by the Criminal Justice and Licensing (Scotland) Act 2010 on 25 June 2012. The term insanity is thus forth replaced by mental disorder.	'... an absolute alienation of reason ... such a disease as deprives the patient of the knowledge of the true aspect and position of things ... hinders him from distinguishing friend or foe,—and gives him up to the impulse of his own distempered fancy' (Hume I, 37). *HMA v Kidd* 1960 JC 61 K murdered wife and child and pled special defence of insanity at time of offence. *Held* to be insane at time of offence. Per Lord Strachan: 'Must have been some mental defect ... by which his reason was overpowered and he was thereby rendered incapable of exerting his reason to control his conduct and reactions.'	Criminal Justice and Licensing (Scotland) Act 2010, s 171 – Abolition of common law rules: Any rule of law providing for— (a) the special defence of insanity, (b) the plea of diminished responsibility, or (c) insanity in bar of trial, ceases to have effect.
Acquittal involving cases of mental disorder		Criminal Justice and Licensing (Scotland) Act 2010, s 169 Before s 54 of the Criminal Procedure (Scotland) Act 1995 insert— s 53E – Acquittal involving mental disorder: (1) Where the prosecutor accepts a plea...of the special defence set out in section 51A of this Act, the court must declare that the person is acquitted by reason of the special defence. (2) Subsection (3) below applies where— (a) the prosecutor does not accept such a plea, and (b) evidence tending to establish the special defence set out in section 51A of this Act is brought before the court. (3) Where this subsection applies the court is to— (a) in proceedings on indictment, direct the jury to find whether the special defence has been established and, if they find that it has, to declare whether the person is acquitted on that ground, (b) in summary proceedings, state whether the special defence has been established and, if it states that it has, declare whether the person is acquitted on that ground."

COMMENTARY	CASE LAW	STATUTE LAW
Note: **Automatism**		
Voluntary intoxication has never successfully founded a special defence in Scots Criminal Law	*Brennan v HMA* 1977 SLT 151 B convicted of murdering his father. Defence of insanity founded upon the ground of acute intoxication rejected. Opinion of the court: 'There is nothing unethical or unfair or contrary to the general principle of our law that self-induced intoxication is not by itself defence to a criminal charge.'	
However, when it can be established that the accused suffered an alienation of reason due to factors out with their control the complete defence of Automatism may be successfully founded *Ross v HMA* criteria: (1) Total alienation of reason (2) caused by external factor (3) which was not self-induced (4) nor foreseeable	*Ross v HMA* 1991 SCCR 823 Assault. automatism, spiked drink – involuntary intoxication. *Held* (Five-judge bench), automatism due to an external factor (not disease of the mind), which is not self-induced and which leads to total alienation of reason amounting to a complete absence of self control, is something which the accused is not bound to foresee and is a defence. Crown must always establish mens rea. *HMA v Cunningham* 1963 JC 80; *Clark v HMA* 1968 JC 53 and *Carmichael v Boyle* 1985 SCCR 58 overruled as far as they hold that any mental condition short of insanity relevant only to mitigation.	
Criteria set out in *Ross v HMA* are stringently applied with direct evidence required on each point.	*Sorley v HMA* 1992 SCCR 396 Automatism, spiked drink. Held that the evidence fell far short of what will be sufficient for this defence. Need expert evidence on state of the accused, total loss of control backed up by eye witnesses.	

SELF-DEFENCE

This **special defence** is that the use of **reasonable force** against a person is **not criminal** if done in **self-defence** or **defence of others**. **Provocation** is not such a defence.

COMMENTARY	CASE LAW	STATUTE LAW
Reasonable force Retaliation must not exceed what is necessary in the circumstances although the matter will not be weighed too finely by the law.	*Fraser v Skinner* 1975 SLT (Notes) 84 F, a police officer, 'handed off' an aggressive motorist stopped for speeding believing himself to be under attack. Opinion of the court: 'It is only *cruel excess* which will defeat a plea of self-defence.'	
	HMA v Doherty 1954 JC 1 Culpable homicide. C attacked D with a hammer and D responded by striking C in the face with a bayonet supplied to him during the affray by another. Defence of self-defence fell and D convicted of culpable homicide and sentenced to twelve months' imprisonment. Per Lord Keith's charge to the jury: 'Let me remind you ... of the limits of self-defence ... two fundamental things you will keep in mind, that there is imminent danger to life and limb and that the retaliation used is necessary for the safety of the man threatened.'	
	Whyte v HMA 1996 SCCR 575 Accused punched victim as thought complainer going to punch mother. He admitted using excessive force and said he did not mean to. Conviction quashed on appeal as should have been left to jury, since excessive blow due to error of judgment in circumstances where hard to judge how strong the blow needed to be. Per LJ-G Hope: 'It is always difficult to judge precisely the force with which a blow may strike a victim.'	
	Hillan v HMA 1937 JC 53 Assault. H accused of a minor assault. However, he claimed he was merely acting in self-defence, the case having a sexual connotation. *Held*, on appeal, that H had been acting in self-defence and acquitted. Per Lord Wark, quoting Hume: 'In deciding on pleas of this sort the judge will not insist on an exact proportion of injury and retaliation, but rather be disposed to sustain the defence unless the panel has been transported to acts of cruelty or great excess.'	
Cruel excess of violence used.	*Fenning v HMA* 1985 SCCR 219 F killed P on a fishing trip. Alleged that P had become suspicious that there was a relationship between F and deceased's wife. P had thus threatened F with knife and in response F smashed P's head several times with rock. On appeal conviction for murder upheld as there was cruel excess of violence used. Per trial judge Lord Mayfield: '... there must be no cruel excess of violence on the accused's part.'	

COMMENTARY	CASE LAW	STATUTE LAW
Where there is a mistaken apprehension of danger, a plea of self-defence is not defeated if there are reasonable grounds for the belief.	*Owens v HMA* 1946 JC 119 Murder. O killed a man whom he maintained he believed to have had a dangerous object in his hand when he sprang at O. On appeal, conviction quashed. Per LJ-C Normand: 'Self-defence is made out when it is established … that the panel believed he was in imminent danger and that he held that belief on reasonable grounds. Grounds for such a belief may exist though they are founded on a genuine mistake of fact.'	
	HMA v Kay 1970 SLT (Notes) 66 Murder. K killed her husband with a knife alleging self-defence. Notable in that Lord Wheatley allowed evidence of previous assaults by deceased on K. Per Lord Wheatley: 'The defence … is to the effect that the accused was acting in self-defence, she reasonably believing that there was imminent danger to her life due to an assault intended by the deceased.'	
Not criminal: If act is done in self-defence it is not of criminal quality.	*HMA v Brogan* 1964 SLT 204 Assault. B accused of assaulting W by striking him on the head with a chair. B claimed in self-defence that he was first assaulted by W. Per Lord Cameron's charge to the jury: 'Although a plea of self-defence may be put forward … the burden of proof remains with the Crown throughout to prove beyond reasonable doubt … the charge.'	
	M'Cluskey v HMA 1959 JC 39 Culpable homicide. M'C claimed he had killed O when acting in self-defence in that O was forcibly attempting to effect sodomy on him. Convicted of culpable homicide on basis of provocation, self-defence being rejected. Decision upheld on appeal. Per LJ-G Clyde: 'I can see no justification at all for extending this defence to a case where there is no apprehension of danger to the accused's life … but merely a threat … of an attack on the appellant's virtue.'	
	Derrett v Lockhart 1991 SCCR 109 Self-defence open in an assaulttype breach of the peace but not where the accused has not looked for an opportunity to retreat before taking pre-emptive strike.	
An 'imminent danger to life' must exist in murder cases	*June Greig (1976)* (unreported) Accused killed her husband while he slept. Accused had previously been seriously beaten by the deceased on a number of occasions but failed in her plea of self-defence. *Held*, G's fear was of the possibility of future violence as no imminent danger to her life existed during her attack on her sleeping husband. See also: *Boyle v HMA* 1992 SCCR 824; 1993 SLT 577.	
Accused must be unable to escape violence	*HMA v Doherty* 1954 JC 1. '… if the person assaulted has means of escape or retreat, he is bound to use them.' (per Lord Keith, at p 6)	

COMMENTARY	CASE LAW	STATUTE LAW
Defence of others The special defence extends to the use of reasonable force to protect another party from unjustified attack.	*HMA v Carson and Anr* 1964 SLT 21 M, C's co-accused, alleged that he had struck D with a bottle, only to protect C from a homicidal knife attack by D. M alleged that he was thus acting in self-defence of C. Per Lord Wheatley: 'If a man sees another man being unlawfully attacked, he is entitled to stop that unlawful attack.' See also: *Boyle v HMA* 1992 SCCR 824; 1993 SLT 577. *Dewar v HMA* 2009 SLT 670	
Prevention of Rape	*Pollock v HMA* 1998 SLT 880 Accused killed victim by inflicting 70 injuries by jumping on his head. Accused said protecting girlfriend from rape by victim whom he believed had a knife. Trial judge withdrew self-defence but allowed provocation and accused convicted of culpable homicide. Upheld on appeal, savagery of attack went far beyond measures reasonably required to protect girlfriend.	
Provocation Where the accused has acted in unjustifiable self-defence, he may be entitled to plead provocation, but it is not a justification of an attack that there has been provocation.	*Crawford v HMA* 1950 JC 67; 1950 SLT 279 C killed his father, stabbing him as he was preparing to shave. There had been a family quarrel the previous night and immediately before the stabbing C had been shouted at by his father. Plea of self-defence failed although plea of provocation accepted in mitigation of sentence. Per LJ-G Cooper: 'Provocation and self-defence are ... often I fear confused ... but provocation *is not* a special defence.'	
To successfully establish a plea of provocation there must be: (1) A loss of self-control	*HMA v Hill* 1941 JC 59 H shot his wife and her lover immediately after they had confessed they had committed adultery. Per Lord Patrick: 'If a man catches his wife and her paramour in the act of adultery and, in the heat of passionate indignation, then and there kills them, his crime is a very serious one, but it is not murder, it is culpable homicide.' *Rutherford v HMA* 1997 SCCR 711 Partner told appellant on Friday she had an affair. On Sunday she said affair more serious than previously disclosed. Trial judge withdrew provocation but on appeal High Court said Sunday's account different and should have been left to jury, conviction of culpable homicide substituted.	
(2) A provoking act (either an initial assault on the accused or the discovery of sexual infidelity) and	*HMA v McKean* 1996 SCCR 402 Accused convicted of culpable homicide: responded to information he had been sharing her lesbian partner. Per Lord MacLean: 'I also see no reason why in the modern context the plea should not also be available to homosexual couples who live together and are regarded in the community as partners bound by close ties of love, affection and faithfulness.' *Graham v HMA* 1987 SCCR 20 G charged with murder. She had quarrel with victim who had knife and threatened to kill her. She successfully disarmed him and killed him. Convic-ted of murder. Per LJ-C Ross: 'What is noteworthy is that by the time the killing took place, the appellant had dis-armed the victim.'	

COMMENTARY	CASE LAW	STATUTE LAW
(3) an immediate and proportionate retaliation	*Drury v HMA* 2001 SLT 1013Five judge bench. Provocation successfully established. Drury had been having an on-off sexual relationship with the deceased with whom he had previously resided with. On the night of the attack, D arrived at the deceased's house but she had refused to answer the door. Sometime later, a blonde haired man was seen by D leaving the premises adjusting his clothes. D approached both the man and the deceased and asked what they had being doing ascertaining from the deceased's answer that they had been having sex. D then grabbed a claw-hammer kept at the side of the house before brutally attacking the deceased about the head. See also: *Gillon* v *HM Advocate* 2006 SLT 799; 2007 J.C. 24	
Test is subjective.	*Jones v HMA* 1989 SCCR 726 J charged with murder. Victim had threatened J with knife previously and when J later met him in the street, he believed he had knife and stabbed him. Trial judge directed jury that test for self defence and provocation was objective. On appeal *held* to be misdirection. Test to apply is the subjective one, whether accused believed on reasonable grounds that deceased had a knife. Conviction of culpable homicide substituted. *Low v HMA* 1993 SCCR 493 Provocation. Deceased inviting L to have sex with him, in following struggle the deceased cut L on the hand, L stabbed deceased 50 times. Provocation withdrawn at trial, upheld on appeal. Gross disproportion between the provocation and the retaliation. 'Gross disproportion' preferred to 'cruel excess' as in *Lennon v HMA* 1991 SCCR 611. *Robertson v HMA* 1994 SCCR 589 Murder, provocation. R had stabbed the deceased 99 times after the deceased had made a homosexual advance to him and had presented a knife at him. *Held* on appeal that the trial judge's direction that there must be a reasonable proportionate relationship between the deceased's actions and R's response was the same in effect as saying the retaliation must not be grossly disproportionate. *Drury v HMA* 2001 SLT 1013 'While the terminology of "reducing murder to culpable homicide" is frequently encountered, it is essentially misleading... In particular, it suggests that the jury would first conclude that, absent provocation, the accused would have been guilty of murder, and only at that stage would they consider provocation. In reality, however, evidence relating to provocation is simply one of the factors which the jury should take into account in performing their general task of determining the accused's state of mind at the time when he killed his victim.' per Lord Justice General Rodger at para 17, p 591.	

NECESSITY

This **special defence** of **necessity** can be pleaded in **certain limited circumstances** whereby the accused has no alternative but to commit an offence in order to prevent death or serious bodily harm.

COMMENTARY	CASE LAW	STATUTE LAW
Certain limited circumstances	*R v Dudley and Stephens* (1884) 14 QBD 273 Two men and a boy cast adrift in open boat. The two men killed the boy, who was ill, after eight days without food and six without water. Fed on flesh of boy. Convicted of murder. Per Lord Coleridge: 'It is not correct to say that there is any absolute or unqualified necessity to preserve one's life.' *Moss v Howdle* 1997 SCCR 215 Accused speeding at over 100 mph on motorway to reach service station as passenger in pain. Pain turned out to be cramp. Accused claimed necessity, but sheriff held he had real choice and was not constrained to commit the offence: he had the alternative of pulling over and finding out what was wrong with passenger. Conviction upheld by High Court, which held that the defence of necessity was available in respect of all offences and the minimum requirement was of immediate danger or great bodily harm to accused or companion and danger may come from a person or natural disaster or illness and that any viable legal alternative must be taken if available.	
Danger must be immediate	*Ruxton v Lang* 1998 SCCR (Sh Ct) 1 Drink driving. Accused returned home after office party with colleague and her boyfriend threw him out and threatened accused with knife so she went off in car intending to drive to brother's house two miles away. She was stopped in street where brother lived. *Held*, defence of necessity available to charge of driving with excess alcohol but not in instance as when stopped by police the danger had already ceased. Accused fined and awarded 11 penalty points, there being special reasons for not disqualifying her. Accused refused leave to appeal. See also: *D v Donnelly* 2009 SLT 476	
Defence Where, in order to preserve a greater value, there is the commission of a crime, eg stealing a fire extinguisher to save a burning building (Williams, p 737).		
Where to ensure personal safety there is the commission of a crime.	*Tudhope v Grubb* 1983 SCCR 350 (Sh Ct) Accused charged under s 6(1) of Road Traffic Act 1972. *Held*, that as accused had attempted to drive so as to avoid further injury following an assault, he had established defence of necessity. Acquitted.	

COERCION

This **special defence** of **coercion** may operate as a defence to a criminal act or as a plea in mitigation where an individual has compelled the accused to perform an act against his or her will by use of psychological pressure, violence, or threats. Similarly, where such coercion takes the form of **superior orders** such a plea will have the same effect.

COMMENTARY	CASE LAW	STATUTE LAW
Coercion 'Crime consists in the intentional violation of the rights of others; it follows it cannot be visited with punishment where it has arisen not from intention or voluntary depravity but such coercion as has deprived the party of the free exercise of his will' (Alison I, 668).	*Thomson v HMA* 1983 SCCR 368 Threat must be of immediate harm in circumstances where resort to protection of authorities impossible, and it is impossible to resist or avoid participation. The defence of coercion can extend even to a person playing a principal part, and the question whether the gain, etc, was disclosed to the authorities matters only as regards the credibility of the accused.	
Coercion may take different forms. It may be of a public nature,	*James Purdie* 1720 Hume I 52 Charge of mobbing. Acquitted on basis that he was forced and compelled to participate by the mob.	
or be issued by one individual to another, the essence of the plea being the existence of such coercion that the accused 'could not resist without manifest peril to his life or property' (Alison I, 672).	*Docherty and Ors* (1976) SCCR Supp 146 Three men charged with armed robbery. Two of them pleaded that they had been coerced by the third who had threatened them and their mothers. Issue of coercion left to jury to decide. Per Lord Keith: 'In order that coercion may be a defence the position must be that the accused acted in a situation created by a threat to him which he had reason to believe would be carried out.'	
The threat must be imminent.	*HMA v McCallum* (1977) SCCR Supp 169.	
Individual's will must be completely overborne: An objective test.	*Cochrane v HMA* 2001 SCCR 665. C had entered the home of the complainer armed only with a candlestick. C had threatened the complainer with the candlestick if she did not hand over her purse which contained her wages. C later claimed he had been coerced into the attack by a co-accused who in turn had threatened to blow up C's house. It was established in evidence that C's IQ placed him in the bottom 4% of the population making him particularly susceptible to manipulation. In affirming the appropriate test to be used in cases of coercion, the High Court *Held*, '[the jury] should consider whether an ordinary sober person of reasonable firmness, sharing the characteristics of the accused would have responded as the accused did…'	
Fear of imminent death or serious injury may operate as a defence even to a serious crime.	*Sayers and Ors v HMA* 1981 SCCR 312 Jury directed that where a person's will is overborne by the will of another so that he is not acting of his own free will, that might be a defence to a criminal charge, but that matter be approached with some caution lest it become an easy answer for those that could not otherwise explain their conduct.	

COMMENTARY	CASE LAW	STATUTE LAW
Superior orders: may form the basis of a plea of coercion where a soldier acts under a lawful order or believes that he is so acting.	*HMA v Sheppard* 1941 JC 67; 1941 SLT 404 Charge of culpable homicide. Private in army part of escort to return a deserter to the regiment. Accused left alone with deserter for a few minutes and deserter attempted to escape. Accused shot and killed him. No clear orders but told by superior officer to 'stand no nonsense and shoot if necessary'. Found not guilty. Per Lord Robertson: 'It would be altogether wrong to judge his actings so placed too meticulously— to weigh them in fine scales. If that were to be done it seems to me that the actings of soldiers on duty might well be paralysed by fear of consequences with great prejudice to national interests.'	

EVIDENCE

ADMISSIBILITY

BEST EVIDENCE

The best evidence rule requires that primary evidence be given but **secondary evi-dence is admissible, *quoad* credibility in *de recenti* statements**: of **taped interview by police**; of statements by an **accused at judicial examination**; of **witness's statements different from those at trial**; but not **statements in precognition**; save on oath or if it is **impossible**, or **not reasonably practicable to produce primary evidence**.

COMMENTARY	CASE LAW	STATUTE LAW
The 'best evidence' rule: 'A party must adduce the best attainable evidence of the facts he must prove…' W.G. Dickson *'A Treatise on the Law of Evidence in Scotland'* (3rd edn, 1887, para 195)		
Secondary evidence is admissible *quoad* credibility in *de recenti* statements	*Harrison v Mackenzie* 1923 JC 61 Illegal trawling. Only evidence of identification that of fisherman who read boat mark through telescope and reported to father immediately. *Held* evidence admissible *quoad* credibility. Appeal sustained *quoad* absence of corroboration.	
A *de recenti* statement is of no corroborative value, it bears only on credibility.	*Morton v HMA* 1938 JC 50 Indecent assault. Only identification that of complainer. *De recenti* statement to brother led in evidence. Objection repelled. *Held* that evidence admissible *quoad* credibility. Per LJ-C Aitchison: 'A statement made by an injured party *de recenti* ... is admissible as bearing upon credibility only, [it is] not evidence of the fact complained of.' (Re: Evidence of distress *de recenti* and corroboration see also Evidence—Sufficiency, p 137.)	
Taped interview by police Better evidence than recollection.	*HMA v McFadden* 1981 *Scolag* 260 Murder. Police interview taped and tape produced as evidence to which defence objected and queried admissibility as to: (1) unfairness, ie accused cross-examined by police; (2) tape contained hearsay statements and matters irrelevant to the indictment. Per Lord Jauncey: 'There is a good deal to be said for the view that where you have a tape recording, that must be the better evidence ... than a recollection of events some months ago.' *Deb v Normand* 1996 SCCR 766 *Held*, best evidence of what a police officer had witnessed was his own recollection and he could not be compelled to produce his notebook which he had referred to prior to going into the witness box.	

COMMENTARY	CASE LAW	STATUTE LAW
	Jones v HMA 1991 SCCR 290 Two accused admitted to police involvement in a robbery but denied being party to murder in the course of the robbery, incriminated another man. *Held* on appeal that such a 'mixed' statement could be evidence. *Morrison v HMA* 1990 SCCR 235 followed. *Thomson (Kenneth) v HMA* 1998 SCCR 683 *Held*, evidential character of mixed statement is not altered when accused gives evidence. *Scaife v HMA* 1992 SCCR 845 'Mixed' statement. S admitted theft but denied violence. On appeal (following *Morrison v HMA* 1990 SCCR 235), *held* the jury should have been specifically directed to determine whether they accepted the whole, or part of it, and whether it caused reasonable doubt. *Earley v HMA* 1995 SCCR 267 E charged with assault. Crown relied on a statement which appellant denied making. *Held*, since no explanation in statements why he could claim self-defence the exculpatory element which is the basis of *Morrison v HMA* 1990 SCCR 235 was absent. *Higgins v HMA* 1993 SCCR 542 H said he had stabbed the deceased but only in self-defence. *Held* that the judge was entitled to tell the jury that they could isolate parts of the statement that they wished to accept.	
Accused at judicial examination	*Howarth v HMA (No 1)* 1992 SCCR 364 Judge entitled to refer to a statement made by the accused to police even though he denied making the statement at judicial examination. *Sutherland v HMA* 1994 SCCR 80 *Held* on appeal that judge correct to give a direction that jury could not draw an inference from S's failure to give evidence but could draw an inference where the facts were crying out for an explanation and none was given. Sufficiently special circumstances. *Robertson v HMA* 1995 SCCR 152 LJ-C: 'Although in *Morrison v HMA* the court was not dealing with statements at judicial examination, there is no reason to think that the principles laid down in that case would not cover statements made at judicial examination.'	Criminal Procedure (Scotland) Act 1995, ss 35–39.
Record evidence without witnesses.		**Record of proceedings at judicial examination as evidence:** CP(S)A 1995, s 278. Record is evidence without witness. Either party can object to the record or part of it being read; witnesses to it can be called. 'Record', each record, in list of productions.

COMMENTARY	CASE LAW	STATUTE LAW
Prior statement of witness (other than accused) evidence of contents where witness gives evidence.	*Jamieson v HMA* 1994 SCCR 610 Crown witness said she could not remember what happened or her statement that appellant was kicking the complainer, but said if that's what she told police then true. Evidence led that she told police appellant had been kicking the complainer. *Held*, her evidence that she told police the truth incorporated her statement to police into own evidence. *Note*: *Jamieson* wider than CP(S)A 1995, s 260 since statement not in document.	CP(S)A 1995, s 260(1). Subject to the following provisions of this section, where a witness gives evidence in criminal proceedings, any prior statement made by the witness shall be admissible as evidence of any matter stated in it of which direct oral evidence by him would be admissible if given in the course of those proceedings. CP(S)A 1995, s 260() (2). A prior statement shall not be admissible under this section unless— (a) the statement is contained in a document; (b) the witness, in the course of giving evidence, indicates that the statement was made by him and that he adopts it as his evidence; and (c) at the time the statement was made, the person who made it would have been a competent witness in the proceedings.
Witness's statements different from those at trial	*Dunsmore v HMA* 1991 SCCR 849 D giving evidence that at an earlier trial a witness had identified his co-accused not D. On appeal *held* that the jury entitled to have regard to the evidence as a direction otherwise would have meant them ignoring part of D's evidence. *Greenhalghse v HMA* 1992 SCCR 311 Crown putting to witness evidence of a statement made to the police which differed from the evidence she was giving at trial. Judge making no comment about the statement in his charge. *Held* on appeal that the judge should have dealt with the statement because some of it was hearsay. *HMA v Hislop* 1994 SLT 333 Witness could not recall what statement she had given police. *Held*, non-recollection sufficed to meet the 'different' requirement under CP(S)A 1995, s 263(4). *Young v HMA* 1995 SCCR 418 Statement made to police when witness patient in hospital. *Held*, wording of section does not exclude possibility that statement unfairly obtained should not be put to the witness, for jury to decide whether fair to take evidence into account. *Paterson v HMA* 1997 SCCR 707 Defence agent sought in cross-examination to lead evidence from police witness as to inconsistencies of B's statement. Court *held* he should have put to B first the specific occasion when statement made and to whom.	CP(S)A 1995, s 263(4). A witness may be examined as to whether he has on any specified occasion made a statement on any matter pertinent to the issue at the trial different from the evidence given by him in the trial; and evidence may be led in the trial to prove that the witness made the different statement on the occasion specified.

COMMENTARY	CASE LAW	STATUTE LAW
	McNee v Ruxton 1997 SCCR 291 Witness adopted statement of another witness. *Held*, sheriff wrong to prevent defence from using CP(S)A 1995, s 263(4) as no grounds for saying that he sought to put a statement other than the witness's own statement. Conviction quashed.	
	Hemming v HMA 1998 SLT 213 Court granted order allowing recovery of police witness statements to allow defence to test credibility in terms of CP(S)A 1995, s 263(4). Granted on grounds of the overriding public interest of fair hearing of accused, and given that Crown made similar use of statements. Observed, need for substantial reasons why recovery necessary in the interests of justice.	
	See also: *McGhee v HMA* 1992 SCCR 324	
Statements in precognition By their nature interviews of defence witnesses are precog-nitions and therefore inadmissible.	*McNeilie v HMA* 1929 JC 50; 1929 SLT 145 Attempted theft. Special defence of alibi. Objection to evidence of statements made to police when they interviewed defence witnesses repelled. McN convicted. Conviction quashed on appeal. Object had been to discover what the witness's evidence was to be, was a precognition, and therefore inadmissible.	
	KJC v HMA 1994 SCCR 560 Rape trial. Complainer examined on inconsistencies in precognition on oath. *Held*, fairness requires that the other party be allowed to put the full statement to show consistency with evidence.	
Statements taken when a case is at the stage of active construction are precognitions.	*Kerr v HMA* 1958 JC 14; 1958 SLT 82 Theft of goods. Employer gave statement to police in interview which was read as evidence in court. K convicted. Conviction quashed on appeal. Per LJ-C Thomson: 'There is no dispute that on authority, if this statement was a precognition, it was inadmissible [a precognition] is filtered through the mind of another ... once the police have begun to build up a case against certain people ... we have passed beyond the stage of preliminary investigations and have got into the stage of preparation for the leading of evidence.'	
	HMA v McSween 2007 SCCR 310 Perjury respondent re-interviewed by police in murder enquiry. Question and answer session, police officer putting answers into sentence construction. Not a precognition as not instructed by procurator fiscal and would have been disclosable.	
Impossible to produce primary evidence To test whether primary evidence is requisite, the questions to be asked are whether the evidence is necessary and available.	*Clements v Macaulay* (1866) 4 M 543 Pursuer wanted to produce copy of letter. Pursuer unable to produce original after due diligence. *Held* that copy admissible. Per Lord Cowan: 'Secondary evidence is admissible only after due exertion is proved to have been made for recovery of the principal document.'	

COMMENTARY	CASE LAW	STATUTE LAW
Real evidence not essential.	*McLeod v Woodmuir Miners' Welfare Society Social Club* 1961 JC 5; (1960 SLT 349) 'Primary evidence is not always essential, and secondary evidence is not necessarily incompetent. Secondary evidence *is* competent if it is not reasonably practicable and convenient to produce the primary evidence.' (Per LJ-G Clyde at 9).	
	Maciver v Mackenzie 1942 JC 51; 1942 SLT 144 Accused took possession of wreck without reporting it to receiver. Wreck not produced. Secondary evidence of condition admissible *quoad* marks on timber. Per LJ-C Normand: 'The question in each case is whether the real evidence is essential for proving the case against the accused.'	
	Friel v Leonard 1997 SLT 1206 Audiovisual equipment allegedly stolen from house not produced at trial. Sheriff refused to allow evidence. *Held*, sheriff's decision recalled, because production of items not necessary for proof of Crown's case and no prejudice to accused from their absence. LJ-G dictum in *Maciver v Mackenzie* 1942 JC 51; 1942 SLT 144 applied.	
Is it reasonably practicable to retain evidence?	*Anderson v Laverock* 1976 JC 9; 1976 SLT 62 Statutory prosecution for unlawful possession of salmon. Fish destroyed by police before defence allowed to examine them. Condition of fish material. Convicted. Conviction quashed. Opinion of the court: 'Whether goods are perishable or whether it is reasonably practicable and convenient to retain them as primary evidence ... will depend on the circumstances and evidence in each particular case.'	
Not reasonably practicable to produce primary evidence Newspapers sold for trading purposes.	*Hughes v Skeen* 1980 SLT (Notes) 13 Stolen newspapers recovered and returned for distribution, but not produced at trial. Per Lord Cameron: 'Production of these newspapers ... neither necessary nor ... practicable in this particular case.'	
No authority to impound whisky bottle and label.	*McLeod v Woodmuir Miners' Welfare Society Social Club* 1961 JC 5; (1960 SLT 349) Statutory prosecution for sale of understrength whisky. Objections to oral evidence of details on label on bottle not produced at trial sustained. Crown appeal successful. No authority to impound the bottle, not reasonably practical to produce it.	
Photographs of fingerprint 'lifts'.	*Hamilton v Grant* 1984 SCCR 263 Objection taken to evidence consisting of photographs of fingerprint 'lifts'. Sheriff held photographs inadmissible and said actual 'lifts' required and best evidence rule contravened. Reversed on appeal. No opinion delivered.	
Blood samples not produced.	*Williamson v Aitchison* 1982 SCCR 102; 1982 SLT 399 Drunken driving. Certification lodged re blood samples' results. Objection by defence that blood samples should have been prodced repelled. Appeal rejected. Shown that the blood analysed had been taken from the accused.	Biological material CP(S)A 1995, s 276. Evidence of characteristics and composition competent notwithstanding neither material nor sample lodged. If party wishes to lead evidence where neither material nor -sample lodged he shall make material/sample available for inspection by other party unless material hazard to health or destroyed in process of analysis.

COMMENTARY	CASE LAW	STATUTE LAW
Printout from breath testing device not available.	*McLeod v Fraser* 1986 SCCR 271 *Held* that best evidence of result of analysis of blood was that of the analyst and it was permissible for him to refer to the register of blood analyses, or the certificate, as an aide-memoire.	
		Documentary evidence CP(S)A 1995, s 279, Sch 8. Provides for certification of documents, in particular business documents (which may contain hearsay) and validates their use as best evidence.
There are statutory exceptions to the rule that hearsay evidence is inadmissible.	*Forrester v HMA* 1997 SCCR 9 Hearsay admissible, but oral evidence preferable. Sufficient reason to extend 12-month time limit (see Statutory time limits).	CP(S)A 1995, s 259(1). Evidence of a statement made by a person otherwise than while giving oral evidence shall be admissible where the judge is satisfied that: (a) the person who made the statement will not give evidence because he— (i) is dead or mentally/physically unable to give evidence; (ii) is outwith UK and it is not reasonably practicable to secure attendance or obtain evidence in any other competent manner; (iii) cannot be found and all reasonable steps have been taken to find him; (iv) is authorised by the court to refuse to answer on grounds of self-incrimination; or (v) is called as a witness and refuses to take oath or affirmation or, having sworn, refuses to give evidence; (b) evidence of the matter would be admissible in proceedings if that person gave direct oral evidence of it; (c) person who made statement would have been a competent witness in such proceedings at time statement made; and (d) evidence would entitle judge/jury to find that the statement was made and either it is contained in a document or the person who gave oral evidence of statement has direct personal knowledge of its making. CP(S)A 1995, s 259(3). Evidence of statement above shall not be admissible where judge is satisfied that evidence is unavailable due to actings of person in support of whose case the evidence would be given (or a person acting on that person's behalf).

ADMISSIBILITY

COMPETENT EVIDENCE

To be admissible, evidence must be competent; **non-compliance with statutory requirements** will make it incompetent. Competent evidence may be **compellable or non-compellable**. In the case of a **witness present during earlier evidence** it is subject to special considerations. By statutory provision evidence in **replication**, and **additional** evidence is competent.

COMMENTARY	CASE LAW	STATUTE LAW
Non-compliance with statutory requirements		Criminal Procedure (Scotland) Act 1995.
Service of (a) copy indictment, (b) list of prosecution witnesses. Declaration or extract conviction.	*Bennett v HMA* 1995 SCCR 471 Service of copy indictment missing page 2. Nothing on page 2 concerned appellant. *Held*, breach of provisions but in absence of claim appellant misled/prejudiced court required by statutory provision to repel objection and appeal refused.	**Solemn procedure:** Section 66(4) (prosecution). Accused to be served full copy of indictment and list of prosecution witnesses. Section 67(2) (prosecution). Not necessary to list witnesses to declaration of accused or extract conviction.
Witnesses, productions, not in list—notice.	*Torres v HMA* 1997 SCCR 491 Charge of importing cocaine. Short report compiled on lodged sample not shown to defence. *Held*, no breach of statutory provisions as samples lodged and original report made clear what comparisons might be carried out. Per LJ-C Cullen: 'evidence did not introduce any genuinely new material or additional source of evidence.'	Section 67(5) (prosecution). Com-petent, with leave, to examine witnesses or put in evidence production not included in list, if written notice given to the accused by the relevant time. 'the relevant time' means: (a) where tried in the High Court– (i) not less than seven clear days before the preliminary hearing; or (ii) such later time, before the jury is sworn to try the case, as the court may, on cause shown, allow. (b) where tried in the sheriff court, not less than two clear days before the day on which the jury is sworn to try the case.
Special defence— seven days' notice normally required.	*McQuade v HMA* 1996 SCCR 347 Murder. S admitted shooting deceased in course of robbery and said M present and armed but they never intended to fire. On appeal, convictions for murder upheld. Notice of incrimination not required, since evidence not calculated to exculpate accused. *O'Connell v HMA* 1996 SCCR 614 Special defence tendered at adjourned first diet not accepted as not in proper form. At further diet tendered in proper form but sheriff said special cause required to be shown. On appeal, *held* continued diet was still first diet and since defence duly lodged in proper form cause not required to be shown.	Section 78 (accused). Not competent for accused to state special defence or to lead evidence calculated to exculpate the accused by incriminating a co-accused unless notice lodged no less than seven clear days before the preliminary hearing in High Court cases (at or before the first diet in Sheriff Court cases) unless on cause shown.

COMMENTARY	CASE LAW	STATUTE LAW
Notice by accused if witness or production not in prosecutor's list.	*Brown v HMA* 1998 SCCR 461 Before the start of the trial the depute fiscal changed the backing number on production without informing the defence. Sheriff granted extension, but overturned on appeal due to accumulation of errors on the part of the Crown.	Section 78(4) (accused). Not competent to examine witnesses or put in evidence productions not included in prosecutor's list unless seven clear days' notice given before the preliminary hearing in High Court cases (at or before the first diet in Sheriff Court cases) unless on cause shown.
Witness or production in other party's list competent.		Section 67(6) (both parties). Competent for prosecutor or accused to exam-ine witness or put in evidence production in other party's list.
Alibi—notice in summary cases.		**Summary procedure:** Section 149B (accused). Not competent for accused to found on alibi unless notice of this plea with particulars as to time and place and of witnesses proposed to prove it are given to prosecutor prior to the first witness being sworn. Prosecutor, on notice, is entitled to adjournment. Section 149B(2A) –statement must be lodged: (i) where an intermediate diet is to be held, at or before the diet, or (ii) where such a diet is not to be held, no later than 10 clear days before the trial diet.
Compellable or non-compellable Accused non-compellable either in his own, or a co-accused's defence although he may elect to give evidence.		Section 266(1), (2). Accused a competent defence witness whether on trial alone or with co-accused but only upon own application.
Co-accused compellable only when giving evidence or pleading guilty.		Section 266(9), (10). If co-accused gives evidence an accused may cross-examine and if co-accused pleads guilty (sentenced or not) prosecutor or accused may call him as witness without notice.
Relatives of accused compellable.		Section 265(3). No objection to admissibility or compellability that witness is father, mother, son, daughter, brother, sister, by consangui-nity or affinity, or uncle, aunt, nephew, niece by consangui-nity of party adducing witness.
Spouse or civil partner may be called by accused.	*Hunter v HMA* 1984 SCCR 306 Murder and assault. H father of deceased child. Special defence of incrimination lodged naming wife *quoad* assault. Wife warned that she need not answer any questions. Intimated that she did not wish to do so. H convicted of culpable homicide. Appeal refused. Opinion of the court that one spouse is a compellable witness in the other spouse's defence.	Section 264(1). Spouse or civil partner of an accused may be called as a witness by accused.

COMMENTARY	CASE LAW	STATUTE LAW
	Bates v HMA 1989 SCCR 338 B and C charged with drugs offences in relation to which spouse is not a compellable witness. B intended to lead evidence incriminating C. Crown called C's wife as witness and she was told by trial judge that she was not obliged to answer questions which might incriminate C. She gave evidence against B but refused to answer any questions put to her in cross-examination. On appeal, *held* that judge's direction was wrong. Ought to have instructed spouse that she could not be compelled to give evidence but that if she did she would have to answer all the questions put to her.	
	Casey v HMA 1993 SLT 33 The term spouse only extends to individuals who are married and does not include cohabitants.	
Spouse compellable in personal injury offences and offences against his or her property.	*Foster v HMA* 1932 JC 75; 1932 SLT 482 Forgery and uttering cheques. Alleged that F forged signature of husband. Husband competent and compellable witness. Per Lord Anderson: 'If the fundamental consideration ... is necessity—the need for the evidence of the injured spouse to secure conviction, this would seem to operate as strongly in the case of offences against property as in the case of bodily injury.'	Section 264(1) – The spouse or civil partner of an accused is a competent and compellable witness for the prosecution, the accused or any co-accused in the proceedings against the accused.
	Hay v McClory 1993 SCCR 1040 CP(S)A 1975, s 348. Spouse compellable where she would have been at common law. Offence by accused against the house of the spouse did not make her compellable because the offence was not against her, council paid for repairs to the house. Spouse should have been warned that she need not give evidence.	
Wife's evidence at previous trial may be admissible even where she is not compellable in present trial.	*Lockhart v Massie* 1989 SCCR 421.	
Socius criminis No warning need now be given to treat the evidence of a *socius criminis* with special care.	*Docherty v HMA* 1987 SCCR 418 Appellant convicted, by majority, of assault and robbery while acting with three others who had earlier pled guilty on separate indictments, and were called as witnesses for the Crown, giving evidence that the appellant had been recruited as driver for a different criminal enterprise (an assault upon a man against whom one of the three sought retaliation for the alleged rape of his step daughter). Appeal that conviction should be quashed because no 'cum nota' warning given. A bench of nine judges was convened to reconsider the soundness of the rule referred to in *Wallace v HMA* 1952 JC 78 in these terms: '(the) evidence [of a *socius criminis*] ought always to be made the subject of a specific and particular warning that ... it is suspect evi-dence deserving of close scrutiny'. *Held* 'Trial judges need only give to juries in all cases, whether or not any *socius criminis* has been adduced as a witness for the Crown the familiar directions designed to assist them in dealing with the credibility of witnesses and any additional assistance which the circumstances of any particular case may require.'	

COMMENTARY	CASE LAW	STATUTE LAW
Witness present during earlier evidence Reasons to hear evidence required.	*Macdonald (Angus) v Mackenzie* 1947 JC 169; 1948 SLT 27 Reckless or careless driving. Witness for defence in court during earlier evidence. No objection by procurator fiscal. Evidence disallowed by sheriff. Per Lord Jamieson: 'It is for the party tendering the witness to satisfy the court that his presence was not due to negligence or, ... that he had not been or was not likely to have been influenced by what he had already heard.'	Section 267(2). Witness need not be rejected because of presence during ear-lier evidence without permission or consent if presence was not through culpable negligence or criminal intent, if witness not unduly instructed or influenced and injustice will not follow. Section 267(1). Court may permit witness to be in court prior to giving evidence if it appears to the court not to be contrary to the interests of justice.
Note: The statutory requirements do not apply to a defence solicitor as witness.	*Campbell v Cochrane* 1928 JC 25; 1928 SLT 394 Licensing Act prosecution. Solicitor conducting defence adduced as defence witness. Ruled inadmissible. Appealed. *Held* that solicitor competent witness.	
Witness not present but informed of earlier evidence.	*Keenan v Scott* 1990 SCCR 470 Person in court hearing evidence and then going to witness room to tell the witnesses what had been said. Trial proceeding, appeal. *Held* that the sheriff was correct to allow the trial to proceed as he had repelled the submission of no case to answer holding that evidence was sufficient without the 'suspect' evidence.	
Replication evidence To contradict defence evidence where it could not have been reasonably anticipated.	*Sandlan v HMA* 1983 SCCR 71 Theft. S and K charged. K lodged special defence incriminating S. S lodged special defence incriminating K. In course of cross-examination by Crown, S gave evidence of shopping visit. Crown allowed evidence in replication to show trip took place two days earlier. S gave further evidence and called solicitor as witness. Argued evidence in replication incompetent on grounds that CP(S)A 1975, s 149A only applied to evidence led to contradict evidence of defence witness in examination in chief. Argument rejected by Lord Stewart: evidence in replication competent. On appeal conviction quashed on other matter. Per Lord Hunter: 'I doubt whether the interpretation contended for on behalf of the appellant is well-founded.' *Campbell v Allan* 1988 SCCR 47 *Held*, allowing appeal, evidence in replication cannot be used by Crown to contradict earlier prosecution evidence. *Neizer v Johnston* 1993 SCCR 772 Statutory offence. Sheriff refused to allow replication evidence of witness who had been precognosced by the Crown but not led. Upheld. Per LJ-C Ross: 'Having regard to the notice which the Crown had been given ... the Crown could reasonably have anticipated the evidence [and] the Crown had in fact precognosced both [witnesses].'	**Solemn procedure:** Section 269. Judge may, after defence case closed and before speeches, permit prosecutor to lead evidence to con-tradict evidence prosecution could not have reasonably anticipated; or to prove witness made different statement to that at trial although witness or pro-duction not listed and witness must be recalled. **Summary procedure:** Section 269. Judge may, before prosecutor's address on evidence, allow him to lead additional evidence to contradict evidence he could not have reasonably anticipated or to prove witness made different statement to that at trial, although witness must be recalled.

COMMENTARY	CASE LAW	STATUTE LAW
Additional evidence	*Cushion v HMA* 1993 SCCR 356 Murder. Before trial began, appellant told advisors of rumours that co-accused, T, had offered two men money to give evidence against him. Appellant unable to provide their names until trial had started. T cross-examined on these allegations, then application made to call the men. Not disputed that evidence material and unavailable when jury sworn, but application refused, since trial judge not satisfied evidence could not reasonably have been made available, and no information given to court of attempts to investigate rumour before trial. Conviction upheld on appeal.	**Solemn procedure:** Section 268. Judge may, before speeches, permit either party to lead additional evidence if he considers that it is prima facie material. Judge must consider that at time when jury sworn the evidence was not reasonably available or its materiality could not reasonably have been foreseen, although witness or production not listed and witness must be recalled.
If material, and not previously available.	*Wotherspoon v HMA* 1998 SCCR 615 *Held*, since evidence was of a prior consistent statement which was not challenged by the Crown, it would not have been material and if sheriff had applied CP(S)A 1995, s 268 he would have refused the motion.	**Summary procedure:** Section 268. Judge may, before prosecutor's address on the evidence, permit either party to lead additional evidence if he considers that it is prima facie material. Judge must consider that at time when first prosecution witness sworn the evidence was not reasonably available or its materiality could not reasonably have been foreseen, although witness or production not listed and witness must be recalled.

FAIRLY OBTAINED EVIDENCE

To be admissible, evidence must have been **fairly** obtained. In the case of the **accused**, in determining **fairness**, it will be considered whether the evidence has been obtained **before suspicion: after suspicion but before charge**; or **after charge**. If **statements to persons other than the police** are made, the particular circumstances will be considered, as will **evidence disclosing previous convictions,** or **evidence of bad character**; and **illegally obtained evidence** can be admissible.

COMMENTARY	CASE LAW	STATUTE LAW
Accused, before suspicion Admissibility will be assessed on fairness and whether evidence was volunteered or elicited. Search uncovering evidence of different crime	*HMA v Hepper* 1958 JC 39; 1958 SLT 160. Theft. H gave police consent to search property in connection with a crime. While searching they found attaché case unconnected with matter under investigation. They took this suspicious article away and it founded charges re the case reported here. Evidence held to be admissible as the police had a duty to inquire further in the circumstances.	
	Brown v Glen 1997 SCCR 636 Police asked if they could search appellant and he agreed. Found drugs concealed in his clothing. Allowing the appeal by the procurator fiscal, Lord Sutherland stated that so long as consent sought of person not suspected of a specific crime, any request need not require a specific warning that the person can withhold consent. *Normand v Cox* 1997 SCCR 24 (Sh Ct) overruled.	
	Graham v Orr 1995 SCCR 30 Appellant's breath test was below statutory limit, but car held until clear test produced. Released from arrest, he became agitated and constable searched car. *Held*, no suspicion of any offence and no power to search; evidence from search inadmissible and conviction quashed.	
Confession blurted out at early stage of investigation.	*Bell v HMA* 1945 JC 61; 1946 SLT 204 Rape. B, interviewed during enquiry, blurted out confession. *Held* admissible evidence. Until confession police had no reason to caution or charge B.	
Admission by family member at start of investigation.	*Thompson v HMA* 1968 JC 61; 1968 SLT 339 Murder. Members of victim's family were interviewed, including T who remained at police station while accommodation was being found for him. T blurted out, 'It was either her or me.' *Held* admissible evidence. Per LJ-G Clyde: '[T] had not been cautioned or charged, nor was he being asked questions by the police at the time. Nothing in the nature of bullying or cross-examining had occurred.'	
Accused, after suspicion but before charge Where there is urgency, search without a warrant may be justified.	*Lord Advocate's Reference (No 1 of 1983)* 1984 SCCR 62 Per LJ-G Emslie: 'A suspect's self-incriminating answers to police questioning will indeed be admissible in evidence unless it can be affirmed that they have been extracted from him by unfair means ... In each case ... it will be necessary to consider the whole relevant circumstances in order to discover whether or not there has been fairness.'	

COMMENTARY	CASE LAW	STATUTE LAW
	HMA v McGuigan 1936 JC 16; 1936 SLT 161 Murder, rape. Evidence obtained during search without warrant led to charges of murder, rape and theft being brought. Evidence held admissible on ground of urgency.	
	Edgley v Barbour 1995 SLT 711 Police stopped and searched the car of a man they had suspected of using an illegal radar detection device. Without obtaining a warrant, one officer searched the vehicle where he found the device within the glove compartment. The sheriff in the case admitted the evidence, as was upheld in the appeal, as to expect the officers to obtain a warrant would have given the driver ample time to dispose of the illegal device which they had good reason to believe was in the vehicle.	
Search without consent or warrant justified if evidence could have been lost.	*Walsh v MacPhail* 1978 SLT (Notes) 29 Possession of drugs. Servicemen on an air base were suspected of possessing drugs. Search made without consent and on an invalid warrant. Evidence held admissible on ground that drugs could have been disposed of or lost.	
Evidence obtained improperly but in good faith admitted.	*Fairley v Fishmongers of London* 1951 JC 14; 1951 SLT 54 Salmon poaching. Evidence against F was discovered by a private inspector and a government official. *Held* that although the evidence was improperly obtained it was admissible, as they had acted in good faith.	
Genuine but mistaken belief that search authorised.	*Lawrie v Muir* 1950 JC 19; 1950 SLT 37 Illegal use of milk bottles. Two inspectors of the Scottish Milk Bottle Exchange searched L's premises believing mistakenly although in good faith that they had authority to do so; incriminating evidence found held inadmissible. Opinion of the court: 'Persons in the special position of these inspectors ought to know the precise limits of their authority and should be held to exceed these limits at their peril.'	
Reasonable belief that obtaining of warrant is necessary.	*HMA v Rae* 1992 SCCR 1 *Held* that a police officer swearing that he has reasonable grounds is sufficient to allow a justice to grant a warrant under s 23(3) of the Misuse of Drugs Act 1971.	
Scope of warrant exceeded.	*Leckie v Miln* 1981 SCCR 261; 1982 SLT 177 Theft. Police told householder of L's arrest on warrant and said they wished to search house. She consented. Incriminating evidence found. *Held* inadmissible. Officers unaware of scope of warrant, consent not given for active unlimited search.	
	Innes v Jessop 1989 SCCR 441 I charged with reset of driving licence and tax exemption certificate found by police while searching for firearms and ammunition. Justice repelled objection to evidence having been irregularly obtained and convicted. On appeal *held* that removal of other articles carried implication that search was random one and it would be unsafe to sustain conviction.	

COMMENTARY	CASE LAW	STATUTE LAW
	Tierney v Allan 1989 SCCR 334 T charged with reset of gas cylinders and a typewriter. Police officers had searched T's house on a warrant referring only to gas cylinders. In course of search typewriter found under cot, similar to some typewriters known to have been stolen. *Held* that the evidence was admissible. Per LJ-G Emslie: 'This was not a case of random search as in *Leckie v Miln* [1981 SCCR 261; 1982 SLT 177]. It was the unexpected discovery of an article which aroused suspicion during the course of a lawful search for material listed in warrant.'	
	HMA v Turnbull 1951 JC 96 Fraud. Police obtained warrant and searched T. Removed property in relation to another alleged crime and kept it for six months. Inadmissible because police had acted outwith the scope of warrant.	
	Davidson v Brown 1990 SCCR 304 Illegal search. Police stopping car of known shoplifters asking to see contents of a bin. *Held*, not an illegal search as the request had been voluntarily complied with.	
	Burke v Wilson 1988 SCCR 361 Police obtained warrant for search of premises for video recordings for which no classification certificate had been obtained. In course of search they removed unlabelled videos which they subsequently found to be obscene. B charged, objected that evidence irregularly obtained. *Held* that the police had come upon videos by accident in course of authorised search and had not acted improperly.	
Dental impressions taken under warrant.	*Hay v HMA* 1968 JC 40 Murder. H inmate of List D school suspected. Police took dental impressions for comparison with bite marks on body. Applied for warrant to take further impressions, granted. Upheld by High Court. '... obtaining of the warrant prior to the examination in question rendered the examination quite legal ... evidence which resulted from it was therefore competent.'	
Note: Police powers with regard to persons in detention under the Criminal Procedure (Scotland) Act 1995. Invasive searches.	*Grant v HMA* 1989 SCCR 618 G questioned by police during six-hour period, but detention not terminated until arrest after the expiry of six hours. *Held* that fact that detention exceeded six hours did not invalidate things done lawfully within period. *Walker v Lees* 1995 SLT 757 Theft. *Held*, on appeal, that warrant to take blood samples involved some degree of loss of liberty, but allowed because crime serious and samples necessary, provided warrant modified to exclude detention of suspect.	Criminal Procedure (Scotland) Act 1995. Section 14. Police may question suspect detained under s 14. Ordinary detention must not exceed 12 hours. (Section 14A authorises a custody review officer to extend a period of detention for a further 12 hours subject to s 14A(4). Section 18(1). This section applies where a person has been arrested and is in custody or is detained under CP(S)A 1995, s 14(1). Section 18(2). Constable may take fingerprints, palmprints or other external prints.

COMMENTARY	CASE LAW	STATUTE LAW
		Section 18(6). With the authority of an officer not below the rank of inspector, may take sample of hair, nail cuttings or blood, body fluid, tissue or other material, or saliva, by means of swabbing or rubbing. Section 19. Briefly, gives police power within one month of (a) conviction; (b) written intimation that sample was unsuitable or insufficient, to obtain prints, samples.
The juncture at which questioning should be discontinued unless a caution is given is determined by the extent to which suspicion has been focused and having regard to fairness.	*Manuel v HMA* 1958 JC 41 Murder. M confessed. Gave location of corpse and commented on its condition. Convicted. Appealed. Alleged his condition motivated by inducements. Appeal rejected, no evidence of inducement.	
Statement containing discrepancies, further questioning allowed.	*HMA v McPhee* 1966 SLT (Notes) 83 Assault and culpable homicide. McP gave statement containing discrepancies. Came under suspicion of having committed offence. No caution given. McP blurted out admissions when questioning was resumed. Evidence held admissible, mere suspicion does not mean that caution is required.	
Person arrested but not yet charged.	*Johnston v HMA* 1993 SCCR 693 Questioning need not cease when person arrested but not yet charged. *HMA v Penders* 1996 SCCR 404 Break in interview of robbery suspect to formulate charge. On resumption caution administered, accused admitted guilt and then questioned on details and cautioned and charged. *Held*, only when formal charges levelled are further questions precluded, and whether it was fair for police to renew interview should be left to the jury. Jury by majority found charges not proven. *Codona v HMA* 1996 SCCR 300 distinguished. *Miller v HMA* 1997 SCCR 748 Police informing accused that they were going to charge him and asking him twice if he had anything to say. Appellant confessed and made further admissions. Conviction upheld on appeal. *Held*, it is only when a charge is made, as opposed to an intention to charge, that further questions with regard to that charge are precluded. Compare with: *Johnston v HMA* 1993 SCCR 693 Gives police right to question arrestee who has not been charged.	
When does a person become 'a suspect'?	*Miln v Cullen* 1967 JC 21; 1967 SLT 35 Drunken driving. C pointed out as one of the drivers involved in a collision. Police officer asked C whether he had been the driver. Response held admissible.	

COMMENTARY	CASE LAW	STATUTE LAW
	Per Lord Wheatley: 'The point at which a person becomes a "suspect" in the eyes of a police officer may be difficult to define with exactitude. The test is basically a subjective one, but the police officer may have to justify his attitude by reference to the facts in his possession or the knowledge which he had at the given point of time. ... In each case the issue is—was the question in the circumstances a fair one? ... The question asked ... was merely to discover whether the respondent was the driver of the car, not whether he had caused the accident or was drunk. If a question had been asked without a caution being administered, and the question had been directed to elicit an admission of culpability for the accident or an admission that he was drunk in charge of his car, then the question might have been properly objected to.'	
	Tonge v HMA 1982 SCCR 313 *Held* (1) that it is a requirement of law that a charge must be preceded by a full common law caution; (2) that where a statement is made in reply to an accusation, whether or not in the words of a formal charge, any reply induced by that accusation will be inadmissible unless preceded by a common law caution, or at least that such a caution was given as soon as it became clear that accused might be about to incriminate himself.	
	HMA v Middler 1994 SCCR 838 Murder. First accused not cautioned before being interviewed, despite suspicions by police of inconsistencies between witness's statements and accused's earlier statement, and despite search warrant obtained for accused's house to search for clothing worn by accused at locus. On appeal conviction upheld. Per Lord Marnoch: '... the question of ... at what stage a caution should be given falls to be determined as part of the more general test of fairness.'	
Questioning of a suspect.	*Chalmers v HMA* 1954 JC 66; 1954 SLT 177 Murder. C brought under suspicion to police, cautioned, then interrogated. Replied to caution and charge: 'I did it. He struck me.' Evidence held inadmissible. Conviction quashed. *Held*, that if suspicion is such that the person is viewed as the likely perpetrator of the crime then any further interrogation amounting to cross-examination may render any confession extracted inadmissible.	
	McClory v MacInnes 1992 SCCR 319 McC found asleep in vehicle at side of road, woken up by police, no caution given and asked what had happened. McC said that he had crashed. *Held*, statement unfairly obtained, police were obviously suspicious but gave no caution.	
	Young v Friel 1992 SCCR 567 F interviewed by police. F seeking incentive from police to give a statement. *Held* that sheriff correct to allow interview where the police officer had said that he was not sure whether any such offer could be made. One caution sufficient to cover statements made in relation to two different offences.	

COMMENTARY	CASE LAW	STATUTE LAW
Police questioning during detention and the issue of fairness.	*Cadder v HMA* [2010] UKSC 43; [2010] 1 W.L.R. 2601; 2011 S.C. (U.K.S.C.) 13; 2010 S.L.T. 1125. Cadder had been detained under CP(S)A 1995, s 14(1). He had been asked whether he wished a solicitor to be informed of his detention upon which he declined. C, without legal advice or representation, was then interviewed under caution making a number of key admissions, which the Crown later relied upon in obtaining C's conviction. C appealed this decision on the grounds that his lack of legal representation during the police interview contravened his right to a fair trial under Article 6(1) and 6(3)(c) of ECHR. Previously, the HCJ decision of *HMA v McLean* [2009] HCJAC 97; 2010 S.L.T. 73 held that reliance by the Crown upon admissions made by an accused who had not had access to legal advice while detained, did not of itself constitute a violation of the ECHR due to a multitude of sufficient safeguards within Scots' Law. In hearing the appeal, the Supreme court *held* that despite the present case falling perfectly in line with the previous authority of *HMA v McLean*, the correct approach was detailed by the Grand Chamber in *Salduz v Turkey* (36391/02) (2009) 49 E.H.R.R. 19 which determined a detainee was to have access to a lawyer from the time of his first interrogation, unless there were compelling circumstances rendering such impracticable. The system of detention under s 14 and s 15 of the CP(S)A 1995 was to be carefully struck between public interest and fairness to the accused and as of such the court had no option but to find in favour of C, following the case of *Salduz*.	**Scottish Executive Emergency Legislation following the Supreme Court *Cadder* ruling bringing the CP(S)A 1995 into line with the ECHR.** The Criminal Procedure (Legal Assistance, Detention and Appeals) (Scotland) Act 2010 s 1 Right of suspect to have access to a Solicitor. s 2 Criminal advice and assistance: automatic availability in certain circumstances. s 3 Extension of period of detention under section 14 of 1995 Act.
***Pre*-detention questioning and the issue of fairness.** Note: Following *Cadder*, there has been an apparent effort by the Supreme Court to narrow and confine its ruling in associated cases.	See: *Ambrose v Harris* [2011] UKSC 43; 2011 S.L.T. 1005. Roadside breath test *HMA v G* [2011] UKSC 43; 2011 S.L.T. 1005. Lawful household search where the individual was handcuffed. *HMA v M* [2011] UKSC 43; 2011 S.L.T. 1005. Questioning in the individual's home. 'Strasbourg has not said that a person who is a suspect and is not in custody must have access to legal advice…the *Cadder* requirement only becomes a live issue when the individual is taken into police custody or his freedom of action has been significantly curtailed and is in effect, in police custody.' Per Lord Hope at 64 and 71.	

COMMENTARY	CASE LAW	STATUTE LAW
Threats and inducements.	*Black v Annan* 1995 SCCR 273 Person detailed on a Saturday on charge of reset. Told if he did not co-operate he would be kept in until Monday. *Held*, on appeal, no need for pressure to be the cause of the statement, which was not shown to be fairly obtained, and conviction quashed.	
	Harley v HMA 1995 SCCR 595 Theft by housebreaking. Appellant accused of obtaining information about house from married woman. Told if he spoke up they would phone her: otherwise they would visit the house, which might lead to her husband finding out. *Held*, unfairly obtained: the matter should not have been left to the jury, and conviction quashed.	
	Stewart v Hingston 1996 SCCR 234 Suspect declined to give statement at home and constable said he would have to detain her and take her to a police station and he would arrange for social worker to look after children. *Held*, policeman just being practical and statement fairly obtained.	
Requirement for caution depends on nature of police questioning.	*Custerson v Westwater* 1987 SCCR 389 C accused with having offensive weapon. Evidence consisted of evidence by complainer that C waved knife at him, and statement by C that he had knife with him for protection. C made statement voluntarily in response to question. C appealed on ground that he had not been cautioned (see *Tonge v HMA* 1982 SCCR 313). *Held* that this case distinguishable from *Tonge* in that statement made in response to unobjectionable question rather than an allegation.	
Youthful suspect—is the evidence spontaneous and voluntary?	*HMA v Rigg* 1946 JC 1; 1946 SLT 49 Murder. R reported discovery of body to police and gave a statement. Later his condition being described as excited. R collapsed trembling and shuddering and gave another statement, which was held inadmissible. Statement was not spontaneous and voluntary, more like a detailed precognition. Ultimate test is fairness to the accused.	
	Codona v HMA 1996 SCCR 300 Murder trial. On appeal, statement by 14 year-old girl held inadmissible because it was unfairly obtained due to: the length of interview (over three hours); her distress; her age; and the form of questioning which pressurised her into changing her answers.	
	Blogojevic v HMA 1995 SCCR 570 Appellant denied being at locus. During a break in the interview, told not doing himself any favours with denial. On resumption he admitted being at locus and stabbing man who punched him. At trial appellant never gave evidence but defence produced psychological report that appellant vulnerable to changing story if pressurised. Conviction upheld on appeal, since in absence of evidence from police or appellant on the matter there was no factual basis for the claim.	

COMMENTARY	CASE LAW	STATUTE LAW
Statement by person not only possible suspect.	*Brown v HMA* 1966 SLT 105 Murder. B cautioned. Statement contained discrepancies. B warned of these and cautioned further at which he broke down saying 'I killed her.' B cautioned again and charged. Subsequently, items were recovered from where B had indicated. Evidence held admissible. Police were not cross-examining the accused or treating him as the only possible suspect.	
Admission volunteered.	*Costello v Macpherson* 1922 JC 9; 1922 SLT 35 Theft. C asked by railway police to open parcel he was carrying, which contained coal. C said he obtained it from a bunker. Regular police became involved and C volunteered that he had stolen the coal. Evidence held admissible, not improper to lead evidence of a statement made voluntarily without questioning being required.	
Statutory power to search after 'reasonable suspicion'.	*Ireland v Russell* 1995 SCCR 685 Misuse of Drugs Act 1971, s 23(2). Appellant searched by constable acting on information received two months earlier. On appeal conviction quashed, since no reasonable grounds existed at time of search.	
	Chassar v Macdonald 1996 SCCR 730 Civic Government (Scotland) Act 1982, s 60(1). Appellant's friend arrested on theft charges. On way to station officer told appellant he was going to search turn ups in trousers and appellant co-operated and cannabis resin found. Conviction upheld on appeal: statutory powers of search without warrant negated need for consent far less intimation that consent can be withheld.	
	Cooper v Buchanan 1996 SCCR 448 Police had information B in possession of drugs in car. Passenger found to have them in search. Upheld on appeal: power to search vehicle covered passengers with suspects when stopped.	
Unless there is urgency, physical evidence from the person of an accused should be obtained under warrant or after charge.	*McGovern v HMA* 1950 JC 33; 1950 SLT 133 Safe blowing. McG suspected of safe blowing. Nail scrapings taken. McG subsequently charged. Evidence held inadmissible as the charge should have come before the scrapings.	
	Bell v Hogg 1967 JC 49; 1967 SLT 290 Theft of telephone wires. Verdigris on B's hands. Before any charge had been preferred, police took palm rubbings without warrant but with consent. Evidence held admissible on basis of urgency.	
Conversation taped without the accused's knowledge.	*McIntyre v HMA* 2005 SCCR 380 Racial harrassment by telephone call; use of tape recording of appellant as detainee to corroborate voice identification. Evidence admissible because legitimately obtained.	
	HMA v Graham 1990 SCCR 56 Police secretly taped a meeting between G and a civilian witness with the help of the civilian; flagrant transgression of the rules of fairness. G had previously been interviewed by the police. Should have had the right not to self-incriminate. Situation distinguished from that where police eavesdropping on the commission of a crime.	

COMMENTARY	CASE LAW	STATUTE LAW
There is no defence of entrapment in Scots law.	*HMA v Harper* 1989 SCCR 472 Police officer who suspected drugs being sold approached van, asked for and was sold drugs. Objection taken to evidence as unfairly obtained through entrapment. *Held* no defence of entrapment, and in the absence of any evidence of deception, pressure or encouragement to commit crime, evidence admissible.	
Evidence from accused after charge Questioning at trial re change of plea.	*Williamson v HMA* 1980 JC 22 Assault. W pleaded self-defence initially but later withdrew that plea. Change of plea questioned by Crown in cross-examination. W convicted. Appeal refused. Per LJ-C Wheatley: 'This question was a legitimate and competent one. ... The objection taken by the appellant's counsel was in anticipation of what the answer might be, and not the question itself.'	
Subject to the test of fairness, evidence of the accused's actings or statements after charge is admissible.	*Forrester v HMA* 1952 JC 28 Safeblowing. F arrested, cautioned and charged. Thereafter his hand was examined for cut. Search made without F's consent. F convicted. Appeal refused.	
Grant of warrants depending on the circumstances, including public interest.	*HMA v Milford* 1973 SLT 12 Rape. M charged with rape, refused to give blood sample voluntarily. Prosecutor petitioned for warrant to take sample. Granted as reasonable in these exceptionally grave circumstances.	
	Morris v MacNeill 1991 SCCR 722 Sheriff granting warrant to take blood sample from accused, balancing public interest and the minimal invasion involved. Upheld on appeal.	
	G v Lees 1992 SCCR 252 Warrant granted to take blood sample but limited to finger pricks as the accused had a phobia of needles.	
	Smith v Cardle 1993 SCCR 609 Murder investigation, one of a set of twins suspected. Warrant sought and obtained to measure S and compare this with evidence from a video to eliminate twin brother. Warrant granted, non-invasive procedure, reasonable in the public interest.	
Accused's answer to question not directed to him inadmissible.	*HMA v Leiser* 1926 JC 88 Murder. After being charged, L answered a question which was not addressed to him. Reply held inadmissible. Judge not satisfied accused had not made a mistake.	
Reply to caution and charge re lesser offence.	*McAdam v HMA* 1960 JC 1 McA charged with assault to severe injury and subsequently attempted murder. Objection taken at trial to admissibility of reply to McA to caution and charge quoad lesser crime. Reply admitted. Admissibility confirmed on appeal. As both charges contained the element of assault they could be seen as within the same category.	
	Carmichael v Kinnie 1993 SCCR 751 Objection to statements made to police about the offence charged and a number of similar offences. *Held* that the police could not ask about the offence already charged but could ask about unrelated matters. Interview only inadmissible as far as matters not already charged.	

COMMENTARY	CASE LAW	STATUTE LAW
Entitlement to communicate with solicitor.	*HMA v Cunningham* 1939 JC 61; 1939 SLT 401 Murder. C cautioned and charged. En route to the cells his attention was drawn by police officer to a notice stating that a prisoner was entitled to communicate with a law agent. Made statement after being reminded of earlier caution. Statement held admissible, police observed every requirement of fairness.	
Admission by one accused put to co-accused in presence of first accused.	*Stark and Smith v HMA* 1938 JC 170; 1938 SLT 516 Theft. Two co-accused. Admission by one accused in reply to police interrogation repeated to other accused in presence of first. Both convicted. On appeal, statement held inadmissible against either accused.	
Presence of accused when co-accused cautioned and charged.	*HMA v Davidson* 1968 SLT 17 Attempted murder. D cautioned and charged, brought to bar of police station where co-accused was about to be cautioned and charged. D not advised that his presence would make any incriminating reply by co-accused admissible in evidence against him. *Held* that in effect the accused was providing evidence against himself contrary to the fundamental rule that he need not do so once charged, reply inadmissible.	
Fingerprint taken after arrest.	*Adair v McGarry* 1933 JC 72; 1933 SLT 482 Theft. McG arrested. Fingerprints taken from him held admissible. Per LJ-G Clyde: '... provided a person has been legally arrested by the police, they may search him for stolen goods, or weapons, or other real evidence connecting him with the crime, and ... neither his consent nor a magistrate's warrant is required for that purpose.' *Namyslak v HMA* 1994 SCCR 140 Theft. Fingerprints taken without consent while not under arrest or detention in respect of theft charge led in evidence to prove theft charge. Conviction upheld on appeal. *Held*, irregularity excused: no unfairness, since the police had recently obtained fingerprints lawfully for a different charge and could ask for a further set prior to accused being fully committed on this original charge. *HMA v Shepherd* 1997 SCCR 246 Accused released on bail without fingerprints taken. Then arrested for further offence and fingerprinted. *Held*, fingerprints admissible to prove earlier offence and nothing in CP(S)A 1995, s 18(2) prevents the use to which records of prints lawfully taken may be put in evidence. *Begley v Normand* 1992 SCCR 230 Warrant granted to take palmprints after B fully committed as the original prints taken turned out to be defective. *White v Ruxton* 1998 SLT 105 Theft. Officer destroyed finger and palm prints in belief accused not to be prosecuted. After trial diet fixed, sheriff allowed warrant for fresh prints. *Held*, administrative error: no basis for saying that sheriff wrong in using discretion, and appeal refused.	

COMMENTARY	CASE LAW	STATUTE LAW
No further questioning after arrest.	*Wade v Robertson* 1948 JC 117; 1948 SLT 491 Theft. W arrested for theft of whisky. Police showed him bottle recovered from his lodgings and told him he would be questioned about the offence charged. Without any questions W made a self-incriminating statement. *Held*, statement inadmissible. Police not entitled to question further with regard to that particular charge.	
	Fraser v HMA 1989 SCCR 82 Appellants charged with assault. In separate cells in police station. Visited by police officer, W, with whom they were friendly and made statements to him. At trial evidence of these statements left to the jury by the sheriff. Appellants appealed on ground that statements induced by W and unfairly obtained. It was conceded in the appeal that issue properly left to jury under proper directions. *Held* that in view of the concession it was not possible to say that the jury were not entitled to have regard to the statements, and that they were entitled to hold that they were not procured by inducement. Appeal refused.	
	HMA v Higgins and ORS 2006 SCCR 305 Two accused placed in adjoining cells by police and officers posted to listen. Evidence of conversation inadmissible because unfairly obtained by deception and trap.	
Statements to persons other than the police Questioning by employer.	*Waddell v Kinnaird* 1922 JC 40; 1922 SLT 344 Theft. Quantity of oil in possession of W, a railwayman. Arrested by railway police and cautioned. Later questioned by stationmaster in presence of civilian police. W convicted. Appeal rejected, allowed to seek an explanation so long as there is nothing to suggest improper motive.	
Interview by employers' investigators.	*Morrison v Burrell* 1947 JC 43; 1947 SLT 190 Fraud, attempted fraud. Horseracing bets placed by M, a sub-postmaster, who falsified date-stamping of envelopes. M interviewed under caution as suspect by Post Office investigators. Statement admitted and M convicted. Appeal rejected. *Held*, domestic investigation into public service department. Can be no objection to replies voluntarily given.	
Confidentiality restricted to spouse and solicitor.	*HMA v Parker* 1944 JC 49; 1944 SLT 195 Murder. P, Canadian serviceman, visited in prison by brother to whom he made statement about how death occurred. Objection to admissibility repelled at trial. *Held*, only spouses and solicitors protected by the doctrine of confidentiality.	
Incriminating remark accidentally overheard.	*HMA v O'Donnell* 1975 SLT (Sh Ct) 22 Assault. O'D in custody shouted incriminating remark to a co-accused which was overheard by police officers. Objection to admissibility repelled. Per Sheriff Macphail: 'It is clear that the incriminating statement was voluntarily emitted by the fourth accused, that no inducement was offered to him, that the witness who overheard the statement had not been ordered to do so but spontaneously stopped and listened when the accused shouted, and that the witness neither knew that the fourth accused was in custody, nor had any reason to suspect him of having been implicated in the assault.'	

COMMENTARY	CASE LAW	STATUTE LAW
Prolonged questioning by Customs investigators.	*HMA v Friel* 1978 SLT (Notes) 21 Tax frauds. F, with others, interviewed by Customs and Excise investigators, first for three and a half hours, then, after caution, for another twelve and a half hours. At trial, objection to admissibility of answers in second interview sustained. *Held* that questioning unfair, in the nature of cross-examination and pressure placed on the accused.	
Immigration officers.	*Williams v Friel* 1998 SCCR 649 Immigration officer never accused appellant of offence, but asked to interview him because he believed passport was a forgery. *Held*, statement on way to interview not unfair and therefore admissible.	
Statement made by suspected shoplifter to shop manager.	*McCuaig v Annan* 1986 SCCR 535 Manager saw McC put articles in pocket and leave without paying. Followed her and removed articles. She agreed to return to the office and made statements without having been cautioned. *Held* that evidence admissible as the test was whether what had happened was fair to the appellant.	
Evidence disclosing previous convictions Unless evidence of previous conviction(s) is necessary to prove the offence(s) charged, it is inadmissible to elicit it. Cannot be invoked where accused leads evidence of his own good character from his own witnesses (CP(S)A 1995, s 270 is available).	*Murphy v HMA* 1978 JC 1 M pled guilty to charges of theft, assault and breach of the peace and admitted previous convictions. M induced his solicitor to make false representations which mitigated the penalty and was subsequently charged with perverting the course of justice. *Held* relevant to incorporate reference to admission of previous convictions as evidence in causa of substantive charge and to show the mitigating effect of the false information. *Nelson v HMA* 1994 SCCR 192 Crown leading evidence of N swallowing a substance on being approached by the police, an offence in itself, to prove a charge of supplying drugs. Allowed on appeal. Per LJ-G Hope: 'The Crown can lead any evidence relevant to the proof of a crime charged, even though it may show or tend to show the commission of another crime not charged, unless fair notice requires that that other crime should be charged or otherwise expressly referred to in the complaint or indictment.'	Criminal Procedure (Scotland) Act 1995. Accused cross-examined as to character and previous convictions Section 266(4). Accused not to be asked questions tending to show commission of an offence other than those charged, or bad character, unless— (a) proof of offence admissible quoad offence charged; or (b) evidence of accused's good character led or character of complainer impugned or nature of defence is such as to involve imputations of character of prosecution or prosecution witness or complainer; or (c) accused has given evidence against any co-accused. Section 266(5), (6). If prosecutor wishes to invoke s 266(4)(b) he must apply to the trial judge for permission in the absence of the jury.
CP(S)A 1995, s 270 mirrors CP(S) A 1995, s 266(4)(b), and closes the loophole where accused does not give evidence. Note: In CP(S)A 1995, s 270(1)(b), the definition of nature of defence is wider to also include 'such as tend to establish the accused's good character'.		Section 270. Evidence not to be led that the accused has committed an offence other than those charged or is of bad character unless— (a) evidence of accused's good character led or character of prosecution or prosecution witness impugned; or (b) nature or conduct of the defence to tend to establish the accused's good character or involve imputations on character of prosecution or prosecution witness.

COMMENTARY	CASE LAW	STATUTE LAW
In case of prison breaking dis-closure of previous convictions is inevitable.	*Varey v HMA* 1985 SCCR 425 V and others charged with prison breaking. Indictment specified length of sentences and crimes for which imposed. *Held* that to prove appellants were lawfully confined at date of charge, Crown required to prove date and length of sentences, and appeals dismissed. *Milne v HMA* 1995 SCCR 751 Charge of driving while disqualified and without insurance. In cross-examination appellant changed plea to guilty and was then charged with perjury. At perjury trial Crown led evidence that earlier trial concluded with plea of guilty. *Held*, competent to lead evidence in support of perjury charge and appellant convicted.	**Previous convictions** **Solemn procedure:** Section 101(1), (2). Previous convictions shall not, subject to subsection (2) below and s 275A(2) of this Act, be laid before the jury or reference made to them before verdict unless as evidence in support of a substantive charge or where crown permitted to lead evidence in terms of CP(S)A 1995, s 266 or s 270. Section 101(3). Previous convictions must not, subject to s 275A(1) of this Act, be laid before judge until prosecutor moves for sentence.
Road traffic disqualification listing of previous convictions where not competently supporting substantive charge not allowed.	*Mitchell v Dean* 1979 JC 62; 1979 SLT (Notes) 12 Driving while disqualified and without insurance. Trial evidence included extract conviction *quoad* disqualification which referred to admission of six previous convictions. M convicted. *Held*, on appeal, that evidence in relation to six previous convictions not competent to support substantive charge and conviction quashed. *Boustead v M'Leod* 1979 JC 70; 1979 SLT (Notes) 48 Driving while disqualified and without insurance. Trial evidence included extract conviction referring to public mischief offence. B convicted. *Held*, on appeal, evidence inadmissible and conviction quashed. Prejudice to be confined within the narrowest limits.	**Summary procedure:** Section 166(1), (3)–(8). Previous convictions not to be laid before judge until charge proved unless as evidence in support of a substantive charge or under CP(S)A 1995, s 266 or s 270 of this Act.
Strictly construed.	*Robertson v Aitchison* 1981 SCCR 149; 1981 SLT (Notes) 127 Driving while disqualified. At trial evidence incorporated extract conviction which referred to an offence additional to that which had led to R's disqualification. R convicted. *Held*, on appeal, that reference to previous conviction was a fatal flaw and conviction quashed. Opinion of the court: 'The words of the statute are clear, the risk of prejudice is guarded against by the strictness of its prohibition which operates "in any proceedings".'	
Breach of statutory prohibition not necessarily sufficient to constitute miscarriage of justice.	*McAvoy and Jackson v HMA* 1982 SCCR 263; 1983 SLT 16 Theft by housebreaking. J, in a voluntary statement to police, made reference to 'two guys who I know from the jail'. Statement given in evidence. No direction in charge to jury to disregard implied reference to previous convictions. Jury, on sheriff's suggestion, took voluntary statement to jury room while deliberating. J convicted. *Held*, on appeal, that the reference to previous conviction had been a breach of CP(S)A 1975, s 160(1), but no miscarriage of justice and appeal refused. No objection raised by the defence at the time.	

COMMENTARY	CASE LAW	STATUTE LAW
Disclosure of previous convictions creating no risk of prejudice.	*Moffat v Smith* 1983 SCCR 392 Driving while disqualified. M convicted. Trial evidence incorporated extract conviction referring to two offences (for driving without licence and without insurance) in respect of which M disqualifed. Submission, that reference to one would have been sufficient, repelled and appeal dismissed. No risk of prejudice. *Robertson v HMA* 1995 SCCR 497 Witness referred to helping appellant in SACRO (Scottish Association for Care and Resettlement of Offenders). Judge in charge told jury to ignore extraneous matters. Conviction upheld on appeal, since (1) unlikely jurors knew what SACRO stood for; and (2) if they did, they were covered by the judge's charge. *Harkin v HMA* 1996 SCCR 5 Appellant charged on indictment of driving while disqualified. Procurator fiscal depute in speech to jury said they must ignore fact that disqualification result of previous conviction. Conviction upheld on appeal: no miscarriage of justice, although comment unnecessary and sheriff entitled to take view that less harm to appellant by not referring to it. *Maclean v Buchanan* 1997 SLT 91 Police witness asked by fiscal to read out part of form recording why accused refused Camic breathalyser procedure. Revealed accused had answered he had been convicted earlier of an offence. *Held*, no miscarriage of justice, since witness not pressed unreasonably and sheriff could put it out of his mind.	
Where credibility in issue.	*Graham v HMA* 1983 SCCR 315; 1984 SLT 67 G tried on four charges. Offer of plea of guilty to charges 2, 3 and 4 rejected. On first charge, wife assault, credibility at issue. Evidence elicited of reply to caution and charge *quoad* charge 2 (breach of the peace) which was: 'That cow's got me the jail again.' Jury directed to disregard reply. *Held* deliberate eliciting of evidence irredeemably prejudicial, and conviction on charge 1 quashed. Per LJ-G Emslie: 'So grave was the breach, and so important was the issue of credibility, that we are satisfied that the effect of the breach of the peremptory direction in [CP(S)A 1975,] section 160(1) upon the minds of the jurors could not reasonably be expected to have been obliterated by anything the sheriff tried to do... .'	
Previous convictions elicited by questioning.	*Slane v HMA* 1984 SCCR 77 S tried for conspiracy to rob with two others. During Crown evidence, counsel for one of the co-accused elicited in cross-examination of a Crown witness that S had previous convictions. 'Ample evidence' of S's guilt. Judge gave direction to jury to disregard evidence of previous convictions. *Held* that questions should not have been asked, action of counsel inexcusable, but no miscarriage of justice.	

COMMENTARY	CASE LAW	STATUTE LAW
	McLean v Tudhope 1982 SCCR 555 McL charged with breach of the peace. On cross-examination by prosecutor, McL was asked whether he regarded himself as honest with a previous conviction. No reply. On re-examination by defence solicitor McL stated one previous conviction. Because of revelation of earlier conviction, McL liberated on appeal. Violation of CP(S)A 1975, s 346(1)(f) (replaced by CP(S)A 1995, s 266(4)).	
	Kepple v HMA 1936 JC 76 Assault on wife. Libel evincing previous violence and malice. At trial wife made reference to 'previous convictions'. K convicted. Appeal refused, it being *held* that the information had been volunteered not elicited.	
Special rules re reset.	*Deighan v Macleod* 1959 JC 25 Theft. Two accused. Police witness speaking of accused being 'known thieves'. Conviction upheld, not act of prosecutor. *Watson v HMA* (1894) Adam 355 Reset. W charged with reset. During trial evidence of previous conviction for reset tendered. W convicted. Appeal dismissed. Per Lord Rutherford Clark: 'Under the statute the previous conviction may be given in evidence in order to prove guilty knowledge ... at any stage in the proceedings provided only that evidence has been given that the stolen property has been found in the possession of the accused... .'	Prevention of Crimes Act 1871, s 19. In prosecution for reset competent to lead evidence that accused in possession of other stolen property within previous 12 months. Previous offence of fraud or dishonesty within the preceding five years may be taken into consideration.
Disclosure of manner of accused's identification no reference to previous conviction.	*Corcoran v HMA* 1932 JC 40 Housebreaking. C convicted. Fact that C's arrest based upon identification from a police photograph album disclosed in court. *Held*, on appeal, that disclosure fell short of reference to previous conviction. *HMA v McIlwain* 1965 JC 40 Assault and robbery. Special defence of alibi. Objection to leading of evidence *quoad* identification by police officers repelled. Not always incompetent to lead evidence just because it may incidentally reveal previous convictions.	
Exception to general prohibition: reference rebutting defence of innocence.	*Carberry v HMA* 1975 JC 40; 1976 SLT 38 C and two others charged with conspiracy to rob. Evidence led at trial that co-accused of C had made voluntary statement, before arrest, that he had obtained car, allegedly used in furtherance of conspiracy, from man 'met in Barlinnie'. C convicted. Appeal refused. Opinion of the court: 'The jurisdiction is a delicate one and in its exercise it is necessary to keep firmly in view that the statutory prohibition is designed in the interests and for the protection of accused persons and, therefore, that there is a heavy onus on a prosecutor who seeks to support the competence of evidence which directly or indirectly brings to the knowledge of judge or jury or leads to the drawing of the inference, that the accused has been previously convicted. One of the categories of possible exception from the consequences of breach of the statutory prohibition is where the reference tends to rebut a defence of innocence which might otherwise be open to the accused ... each case must depend on its own facts and circumstances...'	

COMMENTARY	CASE LAW	STATUTE LAW
Police referring to accused as a housebreaker.	*Smith v HMA* 1975 SLT (Notes) 89 S, charged with theft, identified by police witness who referred to him twice as, 'known to me as Smith, a housebreaker'. No warning to jury to disregard evidence. S convicted, quashed on appeal. *Held* that the trial judge should have directed the jury to ignore such evidence.	
Relevant evidence of collateral matters will be admitted if fairness requires it.	*HMA v Kay* 1970 JC 68; 1970 SLT (Notes) 66 Murder of K's husband. Indictment libelled previous evincing of malice and ill-will. At trial K's counsel allowed to lodge hospital records relating to treatment after alleged assaults by deceased. *Held* admissible to lead evidence of these to show the accused had reason to apprehend danger. Departure from general rule justified.	
Accused forced to admit he was in prison at specified time.	*Cordiner v HMA* 1978 JC 64; 1978 SLT 118 Extortion. C, with another, indicted inter alia on a charge of extortion. Special defence of alibi that he was in prison at the time. At trial, evidence of date of conversations grounding charge imprecise and charge withdrawn. C convicted on other charges. *Held*, on appeal, that C had been compelled to disclose record, and conviction quashed. Opinion of the court: 'We cannot say that the jury would have convicted if the Crown had not erred at the outset in forcing the appellant to admit that he was in prison in June 1976.'	
Evidence revealing previous assaults bearing on conclusions in medical reports.	*Gemmill v HMA* 1980 JC 16; 1979 SLT 217 Murder. G's mental condition at issue *quoad* diminished responsibility. Medical evidence disclosed previous assaults on females. G convicted by jury. *Held*, on appeal, that evidence introduced for purposes connected with G's medical history not admissible *quoad* guilt and that the judge should thus have directed the jury to disregard this evidence. However, not misdirection sufficient to require quashing of conviction. *Note:* G was convicted of culpable homicide, not murder.	
Caution and charge referring to previous convictions—insufficient miscarriage of justice.	*McCuaig v HMA* 1982 SCCR 125; 1982 SLT 383 McC convicted on a number of charges. Police witness speaking to caution and charge disclosed to jury that charge referred to previous convictions. *Held*, on appeal, that there had been a breach of the statutory provisions, but miscarriage of justice not sufficient to set aside conviction.	
Disclosure accidental.	*Johnston v Allan* 1983 SCCR 500 Driving without licence. J tried on a number of road traffic contraventions including driving without a licence. During trial a computer printout was production to establish J did not hold a licence. Sheriff asked for and was handed printout he saw on 'production table', which was, however, a different printout disclosing previous convictions. J convicted. Appeal refused, pre-vious convictions not 'laid before the court' by the prosecutor, just an unfortunate accident.	
	Grugen v HMA 1991 SCCR 526 Witness spontaneously implicating G in a crime with which he was not charged. Prosecutor commenting on this matter in his charge to the jury. Conviction upheld on appeal. Prosecutor entitled to make such comment as evidence spontaneous.	

COMMENTARY	CASE LAW	STATUTE LAW
Cross-examination on character.	*Leggate v HMA* 1988 SCCR 391 L charged with assault and robbery. Evidence came from two police officers who spoke to an admission by L and two other officers who said that L took them to where weapon hidden. L alleged that police had 'fitted him up' and were lying. Trial judge, relying on *Templeton v HMA* 1985 SCCR 357, allowed Crown to cross-examine L as to character, and he admitted various analogous convictions. *Held* by bench of seven judges (1) where nature or conduct of defence is such as to involve imputations on the character of Crown witnesses, accused is liable to cross-examination on his character in terms of CP(S)A 1975, s 141(1)(f)(ii), and whether or not it was necessary for an accused to conduct his defence in this way in order to establish his defence fairly is irrelevant, but that s 141(1)(f)(ii) does not apply where the accused merely asserts that a Crown witness is lying; (2) that a trial judge has a wide discretion to refuse to allow an accused to be cross-examined on his character, that the fundamental test is one of fairness, having regard both to the position of the accused and the public interest in bringing wrongdoers to justice, and that a significant factor in the exercise of the discretion is whether the questions asked of the Crown witnesses were integral and necessary to the defence or were a deliberate attack on the character of the witness; (3) that while s 161(1) of Criminal Procedure (Scotland) Act 1975 prohibits the prosecutor from laying a list of the accused's previous convictions before a judge, it does not prevent him making reference to them by giving judge relevant information; and (4) trial judge had erred in not exercising his discretion and there had been miscarriage of justice. Appeal allowed and conviction quashed.	
Separate libelling of charges.	*McGregor v Macdonald* 1952 JC 4; 1952 SLT 94 Theft. McG and others charged with theft and, being 'known thieves' loitering with intent to steal. List of previous convictions annexed to indictment. Conviction on theft charge quashed. *Held* that charges should have been separately libelled. Statutory provision designed to exclude prejudice but effect here was to nullify that purpose since one charge within general rule and other not.	
Inadvertent disclosure of endorsement on licence.	*Clark v Connell* 1952 JC 119; 1952 SLT 421 Comparison drawn between Connell's handwriting and signature on licence. Examination of licence by sheriff inadvertently disclosed endorsement, although not offence for which imposed. Connell's objection to evidence upheld by sheriff and Connell acquitted. On appeal by Crown court held sheriff to have been mistaken in sustaining objection to competency as information not 'laid before' the sheriff, but appeal dismissed on other grounds.	
Evidence of bad character (i) of the accused Cross-examination of wife—who was accused—on fidelity.	*HMA v Grudins* 1976 SLT (Notes) 10 Murder of husband. G asked by Crown whether she had remained faithful to husband during separation. Defence objection on basis that question attempted to impugn G's character sustained.	

COMMENTARY	CASE LAW	STATUTE LAW
	Per Lord Stewart (quoting LJ-C Thomson in *O'Hara v HMA* 1948 JC 90; 1948 SLT 372): '"The fundamental consideration is a fair trial and there may be cases where the price which the accused may be called upon to pay if cross-examined will be out of all proportion to the extent and nature of the imputations cast on the witnesses who testify against him." I would have no hesitation here in using my discretion in favour of disallowing the line of cross-examination. ... There must be a limit to what can be explored.'	
Accused giving evidence against co-accused is open to question on record.	*McCourtney v HMA* 1977 JC 68; 1978 SLT 10 Manufacture of controlled drug. McC convicted along with four co-accused. Appealed on basis that judge had allowed a co-accused's counsel to ask questions of McC which elicited his previous convic-tions, McC having given evidence already against co-accused. Conviction upheld. Opinion of the court: 'Once an accused has given evidence against a co-accused there is no discretion in the trial judge to refuse to the co-accused the right to cross-examine him as to his criminal record.	
	Burton v HMA 1979 SLT (Notes) 59 B and co-accused J tried on charge of attempted extortion. J acquitted, B convicted. B appealed on basis that J's counsel had been allowed to cross-examine B on issue of character, B having given evidence already against J. Appeal dismissed. *Held*, B's evidence against J was damaging, J entitled to cross-examine.	
Reluctant witness—evidence relevant to explain reluctance.	*Manson v HMA* 1951 JC 49; 1951 SLT 181 Assault. M charged with assault (razor slashing). At trial hesitant witness claimed she had been threatened by, allegedly, M's wife about giving evidence. M convicted. On appeal submitted that jury should have been directed to disregard evidence of inti-midation, presumably as suggesting bad character of M. Appeal refused. *Held*, not evidence against M but evidence to explain the reluctance of the witness.	
	Sinclair v MacDonald 1996 SCCR 466 CP(S)A 1975, s 346(1)(f)(ii). Dangerous driving. Witnesses accused of lying. Stated that Mrs P, activated by malice, accelerated to prevent appellant returning to his own side of the road. Sheriff took view that this went beyond suggestions of perjury and involved serious imputations on their characters and granted leave to cross-examine appellant as to character. Upheld on appeal: sheriff used discretion correctly.	
	Bremner v HMA 1992 SCCR 476 Rape. Character of the complainer, CP(S)A 1975, s 141B. B wished to lead evidence of a previous sexual relationship with the complainer. Leave refused, appeal. *Held* that it was a matter for the trial judge to decide in the interests of justice. No interference here. Time gap of eight months between the relationship ending and the alleged offence.	**Sexual character** Criminal Procedure (Scotland) Act 1995. Section 274(1). Briefly, in a trial on sexual offence the court shall not allow questioning by defence designed to show the complainer: (a) is not of good character, sexually or otherwise; (b) is a prostitute; or (c) has at any time engaged with any person in sexual behaviour not forming part of subject matter of charge.

COMMENTARY	CASE LAW	STATUTE LAW
		Section 275(1). There are exceptions to the above rule where— (a) question designed to rebut or explain evidence otherwise than by accused; (b) question under s 274(1)(c) above is relevant to defence of incrimination or relates to sexual behaviour which took place on same occasion as that forming subject matter of charge; or (c) contrary to interests of justice to exclude question. Section 275(2). Where questioning allowed, court may limit the extent at any time as it thinks fit. Section 275(3). Application to be made in course of trial but in absence of jury, complainer, witnesses and public.
Illegally obtained evidence may be admissible. Urgency.	*Bell v Hogg* 1967 JC 49; 1967 SLT 290 Theft of copper wire. Police intercepted van carrying B and others and cautioned but did not charge them. Palm rubbings taken but B not told expressly that he was entitled to refuse. B convicted. Appeal refused. Per LJ-G Clyde: 'The urgency of the matter is its justification.' *Edgely v Barbour* 1994 SCCR 789 Radar device retrieved from car without search warrant. Conviction upheld on appeal: irregularity excusable on grounds of urgency, since impracticable to obtain search warrant by leaving locus for several hours. Unlikely the appellant could have been detained in car for this period, and would have ample time to dispose of the device. *Welbey v Ritchie* 1997 SCCR 472 Charge of theft of three squash racquets. While accused in detention for four hours, police traced car and searched it and found racquets. Police said the reasons for the search were the risk of removal; inexperienced officer available to guard vehicle; and fear that warrant could not be obtained before detention ended. *Held*, urgency excused search and appeal refused.	
Non-urgency.	*McGovern v HMA* 1950 JC 33; 1950 SLT 133 Theft by opening lockfast place. McG not charged or apprehended in connection with safe blowing, but kept in police station for six hours during which police obtained scrapings from fingernails of McG for chemical analysis. McG later charged. *Held* evidence inadmissible, as no question of urgency, and no knowledge by police as to whether scrapings would yield any evidence of McG's connection with offence.	

COMMENTARY	CASE LAW	STATUTE LAW
	Wilson v Brown 1996 SCCR 470 Appellant attended rave and was searched by stewards without consent and found with controlled drugs. *Held*, no authority for search. It could not be excused on grounds of urgency, since stewards could have detained appellant until police arrived. Appeal allowed and conviction quashed. Observed, search for offensive weapon might have been justified in circumstances.	

SUFFICIENCY

As evidence requires to be **sufficient**, there must be **corroboration** of the essential facts of **the identification of the accused** and **the commission of the crime**, except when there is a **statutory non-requirement for corroboration**. There need not be corroboration of **procedural matters** or **incidental matters**. Special considerations apply in the case of **the *Moorov* doctrine** (named after *Moorov v HMA* 1930 JC 68; 1930 SLT 596) and **the circumstantial confession**. There may be **inferential corroboration from *de recenti*** possession.

COMMENTARY	CASE LAW	STATUTE LAW
The identification of the accused It is essential that identification of the accused be explicit.	*Bruce v HMA* 1936 JC 39 Wilful fire raising. B convicted on evidence of witnesses not asked expressly to identify B, but certain of whom referred 'to the accused James Bruce'. On appeal conviction quashed because B not directly identified in court.	
	Wilson v Brown 1947 JC 81 Sale of adulterated whisky. W convicted on evidence of witnesses not asked expressly to identify her. One witness said he knew the owner of the hotel to be Mrs Wilson, another that he knew licence holder to be Mrs J W S Wilson. On appeal convic-tion quashed because no express identification of accused by witnesses.	
During trial, accused under no duty to facilitate ID.	*Beattie v Scott* 1990 SCCR 296 *Held* on appeal that the sheriff erred in requiring the accused to stand up to assist the Crown with the ID. Accused had no duty to do so, so long as not taking positive steps to conceal his identity.	
Evidence of earlier identification is admissible.	*Muldoon v Herron* 1970 JC 30; 1970 SLT 228 Breach of the peace. Witnesses could not identify M in court and one denied having identified M to police previously. Police evidence of previous identification by witnesses held to corroborate evidence by witnesses that identification made to police at the time of the offence. Per LJ-C Grant: 'The evidence of the police as to who was identified is primary and direct evidence of that matter and no question arises of hearsay evidence in the sense of evidence designed to establish the truth of a statement by proving that the statement was made.'	
	Bennett v HMA 1976 JC 1; 1976 SLT (Notes) 90 Assault to severe injury. D identified on day of assault by victim and two other witnesses none of whom able to identify him at the trial. Police officer gave evidence of previous identification of B by witnesses and victim. B convicted. Appeal refused. *Held*, identification need not be visual. Concurrences of independent fact even if each spoken to by only one witness may be enough when taken together.	

COMMENTARY	CASE LAW	STATUTE LAW
	McGaharon v HMA 1968 SLT (Notes) 99 Breach of the peace and assault. Two witnesses unable to identify McG at trial. Police evidence of identification by these witnesses to police at time of the incident held to be sufficient identification. McG convicted. Per Sheriff Middleton: '... evidence by policeman that a particular witness identified a particular per-son at the time may be very much better than identification by a witness himself six months later in the witness box.'	
	Neeson v HMA 1984 SCCR 72 Murder. Two police witnesses gave evidence that N identified at identification parade by witness. This witness unable to identify N in court. N convicted and appeal dismissed. *Held*, corroborative material from what happened at the identification parade.	
Corroboration of identification normally required unless there is statutory provision to the contrary.	*Morton v HMA* 1938 JC 50; 1938 SLT 27 Indecent assault. M identified by complainer at identification parade and at trial. The only other witness failed to identify M. M convicted. On appeal conviction quashed. *Held*, insufficient evidence. Opinion of the court: '... by the law of Scotland no person can be convicted of a crime or a statutory offence except where the legislature otherwise directs unless there is evidence of at least two witnesses implicating the person accused with the commission of the crime or offence with which he is charged.'	
	Robson v HMA 1996 SCCR 340 Appellant's conviction of using lewd practices towards brother and sister upheld on appeal despite one complainer not asked to point out appellant in court. *Held*, sufficient that man described by children was complainer along with parent's identification and circumstantial detail. Observed, Crown should have complied with rule for identifying accused in court.	
	Harrison v Mackenzie 1923 JC 61; 1923 SLT 565 Illegal trawling. Name of vessel read through telescope by only one witness. H convicted. Quashed on appeal. Per Lord Hunter: '... it is always essential that vital testimony given by a single witness against the person accused should be corroborated, either by the testimony of other witnesses, or by facts and circumstances.'	
	Dudley v HMA 1995 SCCR 52 Appellant convicted of rape. Complainer did not attend identification parade and court was cleared when she pointed out appellant. Conviction upheld on appeal: issue for jury to determine and in any event other evidence overwhelming.	
	Bainbridge v Scott 1968 SLT 871 Criminal damage. B admitted to police that he had damaged car and van with paint stripper. B had also freely admitted to owners of two vehicles that he was responsible for the damage. *Held* that the accused's special knowledge sufficient to corroborate admission to the police but observed that evidence of confession to the owners did not corroborate evidence of confession made to the police.	

COMMENTARY	CASE LAW	STATUTE LAW
	Sinclair v MacLeod 1962 JC 19 Careless driving. Driver of the car owned by S not identified at locus. Later, police arrived at S's house to find wife locking the car door. S in bed admitted to police he was the driver. S convicted. Quashed on appeal, insufficient corroboration. *Reilly v HMA* 1981 SCCR 201 Assault and robbery. Corroboration relied on by Crown consisted of weak sometimes contradictory pieces of circumstantial evidence. Conviction quashed on appeal. Opinion of the court: 'The question ... is whether that evidence, in character, quality and strength, is apt to entitle the jury to treat it as corroborative of the evidence of [the witness]. We have come to be of the opinion that it was not.' *Mair v HMA* 1997 SCCR 44 Robbery conviction upheld on appeal. Held, where positive identification by one witness all that was needed was other evidence consistent in all respects with positive identification. *Ralston v HMA* 1987 SCCR 467 R convicted of assaulting a security guard and attempting to rob him. Evidence consisted of positive identification at identification parade and in court by victim and weak evidence from two other guards that R's face resembled that of the assailant. *Held* that where one starts with a positive emphatic identification by one witness, very little else is required provided that it is consistent with the positive evidence. Appeal refused. *Winter v Heywood* 1995 SCCR 276 Conviction of driving while disqualified upheld on appeal. Appellant registered keeper of car gave false information as to identification of driver. *Held*, reply not simply false denial but giving false information sufficient with fact appellant registered keeper to corroborate eyewitness. *Souter v Lees* 1995 SCCR 33 Accused convicted of careless driving had denied car at locus since he had key. Upheld on appeal since no explanation of theft, and sheriff had not treated reply as admission but held on basis of other evidence that his car involved and he was driver. *Nelson v HMA* 1988 SCCR 536 One positive identification sufficiently corroborated by identification by build. *MacDonald v HMA* 1997 SCCR 116 Convicted of murder, assault and robbery. *Held*, on appeal, complainer's evidence that appellant 'doesn't look unlike' and 'same build, also facially' fell short of amounting to a positive identification (even if treated as equivalent that appellant looked like driver of car). Conviction quashed. *Murphy v HMA* 1995 SCCR 55 Murder. Question of identity. Witness described appellant as 'just the height and the dark hair colour'. Conviction upheld on appeal. *Held*, evidence of resemblance capable of corroborating positive identification (also there was other evidence strengthening witness who spoke to resemblance).	

COMMENTARY	CASE LAW	STATUTE LAW
	Fisher v Guild 1991 SCCR 308 Road traffic. Passenger identifying accused as the driver. Only two in the car and as passenger held to be credible there was sufficient identification.	
	Kelly v HMA 1998 SCCR 660 One positive identification. At identification parade, complainer said 'either number three or four'. Appellant was number four. *Held*, it was not fatal that more than one person was picked out as resembling individual in question. Conviction upheld.	
Contradictory evidence of identifying witnesses.	*Robertson v HMA* 1990 SCCR 142 R identified by two witnesses who differed as to his clothing. Convicted. *Held* on appeal, up to jury to assess reliability, one reliable witness alone would have been sufficient to corroborate the special knowledge admission R had made.	
Evidence of identification can be corroborated by the accused's actings at the time of the offence.	*O'Donnell v HMA* 1979 SLT (Notes) 64 Assault. Evidence of principal eyewitness held by sheriff as corroborated only by circumstantial evidence of O'D being seen at the locus at least ten minutes after crime. O'D convicted. Conviction quashed on appeal. Per LJ-C Wheatley: 'No reasonable jury could have accepted that evidence as corroboration... .'	
	Gracie v Allan 1987 SCCR 364 G convicted of theft by housebreaking. Principal evidence that of Mrs F who identified him as being in the back garden of the house in question. Mrs F said accused very like the person she saw. For corroboration Crown relied on evidence that G found acting suspiciously a quarter of a mile away 20 minutes after the housebreaking. *Held* that it was not necessary that identification witness be 100 per cent certain and there was sufficient other evidence to corroborate that identification.	
	MacNeill v Wilson 1981 SCCR 80 Use of lorry carrying insecure load. W identified by one of his passengers as driver of the lorry, also seen by another witness examining the lorry after accident. W made no admissions to the police but produced damaged strap and said this was being used at the time the load fell from the lorry. W acquitted. On Crown's appeal conviction ordered, evidence that the respondent was the driver.	
	Maclennan v Macdonald 1988 SCCR 133 Road traffic offences. Question of whether M had been driving his car when it collided with parked car. Witness gave evidence of seeing M walking from his car to the parked car. No other traffic present. Damage to parked car consistent with M's car having reversed into it. M's explanation that someone else had been driving his car was not believed by sheriff and witnesses had not heard anyone running off. *Held* that the evidence showed that car involved in collision was the appellant's, seen walking towards the car and no-one else present.	

COMMENTARY	CASE LAW	STATUTE LAW
	Proctor v Tudhope 1985 SCCR 403 P convicted of housebreaking with intent to steal. Clear identification by householder some hours after offence. In addition to this R ran off when pointed out while walking along the street by householder to policeman. *Held*, witness credible and P's reaction sufficiently eloquent of guilt to be corroboration.	
	Stillie v HMA 1990 SCCR 719 Robbery. Complainer identified S. Corroboration in that police officers identified two persons running as or similar to the two accused. Conviction upheld on appeal. Complainer was a debt collector on his rounds, reasonable inference that the purpose of the attack was robbery.	
	Henderson v HMA 1993 SCCR 1005 Mobbing and rioting. Complainer identified H as did a witness who spoke to H telling him of the proposed riot and inviting him to join in. *Held*, sufficient corroboration of H's identification.	
Identification by voice.	*McGiveran v Auld* (1894) 1 Adam 448; 21 R (J) 69 Causing street obstruction. McG alleged to have made statements earlier to witnesses through telephone. Only means of identification of speaker was similarity of voice. McG convicted. Upheld on appeal. Per LJ-C Macdonald: 'The evidence is practically the same as that given by a person outside a house who identifies his voice, and such evidence has never been held incompetent.'	
Identification by video recording.	*Bowie v Tudhope* 1986 SCCR 205 Assault and robbery incident recorded on video tape. Video viewed by two police officers who identified B as one of the men seen committing the offence on film. *Held* that evidence of constables sufficient to identify appellant.	
Fingerprint identification.	*HMA v Hamilton* 1934 JC 1 Opening lockfast place, theft. H convicted on evidence of two fingerprint identification experts who found prints on bottle in shop. No other evidence. Appeal dismissed. Per LJ-G Clyde: '... no chain is stronger than its weakest link. ... Accordingly the strength of the link provided by the fingermark depends on the degree of reliability which—on the evidence presented to them—the jury thought should be attributed to the fingermark method as applied by the police and the experts in the present case.'	
	Langan v HMA 1989 SCCR 379 L charged with murder. Only evidence consisted of bloodstained fingerprint on tap in sink of house where crime committed. Fingerprint identified as L's. L claimed to have never been in the house but offered no explanation for presence of the print. *Held* that in the absence of any explanation the jury were entitled to hold that it was made by the murderer.	

COMMENTARY	CASE LAW	STATUTE LAW
Handwriting identification.	*Richardson v Clark* 1957 JC 7 Forgery and uttering. R and his wife convicted on the evidence of handwriting analysis experts in relation to wife's handwriting. Appeal refused. Per LJ-C Thomson: '... it was for the sheriff, as a jury question, to decide whether and to what extent, the handwriting evidence led before him was careful, reliable and scientific, having in view ... the skill and experience of the investigators and the amount and nature of the materials available to them for comparison.' *Campbell v Mackenzie* 1974 SLT (Notes) 46 Fraud. C convicted of writing letters to chief constable making unfounded allegations about other persons and subscribed by false signature. Appeal rejected, competent and sufficient expert evidence not contradicted.	
Palm print identification.	*HMA v Rolley* 1945 JC 155 Theft by housebreaking. Palm print found in house identified with palm print of R. Police evidence that no case of identity between prints of two different person's palms had ever been found. R convicted. Per LJ-C Cooper: ' . . the evidence in its quality and substance [must be] of a character to carry conviction to the jury, whose duty it is to determine upon its value.'	
DNA identification.	*Welsh v HMA* 1992 SCCR 108 Murder. Blood found at the scene matched to that of W by use of DNA profiling. *Held* on appeal that DNA could be used. While DNA is not unique as with fingerprinting there was only a chance of 1 and between 88 and 99 million that the blood not that of W. No set statistical mark must be reached, up to jury whether to accept an identification using this process.	
Identification by blind person.	*Hill v Copeland* (1976) SCCR Supp 103 H convicted of assaulting a blind person. Complainer said he had been assaulted by person who had brought him home. Threads found in complainer's house similar to those used to repair H's jacket. H had admitted taking complainer home but stated that he had left him in the close and not entered the house. Sheriff believed the complainer and determined that the threads constituted sufficient corroboration.	
Identification by admissions of guilt—unequivocal	*Keane v Horne* (1978) SCCR Supp 225 Theft by opening lockfast car. Accused seen near locus but ran off. Described by owner of car. Two sets of car keys found on the accused's person, who said on apprehension, 'Honest we didn't take anything,' and replied to caution and charge, 'I'm sorry, I didn't mean to take anything.' *Held*, sufficient corroboration. Opinion of the court: 'It has been said time and time again that when you are dealing with an unequivocal and clear admission of responsibility, only a very little evidence in corroboration of such an admission is required in law.'	

COMMENTARY	CASE LAW	STATUTE LAW
	McNab v Culligan (1978) SCCR Supp 222 Careless driving. Collision. Two occupants of car ran off. Later, respondent seen with facial injuries. Car belonged to respondent's father. Registered driver not driving, had handed car over to respondent who said, 'I might as well tell you the truth, it was me', to the police. *Held* sufficient corroboration, even a clear admission requires some element of independent evidence.	
	Meredith v Lees 1992 SCCR 459 Lewd practices. Sheriff holding that the evidence of the four year-old complainer provided the 'very little' required to corroborate the confession of M. *Held*, appeal sustained, even a clear and unequivocal confession required corroboration.	
—equivocal.	*Sinclair v Clark* 1962 JC 57 Careless driving. S admitted to two witnesses that he was the driver. Other evidence showed S one of those in car and that he reported to the police station. S convicted. On appeal *held* sufficient corroboration. Per LJ-C Thomson: '... short of a solemn plea of guilt, an admission of guilt by an accused is not conclusive against him unless it is corroborated by something beyond the actual admission.'	
	Greenshields v HMA 1989 SCCR 637 G charged with murder and attempting to pervert the course of justice. Replied 'You don't think I did it myself do you; but I'm telling you nothing about it until I see my lawyer.' Appealed on the ground of insufficiency of evidence. *Held*, even when confession is not clear and unequivocal it is of evidential value and in present case constituted critical ingredient of case based on circumstantial evidence. Appeal refused.	
Inconsistent account by the accused.	*Wright v Tudhope* 1983 SCCR 403 Careless driving. Collision with parked car. W identified by driver of parked car did not deny then that he was driver. Later W said that he was passenger and actual driver could not be traced. W convicted. Appeal dismissed.	
Identification established by answering summary complaint.	*Smith v Paterson* 1982 SCCR 295 Breach of the peace. Witnessed by two policemen who arrested P but were not asked to identify him in court. Defence submitted 'No case to answer'. Fiscal founded on statutory presumption that per-son who answers summary complaint is person charged by police unless the contrary is alleged and argued that there was sufficient evidence to convict. P acquitted. Crown appeal by stated case allowed. Per LJ-G Emslie: 'In most cases the presumption of limited scope provided by [the statute] will have no part to play at all in proof of the essential facts in a prosecution, viz (i) that the offence libelled was committed and, (ii) that the person who committed it was the accused.'	
Extract conviction and police evidence as proof of disqualification.	*Andrews v McLeod* 1982 SCCR 254 Driving while disqualified. Extract conviction showed disqualification, police evidence identified A as driver. *Held*, sufficient evidence.	

COMMENTARY	CASE LAW	STATUTE LAW
Identification of the accused in the dock	*Holland v HMA* 2005 SLT 563; 2005 SCCR 417. H appealed his conviction on charges of assault and robbery on the basis that his human rights had been infringed by the Crown who had relied upon evidence from two witnesses identifying the accused in the dock during his trial. H had previously been identified by both witnesses from police photographs but neither witness had picked H out of an identity parade. H submitted that the procedure of dock identification compelled the defendant to assist the Crown case against him contrary to his Art 6(1) right against self incrimination and that such evidence was so unfair and unreliable that it was incompatible with a fair trial under Art 6(1). *Held*, despite dock identification lacking certain safeguards offered by other mechanisms of identification, evidence derived from a witness identifying the accused in the dock was not, by its very nature, so unfair as to be incompatible with Art 6(1) ECHR in all cases, nor the present case. *Note:* The appeal in the above case was successful on grounds of the prosecution's non-disclosure of material evidence despite the finding re dock identification. *See also:* *Murphy v HMA* 2007 SLT 1079 *Anderson v HMA* 2010 SCCR 382 *NC v HMA* [2012] HCJAC 139	
The commission of the crime	*Hay v HMA* 1968 JC 40 Murder. Suspicion fell on H because impression of bite marks on deceased's body corresponded with impression of H's teeth. H convicted.	
Cause of death—postmortem evidence desirable.	*Brown v HMA* 1964 JC 10 Causing death by dangerous driving. Evidence of only one doctor that death caused by multiple injuries and shock. Evidence from other witnesses of prior good health provided corroboration of this. Per LJ-C Grant: 'It is unfortunate that the Crown did not follow the normal and proper practice of proving the cause of ... death by medical evidence based on a postmortem dissection. Such evidence, where the cause of death is in issue, is not a sine qua non, but it is highly desirable that it should be led, and grave difficulties may arise if it is not.'	
Police evidence may corroborate evidence of socius criminis.	*O'Hara v Tudhope* 1986 SCCR 283 Car theft. O convicted on evidence of I who pled guilty but incriminated O. Car was stopped after a chase and O was sitting in the back seat. *Held* that I's evidence was sufficiently corroborated by police evidence that O was a passenger in the car.	
It is necessary that there be evidence that the crime was carried out in the manner described.	*McDonald v Herron* 1986 SLT 61 Theft. Witness said McD had been on premises acting suspiciously. No evidence that stolen property found in McD's possession. McD convicted. *Held* on appeal, not enough corroboration to establish that the theft took place and conviction quashed. But see: *Mackay v HMA* 1997 SCCR 743 Robbery. Witness saw complainer and appellant go into lane, heard shouting, and on emerging saw complainer distressed, pleading 'give me it back'. *Held*, corroborated evidence that ring taken by violence or intimidation, and therefore sufficient evidence of robbery.	

COMMENTARY	CASE LAW	STATUTE LAW
	Campbell v Vannet 1998 SCCR 207 Assault. Only part of complainer's account corroborated. Conviction of entire charge upheld on appeal.	
	Miller (J) v HMA 1994 SCCR 377 Murder. Evidence of one witness that appellant stabbed deceased in toilet. Evidence of another witness that accused punched deceased in hall. On appeal conviction quashed: two inconsistent accounts did not provide corroboration.	
	Young v HMA 1997 SCCR 405 Corroboration. Complainer said appellant put hand inside clothing and touched breast. Witness said thought rubbing complainer's tummy. Conviction of lewd practices upheld on appeal: both witnesses' evidence that complainer touched sufficient for conviction.	
	Cassidy v Normand 1994 SCCR 325 Assault. Conviction upheld on appeal. *Held*, evidence of suspicious behaviour (walking along roof at relevant time and jumping down near spot) sufficient to corroborate complainer's evidence.	
	McGrory v HMA 1995 SCCR 237 Assault. Appellant told witness she would be sorry if she gave evidence. Conviction upheld on appeal. Observed, threat to witness is not corroboration, but court can look at remark in light of other evidence.	
	McLeod v Mason 1981 SCCR 75 Forcing open lockfast cars with intent to steal and attempting to steal. Sheriff acquitted, holding complaint should have indicated intent to steal either the contents of the car or the car itself and insufficient evidence to show attempt to steal the car not just drive it away unlawfully. Crown appealed successfully. Opinion of the court: 'There was no need for the Crown in order to establish the commission of a completed crime to show that it was the intention of the respondents to steal the car or its contents or both. It is quite sufficient to libel the opening of a lockfast motor car with the criminal intent of theft and in many cases it will be impossible to prove more.'	
	McCrann v HMA 2003 SCCR 722 A rape was alleged to have been committed early one evening but the complainer had appeared 'happy and relaxed' until 1pm the following day before showing apparent distress. *Held*, there was insufficient evidence to relate her distress to the alleged rape given the lapse of time.	
Other emotional reactions as possible mechanisms of corroboration	*Fulton v HMA* 2000 JC 62 F was convicted of possessing a firearm after his landlord gave evidence stating he had seen the gun in F's possession outside the flat, together with evidence from a police officer that the landlord had appeared 'visibly shocked' when the gun had been discovered during a search of the premises. *Held*, that the landlords genuine emotional response was enough to corroborate his evidence entitling the jury to infer that the gun belonged to F.	

COMMENTARY	CASE LAW	STATUTE LAW
Distress cannot corroborate complainer's evidence of what occurred, but can corroborate withholding consent.	*Fox v HMA* 1998 SCCR 115 Clandestine injury. *Held* (full bench): (1) complainer's distress could corroborate her evidence that she did not consent; (2) corroborative evidence must support or confirm the direct evidence of a witness; (3) it is not the law that circumstantial evidence is corroborative only if it is more consistent with direct evidence of Crown than the account given by the accused; (4) circumstantial evidence can provide corroboration even where the accused puts forward an innocent explanation where the jury rejects this explanation. Conviction upheld on appeal. *Mackie v HMA* 1994 SCCR 277 overruled. See Sheldon, 'Corroborational Relevance' 1998 SLT (News) 115; Brown, 'Two Cases on Corroboration' 1998 SLT (News) 71.	
	Gracey v HMA 1987 SCCR 260 Rape. G charged with rape and his defence was that the complainer had consented to intercourse. *Held* that where evidence is led of the distressed state of the complainer it is for the jury to assess that evidence, and if accepted as genuine, it is capable of corroborating the complainer.	
	Geddes v HMA 1996 SCCR 687 Corroboration. Conviction of assault charge quashed on appeal. *Held*, distress at medical examination of anus five days after incident relied on for corroboration was too remote and could be attributed to intrusive examination.	
	McLellan v HMA 1992 SCCR 171 Lewd practices. Crown leading evidence of child complainer's distress. Judge not directing the jury on a possible alternative source of distress that the complainer was not supposed to be visiting M's house. Conviction quashed on appeal.	
	Smith v Lees 1997 SCCR 139 Accused convicted of using lewd practices towards a young girl, causing her to handle his penis. Distress relied on for corroboration. *Held*, on appeal (bench of five judges): distress cannot corroborate complainer's evidence of what occurred (but can corroborate withholding consent). *Stobo v HMA* 1993 SCCR 1105 overruled. Observed, per Lord McCluskey: mere consistency not enough for corroboration: need evidence pointing positively towards truth of essential facts.	
Distress in non-rape cases.	*Horne v HMA* 1991 SCCR 174 Abduction. *Held* that distress evidence also relevant in cases other than rape. (Following *Mongan v HMA* 1989 SCCR 25 and *Bennett v HMA* 1989 SCCR 608.)	
	Thomson v HMA 1998 SCCR 56 Conviction of assault upheld on appeal despite misdirection of availability of distress as corroboration to fact of assault. *Held*, no miscarriage, since evidence of physical injury at time of distress available for jury to consider.	

COMMENTARY	CASE LAW	STATUTE LAW
Insufficient evidence that an individual committed a specific crime.	*Shannon v HMA* 1985 SCCR 14 Reset. S's conviction of possessing illegal sawn-off shotgun upheld on appeal. *Held*, however, that although S's actings inferred knowledge of possessing the shotgun there was insufficient evidence to infer that he knew gun had been stolen.	
Statutory non-requirement for corroboration		Criminal Procedure (Scotland) Act 1995. **Solemn and summary procedure:**
Autopsy report.	*O'Brien v HMA* 1996 SCCR 238 F gave evidence that actual analysis carried out by C; objection to evidence as hearsay repelled. Conviction upheld on appeal. *Note:* opinion reserved if neither of the two signatories had carried out the work.	Section 281(1). Autopsy report presumed to relate to deceased identified therein unless contrary is alleged by defence by notice not less than six days before trial or later in special circumstances.
Signatories to autopsy or forensic science report.	*Donnelly v Schrikel* 1994 SCCR 640 No statement in certificate that drugs analysed by signatories of certificate. *Held*, on appeal, that parties' joint minute that report was joint report relieved need to rely on statutory provision, and sheriff to proceed accordingly. *O'Brien v McCreadie* 1994 SCCR 516 No statement in report that drugs analysed by signatory of report. Sheriff acquitted respondent. Conviction overturned on appeal, since document was a report and not a certificate, which had different requirements. Sheriff to proceed accordingly.	Section 281(2). Evidence of one of two signatories to autopsy or forensic science report suffi-cient on contents and signatories' qualifications if intimation to accused of intention to call only one specified signatory given when report lodged as production unless notice given by accused requiring other signatory, not less than six days before trial, or later in special circumstances.
Forensic science reports.		Criminal Procedure (Scotland) Act 1995. Section 280(4)–(6). A report purporting to be signed by two authorised forensic scientists shall be sufficient evidence of any fact or conclusion contained in the report and of the authority of the signatories only where notice served and no counter notice issued in terms of s 280(6)(a), (b) above.

COMMENTARY	CASE LAW	STATUTE LAW
		Solemn and summary procedure:
Certificates.	*Law Mining v Carmichael* 1996 SCCR 627 Control of Pollution Act 1974. Test carried out by F using standard laboratory procedures agreed with superior, D. D was not present during analysis, but independently checked results. Conviction upheld on appeal. *McCrindle v Walkingshaw* 1994 SCCR 299 Conviction under s 5(2) of the Misuse of Drugs Act 1971 (possessing cannabis). Sufficient corroboration of principal analyst that second analyst checked the lab reference number against the plate, the slide and lab records, despite the second analyst not present when cannabis removed from bag and put on plate and slide. *Pickard v Carmichael* 1995 SCCR 76 Speeding. *Held*, necessary in circumstances to prove Gatso radar device an approved device. Conviction quashed.	Section 280(1)–(6), Sch 9. Speedometer, odometer, radar meter, measuring apparatus—signatories: two police testers. Substance allegedly controlled drug—signatories: two qualified/authorised analysts. Benefits payments, eg social security, child and supple-mentary benefits—signatory: authorised officer. Certificate signed by person in column 2 certifying matter in column 3 in relation to offence in column 1, shall be sufficient evidence of that matter and of authority/qualification of that person where: (a) copy served on other party at least 14 days before trial; and (b) other party does not challenge matter, qualification or authority, by serving a counter notice within 7 days after service of copy (or as court in special circumstances allows).
Conviction, extract sufficient to show disqualification.		**Solemn and summary procedure:** Criminal Procedure (Scotland) Act 1995 Section 286. Conviction or extract sufficient evidence if copy served on accused at least 14 days before trial diet, purportedly signed by clerk of court having custody of record containing the conviction, unless notice denying conviction given by accused within seven days of service of notice. Criminal Procedure (Scotland) Act 1995 Section 285(6)–(8). Briefly, extract conviction issued by officer sufficient without being sworn to by witnesses, unless challenged by notice and if challenged Crown may prove previous convictions from witnesses not in list. Criminal Procedure (Scotland) Act 1995 Section 285(1)–(5). Provides for proof of previous convictions by fingerprints.
Bail—extract of minutes.		Criminal Procedure (Scotland) Act 1995 Section 28(6). Extract of minutes bearing to be signed by clerk of court sufficient evidence.

COMMENTARY	CASE LAW	STATUTE LAW
Salmon poaching.		Salmon and Freshwater Fisheries (Protection) (Scotland) Act 1951 Section 7(3). Conviction is lawful on evidence of one witness (for illegal possession of sal-mon or trout or means for taking them).
Road traffic.	*Donaldson v Valentine* 1996 SCCR 374 Charge of speeding on a motorway. Only evidence that locus was motorway was from two constables. *Held*, sufficient. *Donnelly v Carmichael* 1995 SCCR 737 Conviction of drinking in prohibited place. Lodging of bylaws without accompanying plans. *Held*, this was insufficient evidence, which could not be made good by evidence from police officers or private knowledge of justice. Conviction quashed.	Road Traffic Offenders Act 1988 Section 21(3). Conviction is lawful on the evidence of one witness for contravention of the Road Traffic Act 1988, s 35(1) (failure to obey traffic direction by police constable or traffic sign).
Routine evidence: controlled drugs and medicinal products.		Criminal Procedure (Scotland) Act 1995 Section 282. Evidence by a forensic scientist that a substance is a controlled drug or medicinal product, by reference either to the label on a sealed container or the characteristic appearance of the substance, shall be sufficient evidence of identity of substance, notwithstanding that no analysis of the substance has been carried out. Notice to be served not less than 14 days before trial diet and counter notice of non-acceptance within seven days, in which case these provisions will not apply. *Note*: There are similar provisions as regards sufficiency and notification procedure for: CP(S) A 1995, s 283 (evidence as to time and place of video surveillance recordings); s 284 (evidence in relation to fingerprints); and s 277 (transcripts of police interviews—accused has 6 days before trial to challenge accuracy of transcripts by counter notice).
Procedural matters Rights re medical examination.	*Farrell v Concannon* 1957 JC 12; 1957 SLT 60 Drunken driving. Sheriff returned 'not proven' verdict. Appeal by Crown allowed. *Held*, on appeal, that the fact that an accused was told he need not consent to medical examination should be proven, but could be done by only one witness.	
Breath test procedure.	*MacLeod v Nicol*; *Torrance v Thaw* 1970 JC 58; 1970 SLT 304 Drunken driving. At trial of N one police witness spoke to circumstances of breath test. At trial of To one policeman spoke to fact he was in uniform and device used was of approved style. Sheriff found charge against N not proven. To convicted. In N's case, Crown appealed and in To's case accused appealed. *Held*, that procedural steps in issue could be spoken to by one credible witness.	

COMMENTARY	CASE LAW	STATUTE LAW
	Per LJ-C Grant: '... in any case any fact can be proved by one witness although the whole case cannot be so proved. ... All that the law demands is that there should be two witnesses to prove a case; and provided that is so, any fact in the case may be provided by the testimony of one credible witness.'	
Incidental matters Security of premises.	*Davidson* (1841) 2 Swin 630 Theft by opening lockfast place. Locking spoken to by only one witness. *Held* only one witness necessary, now fixed law.	
Evidence of real facts.	*Ryrie v Campbell* 1964 JC 33 Driving without due care and attention. No eye witness but tyre marks on the wrong side of the road observed by the police. Paint marks on lamp standard matched car. Appeal refused. *Held* evidence of eyewitness not essential, real facts eloquent of what happened.	
	McGuire v HMA 2003 SCCR 758 Robbery appellant's DNA on mask discarded at locus, no explanation offered. In light of no explanation sufficient.	
	Healey v Vannet 2000 SCCR 35 Assault: unequivocal admission although complainer in evidence denied being assaulted. Corroboration found in disorder at locus and red swelling on complainer's cheek.	
The *Moorov* doctrine The interlinking of evidence on separate charges, if sufficiently idiosyncratic, will furnish corroboration even if there is only one witness speaking to matters.	*HMA v Moorov* 1930 JC 68; 1930 SLT 596 Indecent assault. M convicted of series of indecent assault over a period of years. On appeal, *held* evidence in support of any one charge was competent corroboration of evidence in support of other charges. Per LJ-G Clyde: 'Before the evidence of a single credible witness to separate acts can be used as providing material for mutual corroboration, the connection between the separate acts indicated by the external relation in time, character or circumstance must be such as to exhibit them as subordinates in some particular and ascertained unity of project, campaign, or adventure, which lies beyond or behind, but is related to, the separate acts.'	
	Pettigrew v Lees 1991 SCCR 304 Two charges of indecent exposure. In both incidents only one witness could identify the accused. The presence of others at one incident did not make the doctrine inapplicable as there was only one identification on each occasion.	
	Quinn v Lowe 1991 SCCR 881 *Held* on appeal that *Moorov v HMA* 1930 JC 68; 1930 SLT 596 could apply to two incidents arising out of the same matter in each of which the same complainer was the only witness.	
Offences connected in time.	*Ogg v HMA* 1938 JC 152 Sexual offences. 10 charges over seven years. In first three, complainer the only witness. *Held* that *Moorov v HMA* 1930 JC 68; 1930 SLT 596 not applicable in view of the time between offences and lack of corroboration.	

COMMENTARY	CASE LAW	STATUTE LAW
	Per LJ-C Aitchison: '*Moorov* ... laid down the general proposition in relation to sexual crimes, although not entirely limited to such crimes, that similar sexual crimes each deponed to by a single credible witness may afford mutual corroboration, provided always that they are so inter-related by character, circumstances and time—the presence of all these features is not essential—as to justify an inference that they are instances of a course of criminal conduct systematically pursued by the accused person.'	
	Russell v HMA 1990 SCCR 18 Interval of two years between two incidents held to be fatal to the application of the doctrine.	
	Stewart v HMA 2007 SCCR 303 Thirteen charges of rape, other sexual offences. Complainers all young women or girls. Appellant police officer on uniform duty. "No maximum interval of time . . . if there are compelling similarities" for application of *Moorov* (Latitude of four years).	
	Contrast	
	Sinder v HMA 2003 SCCR 271	
	Beaton v HMA 2004 SCCR 467	
	Turner v Scott 1995 SCCR 516 *Held*, charges of indecent assault separated by three years borderline case, but sufficient coherence in character and circumstance to apply Moorov doctrine (*Moorov v HMA* 1930 JC 68; 1930 SLT 596). Conviction upheld on appeal.	
Offences must be of the same genus.	*HMA v WB* 1969 JC 72 Incest and lewd, indecent and libidinous practices. Five offences over some years. Two incidents separated by interval of fifteen months. *Moorov* doctrine applied despite time interval. *Held*, evidence of incest included indecency and could corroborate evidence of lewd practices but not vice versa as incest much more serious than lewd practices.	
	Smith v HMA 1995 SLT 583 *Moorov* doctrine successfully applied to two charges of lewd conduct and one of sodomy. *Held*, essential element was indecent assault, and similarities meant there was not too great a gap.	
	Compare with:	
	HMA v Cox 1962 JC 27 'Incest and sodomy are different in nature and cannot corroborate each other.'	
	Mackintosh v HMA 1991 SCCR 776 *Held* on appeal that *Moorov* doctrine could not apply to a charge of theft by housebreaking and assault with intent to rob because one incident involved violence and the other did not.	
	Wilson v HMA 2001 SCCR 455 Two charges of theft. *Modus operandi* W. Pretended to be workman/official forced way into house of elderly occupier seized accessible articles (bag, camera) articles not recorded, but because of similar nature *Moorov* removed need for corroboration of their identity.	

COMMENTARY	CASE LAW	STATUTE LAW
	P v HMA 1991 SCCR 993 Trial judge holding that *Moorov* doctrine could be applied to two charges of sexual offences against a young boy and girl. Course of criminal penetrative abuse.	
	Carpenter v Hamilton 1994 SCCR 108 *Moorov* doctrine: offences must be of the same genus. Indecent exposure and jumping out at women making a suggestive noise. *Held*, to have underlying similarity of character and conviction of breach of peace upheld.	
An attempted crime may corroborate a completed one.	*PM v Jessop* 1989 SCCR 324 PM charged with sodomy and attempted sodomy in relation to two boys. Convicted using *Moorov* doctrine. *Held* that the sodomy and attempted sodomy so closely related that evidence of attempted act may corroborate evidence of completed act.	
Moorov doctrine also applied to non-sexual crimes.	*McCudden v HMA* 1952 JC 86 1952 SLT 357;—bribery of professional footballers. *HMA v McQuade* 1951 JC 143—razor attacks *Harris v Clark* 1958 JC 3—reset *McIntosh v HMA* 1986 SCCR 496—supply of drugs	
	Austin v Fraser 1997 SCCR 775 Charge of breach of the peace involved two incidents, 80 days apart on same stretch of road, of obstructing motor car behind by forcing driver to proceed at slow speed and come to a halt respectively. Conviction upheld on appeal: *Moorov* doctrine applicable.	
	Reynolds v HMA 1995 SCCR 504 Two assaults and robberies. Both similarities and dissimilarities. *Moorov* doctrine left to the jury. Conviction upheld on appeal.	
The *Howden* rule If proved both crimes committed by same person and proved one of them committed by appellant, then there is sufficient proof second crime committed by him.	*Howden v HMA* 1994 SCCR 19 Appellant charged with robbery of bank and building society in different parts of Edinburgh 14 days apart. Positive identification in building society, tentative identification in bank. Conviction upheld on appeal: if proved both crimes committed by same person and proved one of them committed by the appellant, then sufficient proof second committed by him.	
The *Townsley* approach Where there are three charges, but only one positive identification on one charge and tentative identification on other two charges, *Moorov* doctrine may be applied to first two charges, and *Howden* rule applied to convict accused of all three charges.	*Townsley v Lees* 1996 SCCR 620 Appellant charged with three offences of theft. Three tentative identifications on first charge; positive identification on second charge; complainer in third charge could only say appellant similar in build and age. Conviction upheld on appeal. *Held*, that the *Moorov* doctrine applied to the first two charges, and since evidence that all three offences committed by same person sheriff entitled to hold appellant involved in all three. *Howden v HMA* 1994 SCCR 19 approved.	
The circumstantial confession Where a confession by an accused or a suspect details information which would have been in the possession of the perpetrator of the crime, the terms of the confession supply corroboration of it.	*Manuel v HMA* 1958 JC 41 Murder. Statement by M as to whereabouts of victim's body which was subsequently discovered by police held sufficient corroboration and conviction upheld on appeal.	

COMMENTARY	CASE LAW	STATUTE LAW
	Beattie v HMA 1995 SCCR 93 Conviction of murder upheld on appeal. Appellant's statement not a circumstantial confession: it displayed special knowledge, and this required corroboration from other evidence in addition to that required to demonstrate accuracy of detailed knowledge of circumstances. *Connolly v HMA* 1958 SLT 79 Theft. Particularised and detailed confession with extraneous evidence of its accuracy. Independent evidence of the accused acting suspiciously in car near locus held sufficient corroboration. *Held*, confession shows crime committed and accused must have been the perpetator or privy to its perpetration. *Mitchell v HMA* 1996 SCCR 97 Corroboration. Attempted murder. Two witnesses in house spoke to knock at window and shot but unable to identify gunman. C said appellant admitted chap and shot; L said appellant admitted shot to him. Conviction upheld on appeal. *Held*, not necessary for each element of confession said to constitute special knowledge to be spoken to by two witnesses. *Woodland v Hamilton* 1990 SCCR 166 *Held* not to be special knowledge admission where the alleged special knowledge could have been given to W by his co-accused. *Robertson v HMA* 1990 SCCR 345 Art and part assault. Statement by R to police, 'You've got this wrong, I've never stabbed anyone' consistent with R knowing of the incident in question but not sufficient to infer she knew or ought to have known that a knife was to be used. *Smith v HMA* (1978) SCCR Supp 203 Theft by housebreaking. Confession amounting to account of offence and some of the items stolen held sufficient corroboration. Per LJ-G Emslie: 'A confession can receive corroboration if there is not only proof of the commission of the crime to which it related but proof *aliunde* of the truth of the confession.' *Wilson v McAughey* 1982 SCCR 398 Vandalism. Details in confession as to how mechanical digger had been started and what thereafter occurred held sufficient corroboration. Per LJ-C Wheatley: 'The law in the situation here could be summarised in the phrase that the respondent could not have been able to make the statement which he did if he had not been present at the time when the offence libelled had been committed.' *Campbell (T) v HMA* 1998 SCCR 214 *Held*, evidence of appellant expressing thanks in circumstances related to crime should be regarded as incriminating remarks rather than an admission and could corroborate the appellant's admission to police, and appeal on this ground refused.	

COMMENTARY	CASE LAW	STATUTE LAW
Admissions partly consistent with facts.	*Gilmour v HMA* 1982 SCCR 590 Rape and murder. Two admissions of guilt by G incorporating information, some consistent, some inconsistent with the proved facts. On appeal held sufficient corroboration of investigating officers' existing information. *Held* on appeal, corroboration found in that the statement contained material facts, established independently, which accused could have known if he had been present when the offence occurred. See also: *Hutchison v Valentine* 1990 SCCR 569 *Reilly v Fraser* 1996 SCCR 26 Assault. Only corroboration was witness in pub with complainer, who said appellant left ten minutes after complainer and returned and said 'You'd better make sure your mate is OK'. Conviction quashed on appeal, since not entitled to infer that remarks were admission, and insufficient evidence.	
Confession must be corroborated by findings in fact.	*Allan v Hamilton* 1972 SLT (Notes) 2 Theft. A told police where stolen savings stamps were cashed and admitted theft. A convicted. Appeal dismissed. LJ-C Wheatley observed that there had been a very full confession by the accused admitting the theft, and that was corroborated by findings in fact. *McDonald v Normand* 1994 SCCR 121 Conviction of assault upheld on appeal. Appellant admitted kneeling on arm; complainer identified accused as man who twisted her arm. *Held*, description sufficient to corroborate general allegation of assault.	
Admission by one accused may be corroborated by another accused.	*Annan v Bain* 1986 SCCR 60 Theft. B and H charged with theft of car. Respondents seen in car and subsequently chased by police. B admitted that he 'stole white car' before police had indicated that this was the reason for apprehension. H also admitted 'We stole it'. *Held* that confessions contained special knowledge and were sufficiently corroborated by presence in car; and that statement of each respondent corroborated that of the other.	
Inferential corroboration from *de recenti* possession In the absence of an explanation, an inference of guilt can be drawn from the possession in criminative circumstances of recently stolen property.	*Christie v HMA* 1939 JC 72; 1939 SLT 558 Theft by housebreaking. C found in possession of part of stolen property and evidence of *de recenti* pawning of stolen article. On arrest C gave detailed statement that goods were obtained from named person, who denied it. No evidence given by C at trial. Appeal against conviction refused. Per Lord Fleming: 'According to the authorities, which extend over a long period of time, it has in practice been recognised that where there is no reasonable explanation of such possession, the jury are entitled not merely to infer that the accused is guilty of reset, but to go further and hold that he was actor or art and part in the actual theft charged.' *Hamilton v Friel* 1994 SCCR 748 Theft of boat and trailer. Appellant had receipt for articles. *Held*, on appeal, that appellant's inability to give details about seller did not amount to incriminative circumstances and conviction quashed.	

COMMENTARY	CASE LAW	STATUTE LAW
Corroboration not necessary to establish that items stolen (Alison p 324).	*Findlay v HMA* (1953) SCCR Supp 1 Theft by housebreaking. Crown relied on evidence of recent possession of stolen articles, the only evidence that the articles were stolen being that of the householder. *Held* that the finding of articles in accused's possession in suspicious circumstances sufficient to corroborate evidence of owner as to their having been stolen.	
Other criminative circumstances in addition to possession necessary.	*Watt v Annan* 1990 SCCR 55 Six months is too great an interval for application of doctrine of recent possession, but may be sufficient to convict of reset.	
De recenti possession must not merely be transporting of items on another's behalf.	*HMA v Simpson* 1952 JC 1; 1952 SLT 85 Theft by opening lockfast place. Stolen goods found in possession of dealer to whom S had taken them as another's servant. Conviction quashed on appeal because no presumption of guilt to be rebutted as S not in 'possession' of the goods.	
	Gilchrist v HMA 1992 SCCR 98 Theft. G spotted by police driving car similar to one seen at the scene of a crime, pursued by police. Car slowed to allow a person to jump from the car. G stopped and jewellery found in the back seat. *Held* on appeal that given the discovery of the jewellery and the manner in which G drove the car there was sufficient evidence to infer that G was aware of the stolen goods.	
Present possession not required—past possession sufficient.	*Brannan v HMA* 1954 JC 87; 1954 SLT 255 Theft by housebreaking and opening lockfast place. Evidence that B had possession of stolen goods initially although recovered elsewhere. B convicted. Appeal refused because held that presumption of guilt arising from recent possession had not in this case been rebutted. Per LJ-G Cooper: 'Possession may be constructive, and it does not necessarily follow that possession which has been parted with need not be explained.'	
Stolen goods not 'in person's possession' as premises open to other people.	*Cryans v Nixon* 1955 JC 1; 1954 SLT 311 Theft. C occupier of two sheds kept unlocked, with customers having access. Part of stolen property found concealed in C's premises. C denied all knowledge. C convicted. Conviction quashed on appeal. *Held* no presumption of guilt to be rebutted, other people had access to premises, goods not in accused's possession.	
Silence, when charged, not a criminative circumstance.	*Wightman and Anr v HMA* 1959 JC 44; 1959 SLT (Notes) 27 (*sub nom* Collins) Theft. Scrap metal found in W's possession. When cautioned and charged W replied: 'I am saying nothing, not one iota.' Other appellant did not reply, neither did he give evidence. Both convicted. On appeal, held that neither the failure to reply nor the failure to give evidence could constitute a criminative circumstance and no presumption of guilt to be rebutted. Per LJ-G Clyde: (quoting LJ-G Cooper in *Robertson v Maxwell* 1951 JC 11): '... no legitimate inference in favour of a prosecutor can be drawn from the fact that a person, when charged with crime, either says nothing or says that he has nothing to say. He is entitled to reserve his defence, and is usually wise if he does so.'	But note: Criminal Justice (Scotland) Act 1995, s 32, repealed Criminal Procedure (Scotland) Act 1975, s 141(b): ie prosecutor can now comment on accused's failure to lead evidence. See also Criminal Procedure (Scotland) Act 1995, s 36(8), and page 127 above: declining to answer a question at judicial examination can be commented on. Criminal Procedure (Scotland) Act 1995 Section 14(9). Detained person under no obligation to answer any question other than to give name and address.

COMMENTARY	CASE LAW	STATUTE LAW
Fingerprints and attempt to dispose of items—*de recenti* possession.	*Cameron v HMA* 1959 JC 59 Theft by opening lockfast place. Box of stolen goods thrown out of window when police arrived at C's house. C's fingerprints found on stolen articles in box. C convicted. Appeal refused. *Held*, evidence of the box confirming evidence as regards possession.	
	Crowe v Dealsey 1996 SCCR 1 (Sh Ct) Location of accused's fingerprints on cheques shortly after being stolen sufficient for conviction of reset and uttering.	
Fingerprint evidence alone—not *de recenti* possession.	*Reilly v HMA* 1959 JC 59 Theft. R co-appellant with Cameron (see *Cameron v HMA* 1959 JC 59). Only evidence of possession fingerprints on sheets of stamps. Conviction quashed on appeal because no presumption of guilt to be rebutted. Per LJ-G Clyde: '... the presence of fingerprints alone is not sufficient to establish possession ... of the articles alleged to have been stolen ... one of the three necessary conditions for applying the doctrine of recent possession has not been satisfied.'	
Uncontroversial evidence.		Criminal Procedure (Scotland) Act 1995 Section 258. Where party considers facts unlikely to be disputed by other party he can prepare and sign a statement specifying facts. Not less than 14 days before trial diet he can serve copy on other party. Other party has seven days (or longer if court allows in special circumstances) to serve counter notice challenging statement. Otherwise, facts deemed conclusively proved. Court may, on application of either party, if special circumstances, and shall on joint application, direct that presumption shall not apply. Applications to be made after commencement of trial and before prosecutor's address on the evidence. If direction then court shall adjourn unless parties agree otherwise and will permit leading of evidence notwithstanding not in list nor notice as required by CP(S)A 1995, s 67(5) and s 78(4). Note: see CP(S)A 1995, s 257 for general duty of each party to take reasonable steps to secure agreement of evidence which they consider unlikely to be disputed.

SENTENCING

ABSOLUTE DISCHARGE

An absolute discharge may be granted for offences where the sentence is not fixed by law, if the circumstances of the offence and/or the offender make it appropriate. A right of appeal is not affected. Although not a conviction, it can be laid before a court in subsequent proceedings.

COMMENTARY

In solemn procedure, absolute discharge follows upon conviction. In summary procedure, it comes after the court is satisfied the offender committed the offence.

Not available where sentence is fixed by law.

Nature of offence to be considered.

Nature of offender to be considered.

Inexpedient to inflict punishment.

Probation order not appropriate.

While not a conviction, an absolute discharge can be referred to in subsequent proceedings.

CASE LAW

Kheda v Lees 1995 SCCR 63
Nurse convicted of breach of the peace and fined. On appeal High Court said sheriff never attached sufficient weight to appellant's good character and repercussions conviction would have on career, and absolute discharge substituted.

Galloway v Mackenzie 1991 SCCR 548
Careers officer convicted of minor assault and admonished. He appealed, since occupation exempt from provisions on convictions becoming spent, which meant he would have to disclose conviction. High Court substituted absolute discharge.

Husband v Russell 1997 SCCR 592
Fireman on emergency run, minor careless in driving

STATUTE LAW

Criminal Procedure (Scotland) Act 1995

Solemn procedure:

Section 246(2). Where a person is convicted on indictment of an offence (other than one for which sentence is fixed by law), if it appears to the court, having regard to the circumstances including the nature of the offence and the character of the offender, that it is inexpedient to inflict punishment and that a probation order is not appropriate it may instead of sentencing him make an order discharging him absolutely.

Summary procedure:

Section 246(3). Where summary offence (other than one for which sentence is fixed by law) and the court is satisfied he committed offence, the court having regard to the circumstances including the nature of the offence and the character of the offender, is of opinion that it is inexpedient to inflict punishment and that a probation order is not appropriate may, without proceeding to conviction, discharge him absolutely.

Section 247(1). Absolute discharge or probation order shall be deemed not to be a conviction, but can be laid before court as previous conviction in subsequent proceedings.

Section 247(2). Absolute discharge (and also probation order) disregarded for the purposes of any enactment which imposes any disqualification or disability upon convicted persons (unless the relevant Act specifically extends to persons granted an absolute discharge).

Section 247(3). Right of appeal not affected.

ADMONITION

A court may, if it appears to meet the justice of the case, dismiss with an admonition any person convicted by the court of any offence.

COMMENTARY	CASE LAW	STATUTE LAW
No statutory limit to the use of admonition. Can be used with other order, eg disqualification.	*Kirk v Kennedy* 2001 SCCR 31 Admonition substituted for custody in case of downloading indecent photographs of children – 'victimless' crime.	Criminal Procedure (Scotland) Act 1995 Section 246(1). A court may, if it appears to meet the justice of the case, dismiss with an admonition any person convicted by the court of any offence.

ANTI–SOCIAL BEHAVIOUR ORDER

The Antisocial Behaviour etc. (Scotland) Act 2004 provides for antisocial behaviour orders which prohibit the subject from doing anything described in that order. The order itself must be raised by a relevant person by way of summary application. It is an offence, if without reasonable excuse the subject breaches the order by doing anything prohibited by that order.

COMMENTARY	CASE LAW	STATUTE LAW
Antisocial behaviour orders		The Antisocial Behaviour etc. (Scotland) Act 2004, s 4(1). On the application of a relevant authority, the sheriff may, if satisfied that the conditions mentioned in subsection (2) are met ... make an antisocial behaviour order. s 4(2) Those conditions are— (a) that the specified person is at least 12 years of age; (b) that the specified person has engaged in antisocial behaviour towards a relevant person; and (c) that an antisocial behaviour order is necessary for the purpose of protecting relevant persons from further antisocial behaviour by the specified person.
Purpose of an order		s 4(5) Subject to subsections (6) and (7), an antisocial behaviour order is an order which prohibits, indefinitely or for such period as may be specified in the order, the specified person from doing anything described in the order. (6) The prohibitions that may be imposed by an antisocial behaviour order are those necessary for the purpose of protecting relevant persons from further antisocial behaviour by the specified person.
When the subject of the order is a child		s 4(4) sheriff is required to arrange and take the advice of a children's hearing panel prior to determining the application.
Relevant person		s 4(13) 'relevant person' means— (a) a local authority or a person within the area of the authority; and (b) registered social landlord— (i) a person residing in, or otherwise in or likely to be in, property provided or managed by that landlord; or (ii) a person in, or likely to be in, the vicinity of such property.
Variation and revocation of orders		s 5 (1) On the application of— (a)the relevant authority that obtained an antisocial behaviour order; or (b) the person subject to such an order, the sheriff may vary or revoke the order.

COMMENTARY	CASE LAW	STATUTE LAW
Breaching orders		s 9(1) Subject to subsection (3), a person who— (a) is subject to an order or an interim order; and (b) without reasonable excuse, does anything that the order to which the person is subject prohibits, shall be guilty of an offence. (2) A person guilty of an offence under subsection (1) shall be liable— (a)on summary conviction, to imprisonment for a term not exceeding 6 months or to a fine not exceeding the statutory maximum or to both; or (b) on conviction on indictment, to imprisonment for a term not exceeding 5 years or to a fine or to both.

CAUTION

Caution consists of a specified amount of money being consigned or bonded as security for good behaviour over a specified period of time. Failure to find caution within specified period allows alternative of imprisonment to be imposed. Caution can be consigned or there can be a bond of caution; if further offence then caution is forfeited; otherwise at end of period caution refunded.

COMMENTARY	CASE LAW	STATUTE LAW
	HMA v B 2006 SCCR 692 £5000 caution as part of more stringent bail conditions	Criminal Procedure (Scotland) Act 1995
Conviction.		**Solemn procedure:** Section 227. Where a person is convicted on indictment of an offence (other than an offence the sentence for which is fixed by law) the court may, instead of or in addition to imposing a fine or a period of imprisonment, ordain the accused to find caution for good behaviour for a period not exceeding 12 months and to such amount as the court considers appropriate.
Caution consists of a specified amount of money as security for good behaviour over a specified period of time.		**Summary procedure**: Section 7(7). In JP court period not exceeding six months and maximum not exceeding level 4 on the standard scale. Section 5(2). In sheriff court maximum amount is the prescribed sum and maximum period for which caution may be required is 12 months.
Caution is consigned.		Section 168(2). Caution may be found by consignation of the amount with clerk of the court, or by bond of caution signed by the cautioner.
If further offence committed, caution is forfeited.		Section 168(3). Where caution becomes liable to forfeiture, forfeiture may be granted by the court on the motion of the prosecutor, and, where necessary, warrant granted for the recovery of the caution.
Failure to find caution.		Section 168(4). If cautioner fails to pay amount under his bond within six days after he has received charge to that effect, court may: (a) order him to be imprisoned for maximum applicable under CP(S)A 1995, s 219 or until payment made; (b) if it considers it expedient, on application of cautioner grant time for payment; or (c) order recovery by civil diligence in accordance with CP(S)A 1995, s 221.

COMMENTARY	CASE LAW	STATUTE LAW
There is no caution by instalments.		**General** Provisions relating to payment of fines and default— CP(S)A 1995, ss 214, 216, 219(2)–(6)—apply equally to caution. *Note*: there is no provision for caution by instalments; the Act sets out the tariffs.

COMMUNITY PAYBACK ORDER

Community Payback Orders (CPO) came into force in Scotland on 1 February 2011 and replaced provisions for Community Service Orders, Probation Orders and Supervised Attendance Orders. A CPO may be comprised of a number of elements tailored at the courts discretion. The order itself is an alternative to custody, ranging between six months and three years in duration, and is available where the offence is punishable by imprisonment and/or a fine. The offender must be over 16 and must consent to the imposition of the CPO.

COMMENTARY	CASE LAW	STATUTE LAW
Community Payback Order:		Criminal Justice and Licensing (Scotland) Act 2010, s 14(1) After section 227 of the CP(S) A1995 insert— s 227A –s 227ZN
CPO is a direct alternative to custody. Offence must be punishable by imprisonment and/or a fine.		s 227A Community Payback Orders – (1) Where a person (the "offender") is convicted of an offence punishable by imprisonment, the court may, instead of imposing a sentence of imprisonment, impose a community payback order on the offender. (2) A community payback order is an order imposing one or more of the following requirements— (a) an offender supervision requirement, (b) a compensation requirement, (c) an unpaid work or other activity requirement, (d) a programme requirement, (e) a residence requirement, (f) a mental health treatment requirement, (g) a drug treatment requirement, (h) an alcohol treatment requirement, (i) a conduct requirement. (3) Subsection (4) applies where— (a) a person (the "offender") is convicted of an offence punishable by a fine (whether or not it is also punishable by imprisonment), and (b) where the offence is also punishable by imprisonment, the court decides not to impose— (i) a sentence of imprisonment, or (ii) a community payback order under subsection (1) instead of a sentence of imprisonment.

COMMENTARY	CASE LAW	STATUTE LAW
		(4) The court may, instead of or as well as imposing a fine, impose a community payback order on the offender imposing one or more of the following requirements— (a) an offender supervision requirement, (b) a level 1 unpaid work or other activity requirement, (c) a conduct requirement.
Duties of the court:		s 227B CPO: procedure prior to imposition - (1) This section applies where a court is considering imposing a CPO.
Court must consider both the need for a CPO as well as,		(2) The court must not impose the order unless it is of the opinion that the offence, or the combination of the offence and one or more offences associated with it, was serious enough to warrant the imposition of such an order. (3)…
Obtaining a local authority report regarding the offender and their personal circumstances.		(4) The court must not impose the order unless it has obtained, and taken account of, a report from an officer of a local authority containing information about the offender and the offender's circumstances. (5)… (6) Subsection (4) does not apply where the court is considering imposing a community payback order— (a) imposing only a level 1 unpaid work or other activity requirement, or (b) under section 227M(2). (7) The clerk of the court must give a copy of any report obtained under subsection (4) to— (a) the offender, (b) the offender's solicitor (if any), and (c) the prosecutor.
Before imposing any CPO the court must also explain the order to the offender before,		(8) Before imposing the order, the court must explain to the offender in ordinary language— (a) the purpose and effect of each of the requirements of the order (b) the consequences which may follow if the offender fails to comply with the order, and (c) where the court proposes to include in the order provision under section 227X for it to be reviewed, the arrangements for such a review.

COMMENTARY	CASE LAW	STATUTE LAW
Seeking their consent to its imposition.		(9) The court must not impose the order unless the offender has, after the court has explained those matters, confirmed that the offender— (a) understands those matters, and (b) is willing to comply with each of the requirements to be imposed by the order.
Failure to comply with CPO:		s 227ZC Breach of CPO: (1) This section applies where it appears … that an offender … has failed to comply with a requirement imposed by the order.
Court may issue a warrant for the offender's arrest Or require the offender to appear before the court.		(2) The court may— (a) issue a warrant for the offender's arrest, or (b) issue a citation to the offender requiring the offender to appear before the court. (3) If the offender fails to appear as required by a citation … the court may issue a warrant for the arrest of the offender. (4)….
Court must also give written details of the offender's alleged breaches to the offender.		(5) The court must, before considering the alleged failure— (a) provide the offender with written details of the alleged failure, (b) inform the offender that the offender is entitled to be legally represented, and (c) inform the offender that no answer need be given to the allegation before the offender— (i) has been given an opportunity to take legal advice, or (ii) has indicated that the offender does not wish to take legal advice. (6) Subsection (5) does not apply if the offender has previously been provided with those details and informed about those matters under section 227X(10) of this Act.
Where the court is satisfied that the offender breached the terms of their CPO – without reasonable excuse – a variety of disposals are available including,		(7) Where the order was imposed under section 227A, if the court is satisfied that the offender has failed without reasonable excuse to comply with a requirement imposed by the order, the court may— (a) impose on the offender a fine not exceeding level 3 on the standard scale,
The revocation and substitution of the CPO with the offender's original offence.		(b) where the order was imposed under section 227A(1), revoke the order and deal with the offender in respect of the offence in relation to which the order was imposed as it could have dealt with the offender had the order not been imposed,

COMMENTARY	CASE LAW	STATUTE LAW
		(c) where the order was imposed under section 227A(4), revoke the order and impose on the offender a sentence of imprisonment for a term not exceeding— (i) where the court is a justice of the peace court, 60 days, (ii) in any other case, 3 months, (d) vary the order so as to impose a new requirement, vary any requirement imposed by the order or revoke or discharge any requirement imposed by the order, or (e) both impose a fine under paragraph (a) and vary the order under paragraph (d). (8)… (9)… (10) If the court is satisfied that the offender has failed to comply with … the order but had a reasonable excuse … the court may, subject to section 227Z(2), vary the order so as to impose a new requirement, vary any requirement imposed by the order or revoke or discharge any requirement imposed by the order.

References: Nicholson, 1–145 to 1–172 and 10–43 to 10–49; Renton and Brown, 23–33.

COMPENSATION ORDER

A Compensation Order (CO) may be made instead of, or in addition to, another disposal. Cannot be made on (a) absolute discharge; (b) community payback order; or (c) deferred sentence. Compensation order requires offender to pay compensation for personal injury, loss or damage caused (other than loss because of death of a person or arising due to a motor vehicle accident). Order is sentence for purpose of appeal or review. Court has power to enforce order generally as if it were a fine.

COMMENTARY	CASE LAW	STATUTE LAW
Conviction.	*Carmichael v Siddique* 1985 SCCR 145 (Sh Ct) Compensation order for £1,000 upheld against shopkeeper selling firework to underage boy who injured eye. *Held*, statute designed to prevent injuries suffered, and no such restrictions as argued by defence (ie defence argued CO competent only where legal position clear and damage capable of precise valuation). *Bruce v McLeod* 1998 SLT 173 Accused person charged with assault but convicted under deletion of words 'repeatedly striking her to her injury' and justice imposed compensation order. On appeal quashed. Per Lord Sutherland: 'the Court requires that the Crown present some information ... which could provide a factual basis for the making of a compensation order.' *HMA v Nelson* 1996 SLT 1073 Accused pleaded guilty on indictment to aggravated assault. Sheriff made CO requiring accused pay £250 to complainer and £1,000 to victim support. *Held*, only competent to make CO in favour of person who had suffered loss, and order quashed. *Wilson v Transorganics* 1996 SLT 1014 Incompetent to suggest to an accused that if donation made to a local trust fund he will be admonished.	Criminal Procedure (Scotland) Act 1995, ss 249–253. Section 249(1). Where person convicted of an offence the court, may instead of or in addition to other disposal make a CO requiring him to pay compensation for any personal injury, loss or damage or direct alarm or distress caused, whether directly or indirectly or direct by the act which constituted the offence. Section 249(2). A CO cannot be made on (a) absolute discharge; (b) community payback order ; or (c) deferred sentence.
Covers personal injury, loss or damage caused by acts constituting offence.	*Nazir v Normand* 1994 SCCR 265 Criminal Procedure (Scotland) Act 1995, s 249(4). Road accidents excluded except damage, not loss, of vehicle. CO to owner of other car damaged by appellant's brother driving without insurance. *Held*, order not excessive and appeal refused.	Section 249(3), (4). COs do not cover loss because of death of a person; or arising due to motor vehicle accident, except where damage caused in case of offence under Road Traffic Act 1988, s 178(1) (taking motor vehicle without authority and property recovered but damaged).
Court to consider means of offender.	*McEvoy v McGlennan* 1997 SCCR 385 Theft by housebreaking. CO of £2,200 at £7.50 a week. He had disposable income of £20 a fortnight. High Court *held* the financial circumstances of the appellant should not be wholly ignored and order excessive and CO for £1,000 substituted. *Storie v Scott* 1990 SCCR 284 Appellant pleaded guilty to theft from employers and CSO made and also CO imposed for £1,137: £100 to be paid in four weeks, and the rest at £5 per week. *Held*, four years' repayment period excessive and CO for £350 substituted. *Note:* repayment period not usually more than two years.	Section 249(5). If going to make compensation order, court to consider means of offender.

COMMENTARY	CASE LAW	STATUTE LAW
Amount.		Section 249(7). Solemn proceedings: no limit to amount. Section 249(8)(a). Summary proceedings before sheriff or stipendiary magistrate: amount not exceeding prescribed sum (£10,000).).
		Section 249(8)(b). District court before lay magistrate: amount not exceeding level 4 on the standard scale (presently £2,500).
		Section 249(9). Payment to clerk of court who shall account for amount to person entitled thereto.
Court has power to enforce order generally as if it were a fine.		Section 249(10). Only the court can enforce CO.
Where order and fine are concurrent, order takes precedence over fine.		Section 252. Court has power to enforce order generally as if it were a fine.
		Section 250(1). Where in respect of offence a court considers a fine AND a CO appropriate but offender has insufficient means to pay appropriate levels of both, a CO should be preferred.
		Section 250(2). Where there is both a fine and a CO, payment shall first be applied in satisfaction of CO.
Appeal.	*Brown v Normand* 1988 SCCR 229 No CO where more than minimal provocation by complainer. Appellant chased by gang including complainer whom he hit with brick. £650 CO quashed on appeal: since not entitled to compensation from Criminal Injuries Compensation Board there was no reason he should get it in a court order.	Section 250(3). Order is sentence for purposes of appeal or review. Section 250(4). Payment to court retained until determination of appeal.
		Review of CO:
Review of compensation order. Reduction of amount possible.		Section 251. At any time before CO complied with or fully complied with, on application of person against whom order made, court may discharge the CO or reduce the amount if it appears to the court that: (a) ... (b) property, the loss of which is reflected in the CO, has been recovered.
		Section 252. All the provisions of CP(S)A 1995 relative to the payment, remission, transfer and enforcement of fines apply to CO, as appropriate.

COMMENTARY	CASE LAW	STATUTE LAW
Alternative disposal.	*Ely v Donnelly* 1996 SCCR 537 Appellant on income support given CO of £540 at £7 a week for breach of peace and vandalism. Appealed on grounds that sentence excessive, and asked for case to be continued to find out if complainer were recovering money from insurers. Motion for continuation refused. *Held*, (1) fact victim insured irrelevant; (2) CO not same as fine and guidelines on time to pay fine did not apply. *Landsborough v McGlennan* 1997 SCCR 464 Housebreaking. CO of £1,360 at £10 a week. *Held*, LJ-G Rodger dismissing appeal against CO, CO unlike fine, and fact repayment period longer than appropriate in case of fine not in itself reason to say order is inappropriate. (Repayment period here of two years.)	But note: guidelines which apply to length of time within which a fine should be paid do not apply to CO (see eg Ely v Donnelly 1996 SCCR 537; Landsborough v McGlennan 1997 SCCR 464). Section 252(3)(a). A court may impose imprisonment in respect of a fine and decline to impose imprisonment in respect of a CO, but not vice versa. Section 252(3)(b). Where a court imposes imprisonment both in respect of a fine and a CO, the amounts are to be aggregated for the purposes of calculating the maximum period imposed.

DEFERRED SENTENCE

Court can defer sentence after conviction on such conditions as the court may order. No limit on length of period of deferment. If conviction of another offence during period of deferment the court may sentence offender—deferment ends prematurely. At date of deferment court may further defer sentence eg to allow longer period to show good behaviour, otherwise court sentences offender.

COMMENTARY	CASE LAW	STATUTE LAW
On such conditions as the court may order. No limit on length of period of deferment.	*Cameron v Webster* 1997 SCCR 228 Theft. Sheriff deferred sentence for a year and asked appellant to bring £300 to court as compensation at that time. He brought £180 but case continued and he spent it and imprisoned. *Held*, sentence quashed and CO and fine imposed: not appropriate to defer sentence to enable accused to save up for CO ie that is what instalments are for. *Lennon v Copeland* 1972 SLT (Notes) 68 Sheriff sentenced accused to three months on second charge (possessing LSD) but deferred sentence on first charge (possessing cannabis). *Held*, question of sentence not in bill of suspension so court cannot dispose of it. Observed approach contrary to practice ie should have sentenced on both or admonished on cannabis charge. *McElwaine v Cardle* 1993 SCCR 619 Complainer convicted of breach of the peace and committing offence on bail. Sentence deferred on breach of the peace and fined on bail charge. *Held*, approach inappropriate as might fetter judge's discretion as to appropriate penalty on each charge taken as a whole and fine set aside and sentence also deferred. *Note:* offence on bail is now an aggravation.	Criminal Procedure (Scotland) Act 1995 Section 202(1). Competent for a court to defer sentence after conviction for a period and on such conditions as the court may determine.
Conviction for another offence during period of deferment: court may sentence offender—deferment ends prematurely.	*Borland v HMA* 1976 SLT (Notes) 12 *Held*, competent for one sheriff to remit accused to High Court despite fact another sheriff presiding when accused found guilty.	Section 202(2), (3). Conviction for another offence during period of deferment: (a) by court making original order: court may sentence for new offence and original offence; (b) by different court (anywhere in Great Britain): court which originally deferred sentence may compel appearance of accused before it by warrant or citation and may sentence.
Lord Advocate's appeal.		Lord Advocate may appeal against deferment of sentence (on indictment, under CP(S)A 1995, s 108(1)(g)); in summary procedure, under CP(S)A 1995, s 175(4A)(v) on a point of law only).

COMMENTARY	CASE LAW	STATUTE LAW
Date of deferment: court may further defer sentence. Otherwise, court sentences offender.	*Laing v Heywood* 1998 SCCR 458 Complainer placed on deferred sentence in district court and told if of good behaviour then absolute discharge. At end of period in which he was of good behaviour another justice admonished him. *Held*, justice not bound by earlier occasion and no flaw. Observed, if any indication they should be given in ways which do not suggest there will be a definite outcome. *Islam v Heywood* 1999 SCCR 68 Conditions attached to deferred sentence should not unduly hamper day-to-day living.	

DRUG TREATMENT AND TESTING ORDER

A Drug Treatment and Testing Order (DTTO) can be made in relation to an offender (other than where offence for which sentence fixed by law) aged 16 or over who is dependent on or has a propensity to misuse drugs and the court considers a DTTO expedient rather than sentencing. The offender's consent is required. Order must be between six months to three years and contain a treatment requirement that the offender submit to a treatment provider with a view to reduction or elimination of drug dependency/misuse.

The testing requirement requires offender to provide samples to the treatment provider. The offender shall also be under the supervision of a supervising officer who shall receive result from samples and report offender's failure/progress to appropriate court. The order may be amended or revoked on application of offender or supervising officer.

The DTTO shall provide for a periodic review at intervals of not less than one month. There shall be a review hearing in court where offender need attend and the order may be amended with the offender's consent. If progress satisfactory future reviews may be made in chambers in absence of parties. If breach of order without reasonable excuse court may fine or vary or revoke order. If court revokes order it may dispose of offender in any way competent at time order made. DTTO may be combined with a community payback order.

COMMENTARY	CASE LAW	STATUTE LAW
		Criminal Procedure (Scotland) Act 1995, ss 234B–234K, as inserted by ss 89–95 of the Crime and Disorder Act 1998.
		Criminal Procedure (Scotland) Act 1995
Offender 16 years or over.		Section 234B(1). 16 years or over convicted of offence other than fixed by law.
Court may make DTTO if expedient.		Section 234B(2). Court may make DTTO if expedient. (a) Effective for period of six months to three years.
Arrangements must be available in local authority area. Offender must have drug dependency/misuse susceptible to treatment.		Section 234B(3). A court shall not make DTTO unless– (a) notified that arrangements available in area; (b) obtained a report from local authority office about offender and his circumstances; and (c) is satisfied offender is a suitable person for such order and that he has a dependency or propensity to misuse drugs which is susceptible to treatment.
Treatment requirement.		Section 234C(1). DTTO shall include a treatment requirement that offender shall be treated by a treatment provider with a view to reducing or eliminating dependency on drugs.
		Section 234C(2). Nature of treatment need not be specified, only need specify institution, time period and resident / non-resident status.

COMMENTARY	CASE LAW	STATUTE LAW
Testing requirement.		Section 234C(4). DTTO shall include a testing requirement. Offender shall provide samples as required by treatment provider.
		Section 234C(5). Testing requirement shall specify the minimum number of samples required each month.
Appointment of supervising officer.		Section 234C(6). DTTO shall specify area where offender to reside and local authority to appoint supervising officer.
		Section 234C(7). Offender to keep in touch with supervising officer and notify change of address, officer to be given details of test samples.
Reports to court on offender's progress.		Section 234C(8). Supervising officer shall report offender's progress/failure to comply to court.
		Requirement for remote monitoring.
Explanation to offender about order.		Section 234D(1). Court must explain to offender in ordinary language the effect of order, its requirements, the consequences of failure, that order may be varied or revoked, that order will be periodically reviewed at times specified in order.
Copy of order.		Section 234D(2). Copy of order shall be given to offender, treatment provider, chief social work officer.
		Amendment and revocation:
Amendment and revocation of order.		Section 234E(1). Offender or supervising officer may apply to the appropriate court for variation or revocation of order (court may do so if it appears in interest of justice and offender consents).
		Periodic Review:
Periodic review of order (intervals not less than one month).		Section 234F(1)–(4). DTTO shall provide for order to be reviewed periodically at intervals of not less than one month at a review hearing, which the offender shall attend. Super-vising officer to give court progress report before each hearing (includes test results). Court can amend order with offender's consent. If no consent court may revoke order.
		Section 234F(5), (6). If progress satisfactory court may provide for each subsequent review without a hearing (in chambers without the parties present).

COMMENTARY	CASE LAW	STATUTE LAW
Breach: court may fine or vary or revoke order.	*Tweedle v Higson* 2002 SCCR 384 Revocation of order incompetent unless reference to breach is clear.	**Breach:** Section 234G(1). If it appears to court failure to comply it may issue a citation to appear or warrant to arrest. Section 234G(2). If proved (evidence of one witness sufficient) that the offender has failed without reasonable excuse to comply with any requirement of order, the court may vary or revoke the order or impose a fine not exceeding level 3 on the standard scale.
Disposal		**Disposal:** Section 234H(1). If court revokes order it may dispose of offender in any way which would have been competent at time order made. Section 234H(2). Court shall regard to the time the order has been in operation. Section 234H(3). Where court revokes DTTO and offender subject to probation order or restriction of liberty order court shall discharge/revoke those other orders before disposing of DTTO.
Combination of orders.		**Section 234J. Combination of orders.** Section 234J(1). Court can make both DTTO and community payback order concurrent if expedient to do so. Section 234J(2). In so deciding court shall regard circumstances including the nature of offence, character of offender and report as required by s 234B(3)(b). Section 234J(3). Copy of each order to be sent to treatment provider, local authority officer, probation officer. Section 234J(4). Where offender breaches either DTTO or community payback order and either one varied, the court may also vary the other order. Section 234J(5). Where an offender breaches both their DTTO and CPO simultaneously, the court can deal with the breach under either order but not both.

FINES

Court may impose a fine following conviction. Maximum fine depends on jurisdiction of the court. Means of the offender must be considered by court in fixing the amount of the fine. Deductions may be made from income support. Court may allow time to pay or payment by instalments or refuse time to pay if there are reasons for doing so. Offender may be under the supervision of a Fine Supervision Order (FSO) while paying. Court may impose the alternative of imprisonment in default of payment (period depends on amount of fine: see below).

COMMENTARY	CASE LAW	STATUTE LAW
Maximum fine depends on jurisdiction of court.		Criminal Procedure (Scotland) Act 1995, ss 211–226. Maximum fines: Section 211(1). For conviction of common law offence on indictment there is no maximum. Section 211(2). For conviction of a statutory offence on indictment there is no maximum. Section 225(1). For conviction of common law offence triable only summarily, the current prescribed sum £10,000 (by Criminal Procedure (Reform) (Scotland) Act 2007, s 48). For conviction of statutory offence the maximum fine is one which does not exceed the level on the standard scale prescribed by statute.
Standard scale.		Section 225. There shall be a standard scale for offences triable only summarily: Level Amount 1 £200 2 £500 3 £1,000 4 £2,500 5 £5,000
Means of offender must be considered by court in fixing the amount of the fine.	*Milligan v Jessop* 1988 SCCR 137 Appellant on social security pleaded guilty to breach of the peace and police assault. Magistrate said appellant unable to meet level of fine required and imprisoned him. *Held*, approach flawed, as possibility of fine rejected because of appellant's means and fines of £100 on each charge at £5 per week imposed. *Forsyth v Cardle* 1994 SCCR 769 Theft of bird eggs, income of £80 a fortnight. Fined total of £16,000 with three months to pay. *Held*, excessive, and fine of £2,000 at £5 per week imposed. Not proper to impose fines completely beyond capacity of offender, even over very long period (normally, fines payable in not much more than a year).	Section 211(7). Means of offender shall be taken into consideration in determining the amount of the fine.

COMMENTARY	CASE LAW	STATUTE LAW
	Picto Ltd v Lees 1994 SCCR 775 Company breached trading standards over safety claims regarding Christmas tree lights. *Held*, on appeal, £2,500 fine not excessive given means of offender regardless of fact company a first offender. *Reynolds v Hamilton* 1994 SCCR 760 Breach of trade descriptions for falsely claiming engines rebuilt. Appellant, on income support, fined £1,200. *Held*, failure to regard means of offender and not reasonable or proper fines would take six years to pay. Fine of £300 at £5 per week substituted. *Buchan v McNaughtan* 1990 SCCR 13 Appellant pleaded guilty to breach of ss 3 and 5 of the Road Traffic Act 1988. In receipt of £47 per week invalidity benefit. Fined total of £225. *Held*, if appellant could not pay fines he must have recourse to means enquiry court. *Hamilton v Scott* 1987 SCCR 188 Appellants plead guilty to assault and fined £600 at £10 per week. *Held*, that as a result of fines, appellants would almost certainly end up in prison for non-payment, and fines excessive and reduced to £300 at £5 per week.	
Court may allow time to pay.		**Time to pay:** Section 214(1). At least seven days must be allowed to pay fine or first instalment.
Court may refuse time to pay if there are reasons to do so.	*Elder v Crowe* 1996 SCCR 38 Appellant convicted of offering to supply counterfeit perfume with street value of £3,000. More than £2,000 in cash at house seized at time. Sheriff fined appellant £2,000 and allowed no time to pay. Decision upheld on appeal, since appellant had sufficient means. *Note:* court can refuse time to pay if it appears there are sufficient means.	Section 214(2). Court may refuse time to pay the fine if: (a) offender appears to have means to pay immediately; or (b) offender does not wish time to pay; or (c) offender has no fixed abode; or (d) court is satisfied that there is any other special reason to refuse time to pay. If court refuses time to pay and offender fails to pay it may impose imprisonment, stating the special reasons for its decision.
Alternative prison sentence may be imposed.	*Barbour v Robertson* 1943 JC 46 Brothel keeping. Fined £100 and refused time to pay in view of nature of offence. LJ-C Cooper held: 'nature of offence rarely a relevant consideration' as to whether time to pay should be granted. *Note:* special reason does not include the nature of the offence. *Robertson v Jessop* 1989 SLT 843 *Held*, on appeal, magistrate's reason for refusing time to pay ie 'unrealistic since accused in custody' was itself unrealistic and appeal allowed and time to pay allowed for payment of fine.	Section 214(4). On the occasion of the imposition of a fine when allowing time to pay or payment by instalments, the court may only impose the alternative of imprisonment in the event of future default if: (a) the offender is personally present; and (b) the court determines, having regard to the offender's character and nature of offence, or other special reason, that it is expedient to do so. Where a court so determines it shall state the special reason.

COMMENTARY	CASE LAW	STATUTE LAW
Court may allow further time to pay.		Section 214(7). Where time to pay, court may on application by offender, and after giving prosecutor an opportunity of being heard, allow further time to pay. Section 215(4). Such application may be oral or in writing. Section 215(3). Court may only refuse such application if satisfied: (a) that failure to pay is wilful; or (b) that there is no reasonable prospect of securing payment if further time allowed.
Court may allow payment by instalments. *Note*: generally, if instalments, fine payable in a year or so.	*Tonner v Hamilton* 1995 SCCR 469 Road Traffic Act 1988 offence. £350 fine at £5 a fortnight. Upheld on appeal, since appellant had requested this repayment. *Brown v McGlennan* 1995 SCCR 627 Appellant offered to pay £5 per week and ordered to do so on fine for £800. *Held*, £5 per week reasonable but repayment time (over 160 weeks) unreasonable and appealed allowed and fine reduced to £400 at £5 per week. *Paterson v McGlennan* 1991 SLT 832 Criminal Procedure (Scotland) Act 1995, s 214. Accused fined £450 at £5 per week with alternative of 60 days' imprisonment if default on grounds of record (16 previous convictions). *Held*, (bench of five judges): (1) 90 weeks' repayment period excessive; (2) alternative of imprisonment on grounds of accused character not justified since he had paid fines in the past. Fines reduced and default order quashed.	Section 214(8). Where court has imposed fine, court may of its own accord or on application of offender order payment by instalments of such amounts and at such time as it thinks fit. Section 214(9). Where court has ordered payment by instalments it may allow further time to pay or order payment of lesser amounts or at longer intervals than those originally fixed.
		Restriction on imprisonment for default:
Restriction on imprisonment for default.	*Buchanan v Hamilton* 1988 SCCR 379 Drink-driving offence. Fined £250 with default order because of nature of offence. *Held*, nature of offence not a relevant reason for imposing the alternative and appeal allowed and alternative of imprisonment quashed. *Finnie v McLeod* 1983 SCCR 387 First offender fined £100 for shoplifting and imprisonment in default due to 'nature of offence' which sheriff described as 'barefaced shoplifting'. *Held*, very case where appropriate for the sheriff to impose the alternative. Compare with: *Buchanan v Hamilton* 1988 SCCR 379 Difference is that in Finnie the sheriff referred to gravity of offence rather than just merely the nature.	Most sheriff courts issue warning letters on default before issuing citation to a means enquiry court. Section 216(1). Where court has imposed a fine, without imposing imprisonment in default of payment it shall not impose imprisonment for failing to make payment unless on an occasion subsequent to that sentence the court has enquired into the reason why the fine has not been paid, in his presence. Section 216(2). Subsection (1) shall not apply if offender is in prison.

COMMENTARY	CASE LAW	STATUTE LAW
Fine defaulter may be cited to attend a means enquiry court.	*Dunlop v Allan* 1984 SCCR 329 Careless driving, motor cyclist killed. Sheriff fined appellant and imposed alternative of imprisonment. *Held*, not competent to impose alternative of imprisonment on ground of gravity of offence (careless driving) which was not punishable with imprisonment in the first instance.	Section 216(3). A fine defaulter may be cited to attend a means enquiry court, or a warrant may be issued for his arrest. Section 216(7). Where a child would, if adult, be liable to imprisonment in default of payment of any fine, the court may order the child to be detained for period not exceeding one month. Only where court considers no other disposal suitable.
As an alternative disposal, court may make a Fine Supervision Order (FSO).		**Supervision pending payment:** Section 217(1). When given time to pay the offender may be under the supervision of local social work department while paying. Section 217(4). Detention of an offender under 21 as an alternative disposal when a fine is unpaid is not competent unless a Fine Supervision Order (FSO) has been made. Section 217(5). Subsection (4) does not apply unless court is satisfied that it is impracticable to place offender under FSO and states the grounds on which it is so satisfied. Section 217(6). Where an FSO has been made, the court must obtain a report from the supervising authority before imposing the alternative.
Periods of imprisonment for non-payment.		**Periods of imprisonment for non-payment:** Section 219(1). When imposing a fine a court may impose a period of imprisonment in default of payment. If no such order made and person fails to pay fine or instalment in time the court may impose imprisonment for such failure. Section 219(1A) Subsection (1) shall not apply to a fine imposed for an offence under section 107 of the Antisocial Behaviour etc. (Scotland) Act 2004. Section 219(2), (4), (5). Maximum period of imprisonment is determined by amount of fine still unpaid. The Act provides the tariff. Section 219(3). If fines were imposed by same court on same day, the period of imprisonment will be determined by the total of the fines imposed.

COMMENTARY	CASE LAW	STATUTE LAW
		Section 220. In the event of imprisonment being imposed as an alternative, the offender may secure his release or reduce the period spent in prison by making payment in whole or in part while in prison (in proportion to amount of fine outstanding).
		Section 224. All warrants for imprisonment in default of payment of a fine shall specify a period at the expiry of which the sentence shall be discharged, notwithstanding that the fine has not been paid.
		Section 213. Fine may be remitted in whole or part by any court which is at that time responsible for its enforcement (High Court fines enforced by sheriff court). Attendance of accused unnecessary.
Sum may be deducted from income support to secure payment.		Criminal Justice Act 1991, s 24: court may apply to the Secretary of State to have sums deducted from income support to secure payment.

References: Nicholson, 1–64 ff; Renton and Brown, 23–29 ff.

IMPRISONMENT AND DETENTION

Imprisonment is competent only for adult offenders (21 years or over). Detention is competent for young offender (not less than 16 but under 21 years of age). Court may not pass prison sentence on adult offender not previously sentenced unless no other disposal appropriate and must first consider background reports. Court may not sentence young offender to detention unless no other disposal appropriate and must first consider background reports. No court may sentence to imprisonment or detention if offender is not legally represented and not previously sentenced to imprisonment or detention unless refused legal representation or failed to apply.
Note: full bench dealt with question of consecutive or concurrent sentences in *Nicholson v Lees* 1996 SCCR 551 (dealt with under Bail above).

COMMENTARY	CASE LAW	STATUTE LAW
		Criminal Procedure (Scotland) Act 1995, ss 204–210
		Imprisonment:
Imprisonment.	*Nicholson v Lees* 1996 SCCR 551 Full-bench decision on concurrent/consecutive sentences: see Bail above.	Only competent for adult offenders: 21 years or over.
Adult offender not previously sentenced to imprisonment or detention. Alternative? Custodial sentence being considered. Court must first consider background reports.		Section 204(2), (2A) and (3): Court may not pass prison sentence on adult offender not previously sentenced to imprisonment or detention by UK court, unless it considers that no other method of dealing with him is appropriate. For this purpose court shall from an officer of local authority or otherwise obtain such information as it can about offender's circumstances (eg Social Enquiry Report). Court must also take account of any information before it relating to offender's character and his physical and mental condition. It has power to make a hospital order in addition to imposing a sentence of imprisonment. (Summary court must state reason for sentence of imprisonment and enter reason in record of proceedings).
Court must, when taking account of previous sentences, disregard suspended sentences not brought into effect.		Section 204(4). Court must, when taking account of previous sentences: (i) disregard suspended sentence (English/Irish) which has not been brought into effect; (ii) interpret detention as meaning a young offenders' institution or detention centre, but not borstal training (except in England and Wales).

COMMENTARY	CASE LAW	STATUTE LAW
If first sentence, offender should be allowed legal representation, irrespective of offender's age.		Section 204(1). No court may pass sentence of imprisonment or detention (or impose such sentence as immediate alternative to fine under CP(S)A 1995, s 214(2)) if the offender is not legally represented and has not previously been sentenced to imprisonment or detention by a UK court. But legal representation not a prerequisite if offender either: (a) has been refused legal aid on financial grounds; or (b) has failed to apply for legal aid after having been informed of his right and having had the opportunity to do so.
		Section 204(5). These provisions apply to all courts and all sentences of imprisonment or detention, except those fixed by law.
		Detention:
Detention: Young offender. Is there any other method of dealing with offender appropriately?		Section 207(1), (5). Young offender: not less than 16, but under 21 years of age. All young offenders serve sentence in young offenders' institution. Maximum and minimum sentences are same as for imprisonment.
		Section 207(3). A young offender not to be sentenced to detention unless no other way of dealing with that person is appropriate. Reason for imposing detention to be given and, except in High Court, entered in the record of proceedings.
	Bain v Wilson 1998 SCCR 454 On 18 February 1998 sheriff proceeded to sentence appellant to detention without obtaining any further report (as CP(S)A 1995, s 207 requires), since he had dealt with appellant on other matters and appellant was known to sheriff from reports provided in January 1998. *Held*, to allow sheriff to proceed from recollection would ride roughshod over CP(S)A 1995, s 207(4). Observed, per LJ-G Rodger, court can obtain information from up-to-date reports from other proceedings. *Note:* case shows LJ-G Rodger's observations are not to be given wide interpretation.	Section 207(4). For purposes of CP(S)A 1995, s 207(3), court shall obtain information from office of local authority or otherwise (SER) and court must also take into account any information before it relating to offender's character, and his physical and mental condition. Section 207(4A). In forming an opinion under subsection (3) above the court shall take into account its power to make a hospital direction in addition to imposing a period of detention.

COMMENTARY	CASE LAW	STATUTE LAW
Supervised Release Orders	*Fyfe v HMA* 1997 SCCR 755 Breach of SROs. 'Date of first proven failure' is the date on which failure occurred. *Ward v Brown* 2000 SCCR 947	**Additional points:** (i) Supervised Release Orders (SROs): CP(S)A 1995, s 209. Only on indictment cases where period of custody 12 months to four years where court considers it necessary to protect public. Again, court must first consider report from local authority officer about offender and his circumstances. Applies to adult and young offenders and prisoner's consent not required. Breach of SRO (proved by one witness) means that court can vary order or order that offender be returned for whole or part of period beginning with date of order for return and equal to period between first proven failure referred to in statement on oath and date on which supervision under SRO would have ceased (see s 209 for details).
Guilty pleas.		(ii) Guilty pleas: CP(S)A 1995, s 196(1). In determining what sentence to pass on, or what disposal or order to make in relation to, an offender who has pled guilty to an offence, a court may take into account: (a) the stage in the proceedings for the offence at which the offender indicated his intention to plead guilty; and (b) the circumstances in which the indication was given. Section 196(1A) Court shall state what account taken of guilty plea in length of sentence. Where the court does not have regard to a guilty plea, it must state the reasons for not doing so.

OFFENCES RACIALLY AGGRAVATED

Where it is libelled in an indictment or specified in a complaint and proved that an offence has been racially aggravated the court shall take that aggravation into account in determining the appropriate sentence. An offence is racially aggravated if offence is motivated by ill-will or malice towards members of a racial group based on their membership thereof OR if offender evinces towards victim malice and ill-will based on membership (or presumed membership) of that group. Evidence from a single source is sufficient to establish that an offence is racially aggravated.

COMMENTARY	CASE LAW	STATUTE LAW
Court shall take racial aggravation into account when sentencing.		Crime and Disorder Act 1998, Section 96(1), (5). Where it is libelled in an indictment or specified in a complaint and proved that an offence has been racially aggravated, the court shall take the aggravation into account in determining the appropriate sentence.
Racially aggravated Malice or ill-will based upon victims membership of a racial group.		Section 96(2). An offence is racially aggravated if: (a) at time of offence or immediately before or after the offender evinces towards the victim (if any) malice or ill-will based upon the victim's membership (or presumed membership) of a racial group; or (b) the offence is motivated (wholly or partly) by malice and ill-will towards members of a racial group based on their membership of that group. Evidence from a single source sufficient to establish that offence is racially aggravated.
'membership'		Section 96(3). In CDA 1998, s 96(2)(a) 'membership' includes association with members of that racial group; 'presumed' means presumed by the offender.
		Section 96(4). It is immaterial for purposes of CDA 1998, s 96(2)(a), (b) whether or not the offender's malice or ill-will is also based on— a) the fact or presumption that person belongs to any religious group; or (b) any other factor not mentioned in that paragraph.
'racial group'		Section 96(6). 'Racial group' means a group of persons defined by reference to race, colour, nationality (including citizenship) or ethnic or national origins.

References: Renton and Brown, 23–123 ff.

PROCEEDS OF CRIME

Forfeiture

The Proceeds of Crime (Scotland) Act 1995 provides for the forfeiture of property used to facilitate crime and the confiscation of the proceeds of crime. Court may make a suspended forfeiture order in respect of property used to facilitate the commission of any offence. The order is made on application of the prosecutor. In general, property is not forfeited right away. Moveable property is forfeited 60 days after making order unless perishable etc whereby it is forfeited immediately. Heritable property is forfeited six months later.

COMMENTARY	CASE LAW	STATUTE LAW
		Proceeds of Crime (Scotland) Act 1995
Court may make SFO in respect of property used to facilitate the commission of any offence.		Suspended Forfeiture Orders: s 21. Section 21(2). The court may, if satisfied on the application of the prosecutor that any property which was at the time of the offence or of the accused's apprehension in his ownership or possession or under his control— (a) has been used for the purpose of committing, or facilitating the commission of any offence; (b) was intended for that purpose, make a suspended forfeiture order in respect of that property.
Prosecutor must intimate to court interest in property of someone other than accused. SFO shall name person having or suspecting to have interest in property.		Section 21(4). If the prosecutor knows or reasonably suspects he knows that someone other than the accused is the owner, or has an interest in the property to which the SFO relates, he shall intimate that fact to the court on making the application. The SFO shall then name the person having or suspecting to have interest in property. (If prosecutor becomes aware of interest after SFO made, he must intimate to court and can apply to vary SFO).
Facilitation.		Section 21(5). Facilitation under s 21 includes any steps taken to dispose of property or avoid apprehension or detection after the offence.
		Section 21(7), (8). Where a statute prohibits the forfeiture of property for offence for which accused convicted an SFO cannot be made. Where the statute specifies the property which may be subject to an SFO then other property cannot be forfeited.

COMMENTARY	CASE LAW	STATUTE LAW
Court may order compensation order to be paid off first.		Section 21(9). If SFO made along with compensation order court may order CO be paid off first from the sale of the property.
Property placed under control of clerk of court.		Section 21(11). Any property in respect of which SFO made shall be placed under the control of the clerk of the court until— (a) the order is recalled; or (b) the property is forfeited.
Property not forfeited right away:		*Note*: in general property is not forfeited immediately.
moveable ... heritable...		Section 24. Moveable property is generally forfeited 60 days after making SFO. If, however, it is perishable, dangerous, of no commercial value, or cannot be lawfully be sold, supplied or possessed, it shall be forfeited immediately. Heritable property is forfeited six months later.
		Section 23. If reasonable cause to believe property subject to SFO is at specified place or premises the court may grant warrant to search premises and seize property.
Person other than accused with interest in property: SFO shall be recalled unless prosecutor proves knowledge/acquiescence.		Section 25. If person other than accused satisfies court on the balance of probabilities that he is owner or has interest in property subject to SFO, it shall be recalled—unless the prosecutor proves beyond reasonable doubt that: (a) he knew or ought to have known property was used to facilitate the commission of the offence; and (b) the applicant failed to take reasonable steps to prevent this use. If applicant came to own property after commission of offence prosecutor must prove that applicant knew or ought to have known that the property was so used.
Even so, order may be recalled if excessive or inappropriate.		Section 25(3). Even if court satisfied applicant knew or should have known, the court may recall an SFO if it appears to the court in all the circumstances of the case that the SFO is excessive or inappropriate.
		(Forfeiture of motor vehicles: see s 33A of the Road Traffic Act 1988, under RTA. Note PC(S)A 1995 does not apply here).
Appeals.		Section 27(2). SFO appealable as if appeal against sentence.

Confiscation Orders

Part 3 of the Proceeds of Crime Act 2002 substantially replaces the Proceeds of Crime (Scotland) Act 1995 and extends powers of confiscation to the High Court and Sheriff Court in Scotland. A **confiscation order** can only be made at the insistence of the prosecutor, where an accused has benefited from either a **general criminal lifestyle** or a particular piece of criminal conduct. In the event the court decides the accused has **benefited** from his criminal conduct, the court must decide a **recoverable amount** which the accused is required to pay. Confiscation orders are subject to **procedural matters** such as: postponement, variation and appeal.

COMMENTARY	CASE LAW	STATUTE LAW
Confiscation order:		**Proceeds of Crime Act 2002**
Making an order		**Section 92:** (1) The court must act under this section where the following three conditions are satisfied.
Accused must have committed an offence		(2) The first condition is that an accused falls within either of the following — (a) he is convicted of an offence or offences, whether in solemn or summary proceedings, or (b) in the case of summary proceedings in respect of an offence (without proceeding to conviction) an order is made discharging him absolutely.
Duty of the prosecution to seek the order		(3) The second condition is that the prosecutor asks the court to act under this section. (4) The third condition is that the court decides to order some disposal in respect of the accused (absolute discharge is a disposal for the purpose of this subsection)
Duty of the court to: (1) measure the accused's criminal lifestyle, (2) calculate the accused's criminal benefit		(5) If the court acts under this section it must– (a) decide whether the accused has a criminal lifestyle; (b) if so, it must decide whether he has benefited from his general criminal conduct; (c) if it decides that he does not have a criminal lifestyle it must decide whether he has benefited from his particular criminal conduct.
(3) grant or refuse the order,		(6) If the court decides under subsection (5)(b) or (c) that the accused has benefited from the conduct referred to— (a) it must decide the recoverable amount, and (b) it must make a confiscation order requiring him to pay that amount.

COMMENTARY	CASE LAW	STATUTE LAW
Court must also take account of any civil proceedings brought by the victim against the accused (s.92(7)) and the representations of any person whom is likely to be affected by the order.		(7)… (8) Before making an order under this section the court must take into account any representations made to it by any person whom the court thinks is likely to be affected by the order. (9) The standard of proof … is the balance of probabilities. (10) The first condition is not satisfied if the accused is unlawfully at large (but section 111 may apply). (11) For the purposes of any appeal or review, an order under this section is a sentence.
General criminal lifestyle.		**Section 142: Criminal lifestyle** (1) An accused has a criminal lifestyle if … the offence(s) concerned satisfy any of these tests— (a) it is specified in Schedule 4; (b) it constitutes conduct forming part of a course of criminal activity; (c) it is an offence committed over a period of at least six months and the accused has benefited from the conduct. (2) Conduct forms part of a course of criminal activity if the accused has benefited from the conduct and— (a) in the proceedings in which he was convicted he was convicted of three or more other offences, each of three or more of them constituting conduct from which he has benefited, or (b) in the period of six years ending with the day when those proceedings were instituted (or, if there is more than one such day, the earliest day) he was convicted on at least two separate occasions of an offence constituting conduct from which he has benefited. (3) But an offence does not satisfy the test in subsection (1)(b) or (c) unless the accused obtains relevant benefit of not less than £5000. *(please see act for further details)*

COMMENTARY	CASE LAW	STATUTE LAW
Assumptions as to the extent of the benefit: Where the court finds that the accused has a criminal lifestyle they are entitled to make a number of assumptions.		**Section 96: Assumptions to be made in case of criminal lifestyle** (1) Where the court decides that the accused has a criminal lifestyle it must make the following four assumptions for the purpose of— (a) deciding whether he has benefited from his general criminal conduct, and (b) deciding his benefit from the conduct. (2) The first assumption is that any property transferred to the accused at any time after the relevant day was obtained by him as a result of his general criminal conduct. (3) Secondly, that any property held by the accused at any time after the date of conviction was obtained by him as a result of his general criminal conduct. (4) Thirdly, that any expenditure incurred by the accused at any time after the relevant day was met from property obtained by him as a result of his general criminal conduct. (5) Fourthly, that for the purpose of valuing any property obtained (or assumed to have been obtained) by the accused, he obtained it free of any other interests in it.
Subject to certain safeguards		(6) The court must not make any of those assumptions in relation to particular property or expenditure if— (a) the assumption is shown to be incorrect, or (b) there would be a serious risk of injustice if the assumption were made.
Benefited: Calculating the benefit to the accused.		**Section 94: Accused's benefit** (1) If the court is acting under section 92 this section applies for the purpose of— (a) deciding whether the accused has benefited from conduct, and (b) deciding his benefit from the conduct. (2) The court must take account of— (a) conduct occurring up to the time it makes its decision; (b) property obtained up to that time. *(please see act for further details)*

COMMENTARY	CASE LAW	STATUTE LAW
Recoverable amount: Decided by the court based upon the benefit to the accused. Recoverable amount may be restricted by whatever amount is *available* to the accused. Please see s 95 for further details.		**Section 93: Recoverable amount** (1) The recoverable amount...is an amount equal to the accused's benefit from the conduct concerned. (2) But if the accused shows that the available amount is less than that benefit the recoverable amount is— (a) the available amount, or (b) a nominal amount, if the available amount is nil. (3)... (4)... (5) If the court decides the available amount, it must include in the confiscation order a statement of its findings as to the matters relevant for deciding that amount. *(please see act for further details)*
Procedural matters: Postponement, variation and appeals.		Confiscation orders may be postponed or varied on application by the accused, prosecutor or by a motion of the court. Confiscation orders are also appealable by the prosecutor exclusively. *(Please see sections 99, 113 and 115 for further details)*

References: Renton and Brown, 23–72 to 23–120.

RESTRICTION OF LIBERTY ORDER

Court may make a Restriction of Liberty Order (ROLO) where offender 16 or over (and convicted of offence the sentence for which is not fixed by law) if it is the most appropriate disposal. Offender's consent is required. ROLO may restrict offender's movement for up to 12 hours a day in place specified and may run for up to 12 months. ROLO is a sentence for the purpose of appeal. Offender is monitored by person / device approved by the Secretary of State. ROLO can be made concurrent with probation order. ROLO can be reviewed on application of offender / person responsible for monitoring. If breach then ROLO may be varied or revoked, or a fine may be imposed. If revoked, court may dispose of offender as competent at time order made.

COMMENTARY	CASE LAW	STATUTE LAW
		Crime and Punishment (Scotland) Act 1997, s 5 inserts ss 245A–245H into Criminal Procedure (Scotland) Act 1995.
		Criminal Procedure (Scotland) Act 1995
Offender 16 or over.		Section 245A(1). Court can make ROLO on offender 16 or over (where sentence not fixed by law) if most appropriate disposal.
Not more than 12 hours a day.		Section 245A(2A). ROLO may restrict offender's movement to place(s) specified but not for period(s) totalling more than 12 hours in one day.
Not longer than 12 months. Explanation of order.	*Macaulay v Houston* 2005 SCCR 589 Not competent to combine CSO with ROLO	Section 245A(3). ROLO may be made up to 12 months.
		Section 245A(4). Explanation to offender in ordinary language about order, consequences, reviews. Offender's consent required.
Copy of order.		Section 245A(5). Copy of order to offender and monitor.
		Section 245A(6). Court to consider information as to place of enforced presence and those likely to be affected by it.
Appeal.		Section 245A(7). ROLO is sentence for purpose of appeal.
Monitoring		Section 245A(11). No ROLO unless court satisfied compliance can be monitored as specified in order.
		Section 245B. Secretary of State to notify court of class of persons who may be monitors.
Remote monitoring		Section 245C. Court can require offender to wear device for remote monitoring.

COMMENTARY	CASE LAW	STATUTE LAW
Concurrent with community payback order.		Section 245D. ROLO can be made concurrent with community payback order if expedient with regards to circumstances such as nature of offence and character of offender.
Review: offender's consent required.		Section 245E. Offender/monitor may apply for review; offender' consent required.
Breach.		Section 245F. If appears to court offender has failed to comply without reasonable excuse court may fine, or revoke or vary order.
Disposal.		Section 245G. If ROLO revoked, court can dispose as competent at the time order made (having regard to time order in force).
Evidence from automatic statement from device sufficient.		Section 245H. Automatic statement from device of offender's movements accompanied by a signed certificate by nominated person that statement relates to offender shall be sufficient evidence, provided copy of statement served on offender prior to hearing and in any event if appears to court offender has insufficient notice court may adjourn.

SEX OFFENDER ORDER

The Crime and Disorder Act 1998, s 20, provides for sex offender orders, which prohibit the subject from doing anything described in the order. The applicant is the chief constable and the action proceeds by way of summary application (civil procedure). See the Crime and Disorder Act 1998 for details.

See Anti-social behaviour order (p 152 above) for details of offences in connection with breach of both orders.

COMMENTARY	CASE LAW	STATUTE LAW
		Sexual Offences Act 2003, s 105(1) SOPO: effect s 107; Variation renewal and discharges s 108; Interim s 109; Appeals s 110; Breach s 113

BIBLIOGRAPHY

Publications referred to in the text

Alison, A. I *Principles of the Criminal Law of Scotland* (1832).
Bovey, K. *Misuse of Drugs* (1986).
Cubie, A. *Scots Criminal Law* (3rd edn, 2010).
Gane, C. H. W. and Stoddart, C. N. *A Casebook on Scottish Criminal Law* (4th edn, 2009).
Gordon, G. H. *The Criminal Law of Scotland* (2nd edn, 1978, with second supplement, 1992).
Hume, D. *Commentaries on the Law of Scotland Respecting Crimes* (with supplement by B. R. Bell, in two volumes, 4th edn, 1844).
Macdonald, Sir J. H. A. *A Practical Treatise on the Criminal Law of Scotland* (5th edn, 1948).
Nicholson, C. G. B. *Sentencing: The Law and Practice in Scotland* (2nd edn, 1992).
Renton and Brown *Criminal Procedure according to the Law of Scotland* (by G. H. Gordon, Looseleaf, 2012).
Brown, A. and Wheatley, J. *Road Traffic Law in Scotland* (4th edn, 2007).

Books for additional reference

Archbold *Pleadings, Evidence and Practice in Criminal Cases* (43rd edn, 1988).
Dickson, W. G. *A Treatise on the Law of Evidence in Scotland* (two volumes, 1887).
Field, D. *Law of Evidence in Scotland* (1988).
Gane, C. H. W. and Stoddart, C. N. *Criminal Procedure in Scotland: Cases and Materials* (1994).
Harper, J. R. *A Practitioner's Guide to the Criminal Courts* (1985).
Lewis, W. J. *Manual of the Law of Evidence in Scotland* (1925).
Macphail, I. D. *A Revised Version of a Research Paper on the Law of Evidence in Scotland* (1987).
Ross, M. and Chalmers, J. *Walker and Walker: The Law of Evidence in Scotland* (3rd edn, 2009).
Wilkinson, A. B. *The Scottish Law of Evidence* (2nd edn, 2000).
Wilkinson's Road Traffic Offences (Wallis, McCormac, Brown and Swift, 23rd edn, 2007).

Index

www.ingramcontent.com/pod-product-compliance
Lightning Source LLC
LaVergne TN
LVHW080043210926
848481LV00011B/3270